OFF THE BEATEN PATH™ SERIES

Georgia

FOURTH EDITION

by William Schemmel

Old Saybrook, Connecticut

Cover photo: Images © PhotoDisc, Inc.
Cover and text design: Laura Augustino
Maps created by Equator Graphics © The Globe Pequot Press
Illustrations by Carole Drong

Library of Congress Cataloging-in-Publication Data

Schemmel, William.
      Georgia : off the beaten path / William Schemmel. —4th ed.
      p. cm. —(Off the beaten path series)
      Includes index.
      ISBN 0-7627-0264-8
      1. Georgia—Guidebooks. I. Title. II. Series.
F284.3.S34   1998
917.5804´43—dc21
                                    98-29252
                                    CIP

Manufactured in the United States of America
Fourth Edition/First Printing

To Roscoe, La Verne, Johnny, and Mike,
and all my good friends
in the Adair Park Dogfest.

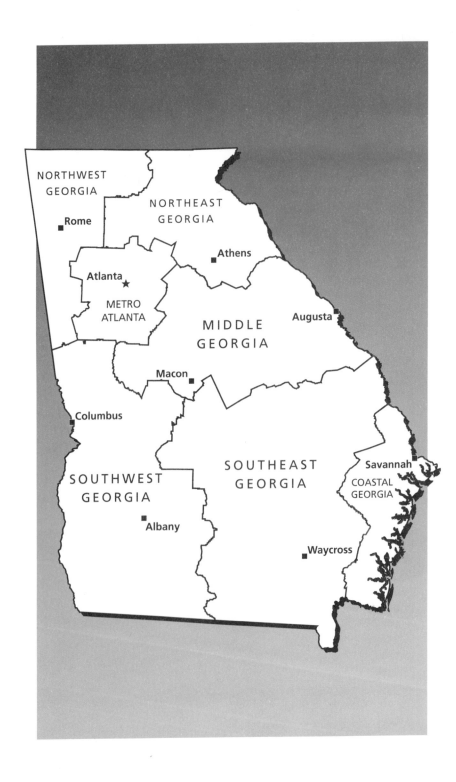

NORTHWEST
GEORGIA

■ Rome

NORTHEAST
GEORGIA

■ Athens

Atlanta
★

METRO
ATLANTA

MIDDLE
GEORGIA

■ Augusta

■ Macon

■ Columbus

SOUTHEAST
GEORGIA

Savannah
■

COASTAL
GEORGIA

SOUTHWEST
GEORGIA

■ Albany

■ Waycross

Contents

About the Author

William Schemmel is a full-time freelance writer and photographer who travels from Paris, Texas, to Paris, France, but most enjoys telling others about his native state of Georgia. His work appears regularly in numerous magazines, newspapers, and guidebooks. A member of the Society of American Travel Writers, he has experienced adventures on Georgia's off-the-beaten-paths for more than twenty-five years. He invites you to get off the interstate highways and make your own fascinating discoveries.

Introduction

After spending a good deal of my life wandering Georgia's byways, I'm happily convinced it will never run out of ways to surprise and delight me. From the Blue Ridge Mountains by the Tennessee and Carolina borders to the Okefenokee Swamp and piney woods bordering Florida, from Savannah and "The Golden Isles" on the Atlantic Coast to Columbus and La Grange and Lake Seminole on the westerly Chattahoochee River, I'm ever amazed at my home state's depth and breadth. It's like an incredible attic stacked floor to ceiling with a never-ending cache of treasures.

I've attended Sunday morning services with Macon County's Mennonites and been transported by the Gregorian chants of the Benedictine monks at Rockdale County's Monastery of the Holy Ghost. I've awakened in the depths of the swamps to the eerie symphony of gators and owls and at sunrise by mountain lakes to the siren songs of loons and geese.

I've encountered ghosts, and tales of ghosts, in antebellum mansions where Sherman and Lafayette once slept, and I've half-believed the outrageous lies of fishermen and small-town sages. I've attended festivals exalting rattlesnakes, chitterlings, sorghum syrup, pecans, autumn leaves, spring dogwoods, and Greek, Chinese, Middle Eastern, East Indian, and American Indian heritage. Along the way I've eaten a fair share of barbecue, catfish, and fried chicken, as well as accomplished European cuisine, in mountain valleys and small-town cafes.

I've beheld a likeness of the Roman she-wolf nursing Romulus and Remus, donated to an embarrassed small town by Benito Mussolini, and best of all, I've met Georgia's proudest monument, her own people, in their natural habitat. A few grouches notwithstanding, they're warm, wise, witty, and when you wander off the beaten path, they'll be tickled to point you in some fascinating directions.

I hope you'll enjoy using this book half as much as I've enjoyed researching it. When you discover some off-the-beaten-path adventures that I've yet to come across, please let me know by writing to me c/o The Globe Pequot Press, P.O. Box 833, Old Saybrook, CT 06475.

Restaurant cost categories refer to the price of entrees without beverages, desserts, taxes, or tips. Those listed as inexpensive are $10 or less; moderate, between $10 and $15; and expensive, $20 and over.

The prices and rates listed in this guidebook were accurate at press time, but I recommend that you call establishments before traveling in order to obtain current information.

INTRODUCTION

Before you launch your Off the Beaten Path adventures, gather information from these sources: Georgia Tourist Division, P.O. Box 1776, Atlanta 30301, (404) 656–3590; and Georgia Department of Natural Resources, Parks and Historic Sites Division, 205 Butler Street, Suite 1352, Atlanta 30334. For general information call (800) 869–8420 from anywhere in the United States; in metro Atlanta call (404) 656–3530.

The Parks Division's new Reservation Resource lets you make one toll-free call for campsites, cottages, picnic shelters, and lodge rooms throughout the system. Rates vary at different parks. Campsites, with electrical and water hookups, range from $12 to $17 a night. Completely furnished cottages are $45 to $55 for one bedroom, $65 to $75 for two bedrooms, and $75 to $125 for three bedrooms. Rates are higher on weekends and in certain seasons. Double rooms at state park lodges are $55 to $75. In metro Atlanta call (770) 389–PARK; anywhere else in the United States call (800) 864–PARK.

If you're interested in a particular area, contact the local convention and visitors bureau or chamber of commerce.

Georgia: OBP Fact Box

State tourism toll-free phone number: (800) VISIT–GA

Major Newspapers:

Atlanta Journal-Constitution, Augusta Chronicle, Macon Telegraph, Savannah Morning News, Columbus Enquirer

Population:

Georgia has 7.1 million people, the tenth largest in the country.

Major metro areas:

Atlanta, 3.4 million	Augusta, 340,000
Savannah, 300,000	Macon, 225,000
Columbus, 250,000	

Size:

With 58,910 square miles, it is the largest state east of the Mississippi, twenty-first in the nation.

Famous People:

- 39th President Jimmy Carter
- Juliette Gordon Low, founder of the Girl Scouts
- Dr. Martin Luther King, Jr.
- *Gone With the Wind* author Margaret Mitchell
- Milledgeville novelist Flannery O'Connor
  (The Violent Bear It Away, Wise Blood)
- Columbus novelist Carson McCullers,
  (Member of the Wedding, The Heart Is a Lonely Hunter)
- Eatonton Pulitzer prize–winning novelist Alice Walker
  (The Color Purple)
- Eatonton folk story author and humorist Joel Chandler Harris
  (Uncle Remus: Tales)
- Moreland novelist Erskine Caldwell
  (God's Little Acre, Tobacco Road)

Popular performers Ray Charles, Lena Horne, Otis Redding, Little Richard Penniman, bandleader Harry James, opera superstar Jessye Norman, songwriter Johnny Mercer, comedian Oliver Hardy

- Danielsville's Dr. Crawford W. Long, who performed the world's first painless surgery with ether in 1842
- Baseball's "Georgia Peach" Ty Cobb, from Royston
- Actress Joanne Woodward, from Augusta
- Actor Burt Reynolds, born in Waycross
- Folk artist Howard Finster, from Summerville
- Western legend John "Doc" Holliday, born in Valdosta

Public Transportation:

Atlanta has a rapid rail and public bus system, called MARTA , for Metropolitan Atlanta Rapid Transit Authority. Other cities with public buses are Macon, Savannah, Augusta, Athens, and Columbus.

Reading for Kids:

Joel Chandler Harris's Uncle Remus Stories

Climate:

Summers are hot and humid, especially in the southern half of the state and the coast; spring is beautiful and balmy; winters are usually mild, with some snow accumulation in the northern mountains; fall, especially in the northern areas and the mountains, is brisk and cool, with colorful foliage.

Georgia Trivia:

Georgia has 159 counties, more than any other state except Texas (which is four times larger), and more than twice as many as almost-the-same-size Florida and Alabama. There'd be even more, but two counties went bankrupt in the 1920s and merged with Atlanta's Fulton County.

Elevations:

Georgia's highest point is Brasstown Bald Mountain, 4,784 feet above sea level; lowest point is sea level on the Atlantic coast.

Georgia's hottest recorded temperature was 113 degrees on May 27, 1978, at Greenville; the coldest was 17 degrees below zero in Floyd County (Rome) on January 27, 1940.

Interesting Information:

You can travel around the world and never leave Georgia. Towns include Vienna (called VIE-enna), Cairo (KAY-ro), Berlin, Boston, Bremen, Hamburg, Rome, Milan, Athens, Arabic, and Sparta. You can shop at Bloomingdale, and try to solve the secret of Enigma. Like Scarlett O'Hara, you'll never be hungry in Peach, Bacon, Baker, and Coffee Counties. Don't stub your toe on The Rock, and don't Bogart that joint, my friend.

Metro Atlanta

Atlanta and Fulton County

With a population of 3.4 million, metro Atlanta is one of the nation's fastest-growing urban centers. New suburbs with cookie-cutter subdivisions and shopping malls sprawl in all directions. Meanwhile, an energetic young population has been busily reviving many of the inner city's older neighborhoods. The 1996 Olympic Games also worked wonders with the city's downtown area. *Centennial Olympic Park* is the most visible souvenir of the Games. The twenty-one-acre park, at Marietta Street, Techwood Drive, and International Boulevard, got a complete makeover after the Games.

All the commercial exhibits and T-shirt vendors are gone, leaving an inviting open space where you can walk, sit in the sunshine, and admire downtown's striking skyline. If the weather's warm, shuck your shoes and splash in the park's Five Rings Fountain and perhaps look for your name on one of the 467,000 bricks that pave the park's walkways. The five Quilt Plazas, made of bricks and varied-colored marble, tell the story of the largest Games in Olympic history. One of the Quilt plazas honors victims of the bomb blast that briefly interrupted the Games. You can play a life-size chessboard and enjoy artworks that range from quirky to classical. Pick up free visitor information at the Atlanta Chamber of Commerce, on the edge of the park.

When you're ready for some quick eats, walk cross Marietta Street to the food court at Ted Turner's CNN Center. You can take the daily tour of the Cable News Network studios and see the news being broadcast around the world.

For a real taste of the South, go west a few blocks to Thelma's Kitchen, 764 Marietta Street, (404) 688–5855, and join working folk, suits, and Georgia Tech students in robust plates of like-your-mama-wishes-she-made-it fried chicken, meat loaf, pork chops, and an array of vegetables cooked Southern style. Lunch Monday through Friday.

The food court and sit-down restaurants in the Peachtree Center office building and hotel complex, on Peachtree Street between International Boulevard and Baker Street, have a wide selection of food to

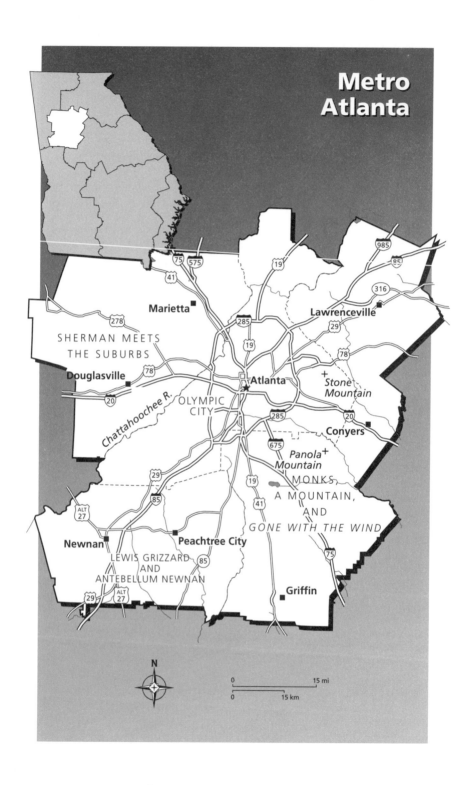

Metro Atlanta

Marietta

Lawrenceville

SHERMAN MEETS
THE SUBURBS

Douglasville

*Stone
Mountain*

Chattahoochee R.

OLYMPIC
CITY

Atlanta

Conyers

Panola
Mountain

MONKS

A MOUNTAIN,
AND

GONE WITH THE WIND

Newnan

Peachtree City

LEWIS GRIZZARD
AND
ANTEBELLUM NEWNAN

Griffin

N

0   15 mi

0   15 km

METRO ATLANTA'S TOP HITS

Centennial Olympic Park

SciTrek Science and
   Technology Museum

Ansley Park

Atlanta Botanical Garden

Piedmont Park

Atlanta History Center

Little Five Points

Zoo Atlanta

Georgia Governors Mansion

Chattahoochee River National
   Recreation Area

Chattahoochee Nature Center

Roswell

Atlanta Preservation Center

Oakland Cemetery

Wren's Nest

Center for Puppetry Arts

Herndon Home

International Boulevard

Michael C. Carlos Emory University
   Museum of Art and Archaeology

Fernbank Museum of Natural
   History/Fernbank Science Center

Stone Mountain Village

Norcross's Historic Old Town

Buford

Yellow River Wildlife Game Ranch

Sugar Hill Municipal Golf Course

Monastery of the
   Holy Ghost

Panola Mountain State
   Conservation Park

Antebellum and Victorian
   Newnan Driving Tour of Homes

Lewis Grizzard Museum

"The Little Manse"

The Buggy Shop Museum

Starr's Mill

Sweetwater Creek
   Conservation Park

Kennesaw Mountain National
   Battlefield Park

Big Shanty Museum

Marietta Town Square

Pickett's Mill Battlefield

go. You can also join the long lines to get into the Hard Rock Cafe and Planet Hollywood, which face each other across the Peachtree-International intersection.

If any inquiring minds are in your party, take them over to the *SciTrek Science and Technology Museum,* 395 Piedmont Avenue, (404) 522–5500, and let them explore 150 hands-on gadgets they can push, pull, stand on, climb into, and revolve around. Open Monday through Saturday 10:00 A.M. to 5:00 P.M. and Sunday noon to 5:00 P.M. Adults $7.50; ages 3 to17 and college students and senior citizens, $5.00.

North of downtown, the *Midtown neighborhood,* along Peachtree Street between Ponce de Leon Avenue and Sixteenth Street, is one of the city's liveliest and most eclectic areas. Straight and gay bars and dance clubs, restaurants of all sorts, shops and live theaters line Peachtree, Tenth and Juniper Streets, and Piedmont Avenue. The Woodruff Arts Center (home of the Atlanta Symphony Orchestra and Alliance Theater) and High Museum of Art (the city's major art exhibition complex) are on Peachtree between Fifteenth and Sixteenth Streets. For clues to what's hot and happening, pick up gay-oriented *Southern Voice and Etc.* and alternative weekly *Creative Loafing,* which is distributed free in street boxes, restaurants, shops, and the Friday Weekend Preview and Saturday Leisure sections of *The Atlanta Journal-Constitution.*

Ansley Park, a lovely neighborhood dating back to the 1920s, is a quiet place to walk, drive, or ride a bike. On Peachtree Street at the Woodruff Arts Center/Colony Square area, turn east onto Fifteenth Street and north onto Peachtree Circle and follow the meandering byways past sumptuous lawns and gardens skirting homes in a spectrum of styles. Stop for a picnic, a walk, or a giddy ride on a swing at Winn Park, at Peachtree Circle and Lafayette Drive. Follow a street called The Prado to Piedmont Avenue. Cross this busy street and you're at the **Atlanta Botanical Garden** (404–876–5859). Take your time strolling through thirty acres of formal gardens, rose gardens, a Japanese garden, and a fifteen-acre hardwood forest with a marked walking trail. Many state, regional, and national flower shows are held in the Day Building at the entrance. The Botanical Garden's centerpiece is the Dorothy Chapman Fuqua Conservatory, with 16,000 square feet of tropical, desert, Mediterranean, and endangered plants. There's also a gift shop and small restaurant. Open Tuesday through Sunday 9:00 A.M. to 7:00 P.M. Adults, $6.00; senior citizens and ages 6 to 12, $3.00; ages 5 and under, free.

After the Botanical Garden, wander into adjoining **Piedmont Park.** The city's largest park has tennis courts, a swimming pool, softball fields, playgrounds, and paved, auto-free roadways for jogging, hiking, biking, and rollerblading. In summer, the park's lawns and hillsides fill up with tanning bodies. You can rent skateboards, rollerblades, roller skates, and bikes at Skate Escape (404–892–1292), across from the park at 1086 Piedmont Avenue.

The *Virginia-Highland neighborhood,* about a mile and a half east of Piedmont Park, is one of the city's favorite dining, shopping, and entertainment areas. It's divided into three parts: From Ponce de Leon Avenue, a lively strip of restaurants, bars, coffee shops, and offbeat shops extends about 3 blocks north on North Highland Avenue; after a 3-block residential break, it comes back to life around the Virginia Avenue–North Highland Avenue corner; and after another residential break, you'll find more fun stuff at North Highland and Amsterdam Avenues and at another strip at North Highland and Morningside Drive.

METRO ATLANTA

The **Buckhead neighborhood,** off Peachtree Street/Road about 6 miles due north of downtown, has long been Atlanta's most splendid residential enclave. West of Peachtree Road, follow the green and white SCENIC DRIVE markers past Spanish and Italian villas, French chateaux, Old English Tudor homes, and white-columned Greek Revival, Georgian, and even Japanese-style showplaces that preside over immense lawns and great stands of trees and flowing shrubbery. Some of the most beautiful homes are on West Paces Ferry, Andrews, Habersham, Blackland, Valley, and Tuxedo Roads.

You'll have a better understanding of what makes Atlanta the kind of city it is after a day at the **Atlanta History Center** (404–814–4000). The tree-shaded, thirty-acre sanctuary at 3101 Andrews Drive includes three fascinating attractions: the insightful and very-well-done Museum of Atlanta History; the circa-1836 "plantation plain" Tullie Smith Farmstead; and the Swan House, an opulent Italian-Palladian villa, built in 1926 and appointed with European and Asian furnishings and set among formal gardens and terraced fountains. Open daily. Adults, $7.00; ages 65 and over and students 18 and over with ID, $5.00; ages 6 to 17, $4.00; ages 5 and under, free.

If you still pine for the flower-child days of the sixties or feel like dyeing your hair electric blue or orange and skateboarding on the sidewalk, **Little Five Points** is your kind of place. You can be totally mainstream and still enjoy an outing at this Southern-style East Village/Soho area. Around the intersection of Moreland and Euclid Avenues, across Ponce de Leon Avenue from Virginia-Highland and about 3 miles east of downtown, you'll find a cluster of good, inexpensive restaurants—Indian, Caribbean, Mexican, Italian, Cajun—coffee bars, bars with and without music, and funky shops selling vintage clothing, new and used CDs, and books on astrology, herbal medcine, and other esoteric subjects. Just like the good old days, street musicians perform for your pleasure and spare change.

TOP ANNUAL EVENTS

Southeastern Flower Show, mid-February, City Hall East, 640 North Avenue, (404) 888–5638

Conyers Cherry Blossom Festival, late March, Georgia International Horse Park, (770) 918–2169

Atlanta Dogwood Festival, early April, Piedmont Park, (404) 329–0501

Georgia Renaissance Festival, April and May, September and October, 7795 Spence Road, Fairburn, (770) 964–8575

Inman Park Spring Festival and Tour of Homes, Euclid and Edgewood Avenues, late April. No phone.

Stone Mountain Village Arts Festival, mid-June, Main Street, Stone Mountain, (770) 498–2097

Peachtree Road Race 10k, Peachtree Road–Peachtree Street, (404) 231–9064

Christmas at Bulloch Hall, throughout December, Roswell, (770) 992–1731

Christmas at Callanwolde, early to mid-December, Callanwolde Fine Arts Center, (404) 872–5338

We Like It Sweet

East Atlanta Village, off I–20 and Moreland Avenue about 10 minutes south of Little Five Points, is the latest given-up-for-dead old neighborhood to get the Lazarus treatment. Young entrepreneurs have turned vacant storefronts around the Flat Shoals Avenue–Glenwood Avenue intersection into kicky shops with unique and offbeat gifts, art, antiques, and imports. Many people come to the neighborhood just to sample the artistic burritos at Burrito Art, 1259 Glenwood Avenue, (404) 627–4433. Owner/chef Ryan Aiken's burritos are definitely not the same old enchilada. They come filled with meat loaf and jasmine rice, pork tenderloin, barbecued and jerk chicken, portobello mushrooms, black beans and rice, Thai curry, and other combinations. Lunch and dinner are served daily. A second location is at 1451 Oxford Road, (404) 377–7786, across from Emory University.

After polishing off your burrito, walk across to Sacred Grounds, 510 Flat Shoals Avenue, (404) 584–5541. The very urbane coffee and dessert shop started the Village's restoration movement. It's the unofficial "living room" for the area's young urban pioneers, who come here to get together, study, read, hang out, and listen to live music. Open daily.

Zoo Atlanta, in Grant Park, 800 Cherokee Avenue, (404) 624–5600, a few blocks from the Village and 3 miles from downtown, is a fun way to spend a day. The most popular area is the Ford African Rainforest, a natural habitat for families of silverback mountain gorillas. The King Kong of the hill is Willie B., who spent nearly thirty years in a solitary indoor cage before being freed in his new home. Now he's a proud papa several times over. Other habitats have big cats, giraffes, bears, birds, and reptiles. Open daily. Adults, $7.50; seniors, $6.50; ages 3 to 11, $5.50; 2 and under, no charge.

Also in Grant Park, the Cyclorama is a colossal painting in the round capturing a crucial hour in the Civil War Battle of Atlanta. Open daily. Phone (404) 656–7625. Adults, $6.00; seniors, $5.00; children, $3.00.

Atlanta has many other off-the-beaten-path attractions. Here are a few:

The *Georgia Governors Mansion* (404–261– 1776), near the Historical Society at 391 West Paces Ferry Road, receives visitors Tuesday through Thursday 10:00 to 11:30 A.M. Public rooms in this modern-day Greek

Bill's Favorites

Atlanta Botanical Garden

Virginia-Highland entertainment area

Little Five Points/East Atlanta Village

Chattahoochee River National Recreation Area

Decatur Square entertainment area

Stone Mountain Park

Old Norcross

Old Buford

Kennesaw Mountain National Battlefield Park

Revival mansion, built in the late 1960s, gleam with museum-quality Federal-period antiques and art. Tours are free.

Georgia's nineteenth-century poet Sidney Lanier sang the praises of the Chattahoochee River in his idyllic "Song of the Chattahoochee." The river rises in the north Georgia mountains and flows through metropolitan Atlanta on its way to the Gulf of Mexico.

The *Chattahoochee River National Recreation Area,* a 48-mile stretch of river and gentle rapids flowing between wooded palisades, is the focus for recreational pursuits of all sorts. From spring through fall, Atlantans love to set their rafts, canoes, and kayaks loose in the river for a lazy day of relaxation. Sturdy four-, six-, and eight-person rafts may be rented from Chattahoochee Outdoor Center, 1825 Northridge Road, (404) 395–6851. If rafting isn't your pleasure, you can also spread a picnic, hike, bike, jog, bird-watch, and exercise on the twenty-two-station fitness trail. The park's main entrance is at Highway 41 and the Chattahoochee River bridge. Contact the Park Superintendent, 1978 Island Ford Parkway, Atlanta 30336; (770) 952–4419.

The river's fauna and flora are celebrated at the *Chattahoochee Nature Center,* 9135 Willeo Road in Roswell, (770) 992–2055. The private, non-profit natural-science center's exhibits of plants and wildlife, special programs, and workshops are in a tranquil fifty-acre setting by the riverbanks, about 25 miles north of downtown Atlanta. Guided walks on Saturday and Sunday at noon and 2:00 P.M. weave through twenty acres of nature trails and a 1,400-foot boardwalk over the river. You can also pick up a brochure and take a self-guided tour. Make a full day of it with a picnic lunch. The center is open Monday through Saturday 9:00 A.M. to 5:00 P.M. and Sunday noon to 5:00 P.M. Admission for adults is $2.00; children and senior citizens, $1.00.

The public square and saltbox-style houses of *Roswell* mirror the Connecticut roots of founder Roswell King, who planned the town in the 1830s. Nowadays the handsome brick buildings, set around a typical New England green, house restaurants and specialty shops. Greek Revival–style *Bulloch Hall* was built in 1840 by Major James Stephens Bulloch. In 1853 the major's daughter, Mittie, married Theodore Roosevelt of New York in the mansion's parlor. Their son-in-law became twenty-sixth president of the United States. Guided tours are given daily (adults, $5.00; senior citizens and children ages 6 to 16, $3.00). Call (770) 992–1731.

Also stop at the **Roswell Historical Society,** 227 South Atlanta Street, (404) 992–1665, for information and a slide show about the town's heritage. Called Allenbrook, the society's saltbox-style headquarters was built in 1845 with brick walls that are 18 inches thick.

Downtown Atlanta's **Woodruff Park** doesn't have a lot of greenery, but on weekdays this open space at Peachtree, Marietta, and Decatur Streets is an A-1 people-watching location. At weekday lunch, the benches and small patches of grass fill up with Georgia State University students, office workers, street preachers, politicians, freelance musicians, and entertainers. Pick up a sack lunch at one of the numerous eateries around the park and sit back and watch the water wall and fountain at the north end of the park. "Phoenix Rising," the large bronze sculpture at the park's south end, symbolizes Atlanta's rebirth after its Civil War destruction.

Gone With the Wind fans may want to see the memorabilia of the movie and book in the **Margaret Mitchell Collection** at the Atlanta Public Library, downtown at Carnegie Way and Forsyth and Peachtree Streets (404–577–6940). The movie made its gala 1939 world premiere across

Get a Bike

*W*ith its varied topography and hundreds of miles of marked and unmarked trails, scenic state parks, and historic sites, Georgia is an ideal place to get on a bike and enjoy a day, a few days, or a week in the countryside. If you're in for a workout, try pedaling through north Georgia's mountains. Or maybe the flatlands of south Georgia and the beaches and forests of the barrier islands suit you best.

If you'd like to join an organized ride, contact the Georgia Bicycle Federation, (770) 422–4840, Web site www.serve.com/bike/georgia. The Southern Bicycle League organizes

about 1,000 yearly rides in Metro Atlanta. Phone (770) 594–8350, Web site www.bikesbl.org. Also, the Southern Off-Road Bicycle Association, (770) 565–1732, Web site www.sorba.org. Atlanta's Stone Mountain Park, (770) 498–5600, and Callaway Gardens at Pine Mountain, (800) 225–5292, have marked trails, splendid scenery, and rental bikes. At Georgia International Horse Park in Conyers (Metro Atlanta), you can bike the same rugged route as the 1996 Olympic mountain bike contenders. Phone (800) 266–9377.

the street at Loew's Grand Theatre, where the Georgia-Pacific sky-scraper now rises.

One of the most interesting ways to delve into the city's history is on a tour led by the **Atlanta Preservation Center** (404–876–2040). The center's half-dozen walking tours from April through October focus on the city's architectural and cultural heritage. The Fox Theatre tour takes you backstage at one of America's last surviving 1920s "picture palaces." Adorned with minarets, Moorish arches, Egyptian hieroglyphics, and a blue-sky ceiling that twinkles with electric stars, the Fox (404–881–2100) hosts a full schedule of touring musicals, concerts of all sorts, and a summertime classic movie festival. It's at 660 Peachtree Street at Ponce de Leon Avenue.

MARTA, the Metropolitan Atlanta Rapid Transit Authority, is an up-to-date way to get around the city. The clean, two-line rapid rail system intersects at Five Points Station downtown and is a swift way of getting to the **Woodruff Arts Center/High Museum of Art** and other attractions. The MARTA bus system is a more comprehensive but much slower way of getting about. Fare for both is $1.50 one way, including transfers; for information call (404) 522–4711.

Oakland Cemetery, 248 Oakland Avenue at Memorial Drive, is a book on Atlanta's past, right behind the ultramodern King Memorial MARTA Station. Established in 1850, Oakland has redbrick walls that enclose a wealth of architectural and cultural heritage. Here is buried *Gone With the Wind* author Margaret Mitchell, struck down by a taxi on her beloved Peachtree Street in 1949. Victorian aristocrats are entombed in templelike mausoleums, embellished with stained glass, gargoyles, and marble busts. You may walk through Confederate and Jewish sections, see the graves of the city's firstborn child and other celebrities, and spread a picnic lunch under the magnolia trees. Open daily. Free tours are conducted on weekends.

A MARTA train to West End Station and a bus connection or 3-block walk will bring you to the **Wren's Nest,** the Victorian home of Joel Chandler Harris, creator of Br'er Rabbit, Br'er Fox, the Tar Baby, and other delightful critters who roam through his 1880s book, *Uncle Remus: His Songs & His Sayings*. Rooms are filled with furnishings and mementos of Harris and his family, editions of his book in many languages, and re-creations of his beloved characters. The house got its name when a mother wren decided that Harris's wooden mailbox would be perfect for her brood. The mailbox now has an honored place among the Wren's Nest's treasures. Especially if you have children, try to

The Wren's Nest

visit when storytelling sessions are scheduled— usually the last Saturday of the month and daily during the summer. Wren's Nest, at 1050 Ralph David Abernathy Boulevard, (404) 753–7735, is open Tuesday through Saturday 10:00 A.M. to 4:00 P.M. and Sunday 1:00 to 4:00 P.M. Adults, $4.00; senior citizens and teens, $3.00; ages 4 to 12, $2.00.

Children, as well as adults, will enjoy the **Center for Puppetry Arts** (404–873–3391), on the northern edge of downtown at 1404 Spring Street. The converted redbrick school building houses a fascinating puppetry museum and puts on a year-round program of puppet theatricals, some aimed at youngsters, others tailored for adults.

West of downtown, **Herndon Home,** at 587 University Place, is a landmark of Black achievement. The dignified Beaux Art–style mansion was built in 1915 by Alonzo Herndon, a former slave who founded Atlanta Life Insurance Company, the nation's largest Black-owned insurance firm. The fifteen rooms showcase his remarkable life. Most of the antique furnishings and family photos are original. The Herndon Home is open Tuesday through Saturday 1:00 to 4:00 P.M. Free admission. For more information call (404) 581–9813.

With a population of 550,000 DeKalb County is the metro area's second most populous. You'll find many off-the-beaten-path attractions among the county's busy streets and freeways, shopping malls, and subdivisions.

There's an **International Boulevard** in downtown Atlanta, but the metro area's real "international" boulevard is Buford Highway (Highway 23). A 10-mile stretch of multilane urban roadway from Lenox Road in the city of Atlanta north through the DeKalb towns of Chamblee and Doraville to Jimmy Carter Boulevard in Gwinnett County is lined with more than 700 businesses and services run by Asian and Hispanic immigrants. Since the early 1980s, old strip shopping centers and newly built malls have filled up with supermarkets where shoppers come from around the Southeast for Korean, Thai, Chinese, Vietnamese,

Caribbean, Mexican, Central American, and South American produce, seafood, rice, spices, and other staples.

Dozens of restaurants offer a selection of authentic cuisines you might expect to find only in Seoul, Bangkok, Saigon, and Lima (or in Los Angeles, San Francisco, or New York). Some of the major hubs include Orient Mall, a revamped outlet mall at the busy Buford Highway–Clairmont Road intersection, where you can explore the exotic wares in the cavernous Hong Kong Supermarket and visit speciality shops and several restaurants. Pho 79, a storefront Vietnamese eatery, serves a variety of pho—hearty soups with beef, pork, and seafood—while you watch Asian music videos on a TV screen; (404) 728–9129.

Further north, Asian Square, 5150 Buford Highway, is anchored by the mammoth Ranch 99 supermarket stocked with Asian and Hispanic goods and about a dozen Taiwanese, Malaysian, Chinese, and Vietnamese restaurants. Asiana Garden (770–452–1677) has Korean and Japanese food and a sushi bar; Little Malaysia (770–458–1818), Malaysian and Singaporean noodle and rice dishes, curries, and seafood. You can also find jewelry, books, videos, clothes, toys, and gifts as well as an Asian bank, accountants, and other services. Atlanta World Journal Chinese Bookstore stocks bilingual Chinese and English books, Chinese newspapers and magazines, Sesame Street workbooks, greeting cards, CDs and tapes, even Chinese editions of *Playboy* and *Penthouse*.

While you're in northeast DeKalb, you can explore an assortment of antiques shops and flea markets around the Peachtree Road–Broad

Where's the Olympic Stadium?

*I*f you'd like to visit Atlanta's Olympic Stadium, you'll have to attend an Atlanta Braves baseball game at Turner Field. The stadium where 1996 Summer Games opening and closing ceremonies and track and field events were held was ingeniously constructed so that about half of the 85,000 seats could be easily taken out after the games and the stadium converted to a new high-tech 50,000-seat home for the Braves. If you get bored with the game, the stadium has plenty of other bells and whistles. You can play a host of virtual reality games or Nintendo, shop, visit the Braves Museum, and have dinner and drinks in food courts and the centerfield restaurant and bar.

TV screens all over the place let you enjoy the game just as you would in the comfort of your own living room. It was renamed for Braves owner Ted Turner, whose TBS Superstation puts the Braves in living rooms from coast to coast.

Street Junction in "old" downtown Chamblee. You're bound to find something you can't resist at Moosebreath Trading Company (770–455–0518), Broad Street Antique Mall (770–458–6316), and Whipporwill Co. (770–455–8357).

Since the Olympics, Decatur, the DeKalb County seat, has enjoyed an ongoing renaissance. Vacant storefronts on Court Square, across from the historic county courthouse, are now filled with upbeat restaurants, taverns, coffeehouses, and shops.

In a cul-de-sac, off main-stem East Ponce de Leon Avenue, there is a choice of these popular eateries. You'll probably have to wait for a table on weekends. In warm weather, you can sit at outdoor tables that line the sidewalks. Restaurants are right outside the Decatur MARTA rail station, about a fifteen-minute ride from downtown Atlanta. On summer Saturday nights, Decaturites spread blankets and picnic suppers on the courthouse lawn and enjoy live music playing in the bandstand.

Emory University's **Michael C. Carlos Emory University Museum of Art and Archaeology** (404–727–4282) holds a trove of antiquities from around the world. Treasures in this beautifully planned building on the Emory Quadrangle include Greek and Roman coins, statuary, and amphorae; an Egyptian mummy with a gilded face; and European, pre-Columbian, and Asian art objects. Floors are inlaid with diagrams of ancient temples and palaces. Special exhibitions are held regularly. A $3.00 donation is requested. Open Tuesday through Saturday 11:00 A.M. to 4:30 P.M. The museum is near the university's main entrance at North Decatur and Oxford Roads. On-campus paid parking is available.

Across from the campus on North Decatur and Oxford Roads, you'll find a row of popular student-oriented eateries, including Everybody's Pizza, Jaggers, Caribou Coffee, Starbucks, Go-Go Gumbo, and Burrito Art. If you're into vegetarian and organic foods, hie on up to Rainbow Grocery, North Decatur Plaza, 2118 North Decatur Road, (404) 636– 5553. The compact little store stocks organic and nonorganic fruits and vegetables, cheese, frozen food, bread and other staples, and herbal vitamins. Help yourself to the salad bar and carryout sandwiches, desserts, and prepared dinners. The cafe in the rear of the store serves delicious vegetarian burritos, lasagna, chili, sandwiches, and soups. Open daily.

Two bed-and-breakfast inns are close to the campus. The 1223 at Emory, 1223 Clifton Road, Atlanta 30307, (404) 377–4987, fax (404) 377–8036, e-mail bbemory1@aol.com, is a four–guest room Colonial Revival home, built in 1925, in the Druid Hills National Register Historic District, adjacent to the campus and the National Center for Disease Control (CDC). Some rooms have a shared bath. All rooms have a TV and phone. Guests can relax in owner Dennis Pitters's large back garden. Reservations only, no walk-ins. Rates are $70 to $100.

Houston Mill House, 849 Houston Mill Road, Atlanta 30329, (404) 727–7878, fax (404) 727–4032, is an historic fieldstone home in a peaceful garden setting, a short walk from the Emory campus, hospitals, and the CDC. One suite has twin beds, the other a queen-size bed. Both have a TV, fridge, and full bath. Breakfast comes with the $75 rate.

Whatta you do on a rainy day in Atlanta? Rain or shine, you could spend all of it at the *Fernbank Museum of Natural History* and the companion *Fernbank Science Center.* The museum's attractions include the hands-on "Walk though Time in Georgia" and "The Maurer World of Shells and Living Coral Reef Exhibits," children's discovery rooms, lifelike dinosaurs, and an IMAX Theater. They are located at 767 Clifton Road between downtown Atlanta and Decatur. The museum is open Monday though Friday 10:00 A.M. to 9:00 P.M. and Saturday and Sunday noon to 5:00 P.M. Adults, $8.95; students and senior citizens, $7.95; ages 3 to 12, $6.95. IMAX Theater: adults, $6.95; students and seniors, $5.95; ages 3 to 12, $4.95. Combination museum-IMAX: adults, $13.95; students and seniors, $11.95; ages 3 to 12, $9.95.

Fernbank Science Center, in a sixty-five-acre hardwood and pine forest threaded with walking trails, has a 500-seat planetarium offering sea-

Nose-to-Nose with Bobby Lee

I'm one of the few people who's actually been close enough to touch the monumental sculpture on the face of Stone Mountain. When the 90-foot-high-by-190-foot-long carving of Jefferson Davis, Robert E. Lee, and Stonewall Jackson was nearly completed in 1970, politicians, VIPs, and news media were invited to a fried-chicken lunch on the scaffolding in front of the figures, which are about halfway up the sheer side of the 825-foot-high, 6-miles-in-circumference chunk of granite. The event commemorated a similar fund-raising lunch during the first attempt at creating the Confederate memorial in the 1920s. I don't remember anything about the fried chicken, except feeling queasy at the thought of it. I do remember the awe at actually standing nose-to-nose with the carving and thinking how fine the workmanship was, even at such close range. I only regret not getting a picture of myself standing up there next to Jeff Davis, Stonewall, and Bobby Lee.

sonal looks at the heavens. You can also look at far-flung galaxies through the Southeast's largest telescope. Other exhibits focus on Georgia's varied plant and animal life. Open daily, charges only for planetarium shows: $2.00 for adults and $1.00 for students. Located at 156 Heaton Park Drive, (404) 378–4311.

A granite monolith 825 feet high and 6 miles around, with numerous attractions and six million visitors yearly, is hardly off the beaten path. However, many Stone Mountain Park visitors miss *Stone Mountain Village*. Outside the park's gates, the Village's nineteenth-century Main Street is flanked by covered sidewalks and 3 blocks of stores stocked with vintage books, arts and crafts, Civil War artifacts, antiques, geodes, apparel, jewelry, and oddities. You can get a haircut in an old-fashioned barber shop and buy an ice cream, a sandwich, or a full meal at several cafes and restaurants.

If you love to rummage through old bookstores, lose yourself in the crowded aisles of *Memorable Books,* 5380 Manor Drive, (404) 469–5911, a few steps off Main Street. Shelves are stacked to the ceiling with books on Americana, Georgia, and the South. You can also find scholarly books and books on cooking, gardening, medicine, the military . . . you want it, chances are it's in here somewhere, and the owner will know exactly where to find it. Next door to the bookstore, ART Station Scene Shop, (404) 498–3870, exhibits paintings, sculpture, and other works by local and regional artists.

Monks, a Mountain, and Gone With the Wind

ike other Metro Atlanta counties, Gwinnett (population about 400,000) has grown so rapidly the past twenty-five years, it seems to be one vast, unbroken lansdcape of mammoth shopping malls, subdivisions, and apartment complexes. But if you peek behind the "new" Gwinnett, you'll find that many of its old towns and cities have become walkable havens with unique shops, restaurants, and art galleries.

Norcross's Historic Old Town is a pleasant throwback to yesteryear a few minutes off traffic-crazy I-85 and Jimmy Carter Boulevard. Take North Norcross-Tucker Road off Jimmy Carter and follow the HISTORIC NORCROSS signs to South Peachtree Street. Antiques and gift shops include Taste of Britain, (770) 242–8585, with imported teas, biscuits, jams, china, and gifts; and Old Norcross Antiques Market, (770) 840–7740. There are also an old-fashioned barber shop, a vintage hardware store, and other small businesses in the well-preserved nineteenth-century buildings grouped around the old wooden train depot.

For more than a century, the small north Gwinnett County town of **Buford** was Georgia's leather-making capital. Leather processed at the town's large Bona Allen tannery was turned into shoes and saddles that were then sold all over the world. When the tannery closed in 1981, most of the businesses on Main Street were forced to close. But thanks to an enterprising small army of artists, Main Street has come back to life. About twenty-five art, antiques, gift, apparel, and other shops now occupy the historic nineteenth-century mercantile buildings. Take I–85/985 to Highway 20 and follow South Lee Street to Main Street.

Stop first at A.R. Wood Studio, 37 Main Street, (770) 945–1660. Randy Wood and Sandy Sumner pioneered the revival when they opened their studio in 1986. The gallery also has a historical museum where you can find out about Buford's leather industry and see many of the beautiful saddles that were made there. Strolling down the block, stop and chat with April Fields and Holly Gray at the Open Windows art/gift/home accessories shop, (770) 614–1422; Allen Rogers at Main

Carter Custard

*M*argaret Lupo, who presided with grace and classic Southern charm over Mary Mac's Tea Room in Midtown Atlanta for more than three decades, died in 1998. Renowned as Atlanta's "Queen of Greens" and "Grande Dame of Yeast Rolls and Sweet Tea," Mrs. Lupo was a perfectionist who treated her guests like royalty and put the fear of God in surly servers and cooks who oversalted the green beans. She added a bar in 1964, explaining that, "A lot of little old ladies enjoy a Manhattan before dinner, unless their preacher's sitting at the next table." Preachers found comfort in her fried okra, country fried steak, and smothered chicken. So did politicians like Jimmy Carter, whom she immortalized with the peanut custard named for him.

Beat together 6 ounces room temperature cream cheese, ¾ cup milk, ½ cup peanut butter, and 1 cup confectioners sugar.

Beat in a separate bowl 1 cup whipping cream and fold very gently into the cheese mixture.

To make the pie crust, mix in a bowl 1½ cups graham cracker crumbs, ¾ cup sugar, and 6 tablespoons melted butter. Pat mixture on bottom and sides of a 9-inch pie plate. Pour the custard onto the graham cracker crust. Top with chopped dry roasted peanuts to cover. Freeze the custard and serve.

Mary, Mary

Since the late 1980s, thousands have flocked to the Rockdale County farm where Nancy Fowler claims to have visitations from the Virgin Mary. Skeptics have responded with this bumper sticker: COME TO CONYERS, GA.— EAT, DRINK, AND SEE MARY.

Street Gallery, (770) 945–9718; and Donna Patrick at Gallery of Fine Wood, (770) 271–3300, who offers art objects and furniture beautifully crafted by thirty-five local artists. Stop for lunch at The Main Street Gourmet, (770) 271–0537, a sunny room splashed with modern art, and lunch on contemporary sandwiches, salads, soups, and light plates Monday through Saturday. "Artrageous" is a festive open house the second Saturday and Sunday of every month. Main Street shops have extended hours—the only time most are open on Sunday— and there's always a seasonal theme.

Yellow River Wildlife Game Ranch is a peaceful place in the woods in the midst of south Gwinnett County's suburban explosion. Just off very busy Highway 78, 3 miles east of Stone Mountain Park, the twenty-four-acre privately owned nature preserve is home for dozens of free-roaming brown deer, huggable bunnies, goats, sheep, coyotes, ducks and geese, pigs and porcupines, foxes, wolves, donkeys, a skunk named William T. Sherman, and a spring-forecasting groundhog named Robert E. Lee.

Deer are Yellow River's self-appointed reception committee. You're no sooner on the tree-shaded walking trail than whole families of gentle does, bucks, and fawns are ambling up for handouts of bread and crackers and a scratch behind the ears. During summer, fragile newborn fawns are an especially appealing sight. Lambs, piglets, baby ducks, and goat kids are also very much in the spotlight.

Small children get a kick out of the Bunnie Burrows, an enclosed area where rabbits of all sizes and colors seem to enjoy being petted and hand-fed raw carrots and celery.

What's purportedly the largest herd of American buffalo east of the Mississippi roams a back meadow. Black bears, bobcats, mountain lions, foxes, and wolves are secured in open-air enclosures, out of the reach of little fingers. If you spread a picnic lunch in a grove by the Yellow River, expect some "deer" friends to drop by for a treat.

You may reserve Yellow River's *Birthday House* for your youngster's special day or for a family reunion or other group activity. Yellow River Wildlife Game Ranch, at 4525 I–78 in Lilburn, (770) 972–6643, is open daily 9:30 A.M. to 5:00 P.M. Admission for adults is $6.00; ages 3 to 11, $5.00; 2 and under, no charge.

The *Sugar Hill Municipal Golf Course* (8 miles north of the Suwanee exit off I–85), (770–271–0519), is a sweet layout for those who'd like to play like the pros but have an amateur's budget. Spread over 300 acres at the north Gwinnett County town of Sugar Hill, the well-maintained par-72, 18-hole course offers plenty of challenges as it swoops up and down hills and around six lakes and forty-five traps.

Amid the burgeoning suburbs of Rockdale County, a short drive off the busy lanes of I–20, about 25 miles east of downtown Atlanta, the *Monastery of the Holy Ghost* is a place of inordinate peacefulness. Since the late 1940s, Benedictine Trappist monks have dwelt and prayed in this cloistered sanctuary at 2625 Highway 212 in Conyers, (770) 483–8705. The Spanish Gothic–style buildings, even the stained glass in the main church, are all products of their labors.

Men and women may attend Sunday morning mass in the church, which is highlighted by the monks' chants and prayers. Men may make retreats at the modern guest house nearby. A small shop sells bread, cheese, jam, religious items, and produce and herbs grown in the monastery's fields. You may also bring a picnic lunch to tables that sit by a lake beside the cloister.

The abbey does not observe a strict rule of silence, and most monks may converse with visitors.

Just east of Conyers on I–20 is Covington in Newton County. Fans of TV's *In the Heat of the Night* will recognize many of the show's locations around the *Covington* courthouse square. Many beautiful white-columned homes are on the tree-shaded streets radiating from the square.

You'll also find a trove of antebellum treasures around nearby Oxford College of Emory University, which welcomed its first freshman class in 1839.

Twenty miles southeast of downtown Atlanta, via Highway 155, *Panola Mountain State Conservation Park* is a peaceful 585-acre day-use park where you may have a walk in the woods, enjoy a picnic, and wonder at a 100-acre granite outcropping that's been part of the Henry County landscape for about a million years. The lichen-covered monadnock is part of a major belt of granite, most dramatically evidenced by Stone Mountain, a few miles away.

Stop first at the park's Nature Center for information on trails leading through the woodlands and around the mountain. Meandering through hardwood and pine forests, the 1¼-mile Microwatershed Trail is a moderately strenuous course. Several stations along the way have benches and markers describing the park's fauna and flora. At the base of Panola Mountain, a three-acre pond is alive with turtles, frogs, fish, and small reptiles.

The ¾-mile Rock Outcrop Trail takes you through the woods to an overlook on one of the mountain's major outcroppings. On Saturday and Sunday afternoons, park naturalists conduct walks and give talks at the small amphitheater close to the Nature Center. Picnic tables are located near rest rooms and soft drink machines. Pets on leashes may be walked in the picnic area but aren't allowed on the nature trails.

The park is open daily from 8:00 A.M. to sundown. There is a $2.00 parking fee. Contact the superintendent, Stockbridge 30281, (770) 389–7801.

South of the park, via Highway 155, you'll find small cafes and shops around the pretty little courthouse square in **McDonough.** On the third Saturday of May, the Geranium Festival fills the square with arts, crafts, and entertainment. The popular Indian Springs State Park is a short drive south of McDonough.

Bargain lovers should put the Spalding County seat of **Griffin** high on their shopping lists. The textile town of 20,000, on Highways 19/41, 40 miles south of Atlanta, has some especially tempting values in towels and socks.

Dundee Direct Bath, Bed, and Baby Shop (770–227–4165) is an attractive, modern outlet for Springs/Dundee Corporation's products. First-run and irregular bath, bed, and baby products are available in a big variety of styles, colors, and fabrics at prices much lower than you'll find at retail stores. The shop, at 1440 North Expressway, Griffin 30223, is open Monday through Saturday 9:00 A.M. to 6:00 P.M. Major credit cards are accepted.

Spalding Hosiery Shoppe (770–227–4362) has the answer to virtually all your hosiery needs. Aisles are jammed with colorful argyles, athletic socks, dress socks, heavy-duty work socks, as well as pantyhose, sweatshirts, and other items made by major manufacturers. Irregulars, with all but impossible to discern blemishes, go for at least half the price you'd normally pay. First-run items are more expensive, but still very much a bargain. It's open Monday through Saturday 8:30 A.M. to 5:30 P.M. No credit cards accepted. On East Broad Street, across from the redbrick Spalding Mills, a block from the center of town.

You can sleep in antebellum history at two unique Griffin area bed-and-breakfasts. **Double Cabins Plantation,** a Doric-columned 1842 Greek Revival home lived in by seven generations of builder Shateen Mitchell's descendants, is set among gardens, old trees, and pre–Civil War outbuildings. Three guest rooms in the main house have many original furnishings and period pieces. Two have private baths. Rates are $55 for a double, including full breakfast. Group tours are available. Contact Mrs. Douglas Holberg, 3335 Jackson Road (Highway 155), Griffin 30223, (770) 227–6611.

Buckhead, Atlanta's most affluent, most fashionable neighborhood, owes its unique name to an early settler. In 1838, Henry Irby paid a few dollars for a small piece of wilderness near the modern-day intersection of Peachtree, Roswell, and West Paces Ferry Roads. He put up a tavern and a general store that became a meeting place for farmers, hunters, and tradesmen. One day while hunting in the dense woods, he shot a buck, posted the deer's impressive head on his door, and christened the establishment The Buck's Head Tavern. In time, the tavern gave its name to the entire neighborhood. Irby Avenue remembers the founding father.

Inn Scarlett's Footsteps, at 40 Old Flat Shoals Road, Concord 30206, (770) 884–9010 and (800) 886–7355, is a must for *Gone With the Wind* fans. Innkeepers K. C. and Vern Bassham, former Ohioans, have turned a majestic white-columned mansion, a "Twelve Oaks" lookalike, into a nostalgic trip through the novel and the movie. Ten bedrooms are named for Scarlett, Rhett, Melanie, Ashley, and Gerald. Each has appropriate decor and a private bath. The Museum Room displays thousands of pieces of GWTW memorabilia collected by the Basshams. Rates are $79 to $125 for a double, including full Southern breakfast. Group tours are by appointment at $5.00 a person.

Lewis Grizzard and Antebellum Newnan

oweta and Fayette Counties, on metro Atlanta's southwest periphery, are perfect for a one-day getaway from the big city, and they have more than enough to keep you happily occupied for much longer than that.

Take I–85 exit 9, 40 miles south of Atlanta, and follow Bullsboro Drive/Highway 34 into downtown Newnan. First stop at the Coweta County Welcome Center, 100 Walt Sanders Memorial Drive, Newnan, 1 mile off I–83, exit 9. Phone (800) 8–COWETA. They'll fill you in on every place to see, do, eat, and sleep in and around the city of 15,000. Be sure to pick up an *Antebellum and Victorian Newnan Driving Tour of Homes* guide, which describes twenty-three pre–Civil War landmarks. Many of the homes welcome visitors during the annual *Tour of Homes and Arts and Crafts Show* the third week of April. Before your driving tour, park around the majestic old courthouse in the center of the square and browse the many antiques, gift, and bookshops that lure locals away from the ubiquitous malls on the outskirts. The Alamo Gift Shop used to be Newnan's first-run movie house. Owner Elizabeth Crain spent many childhood hours in the old theater, and she's left the Alamo's stage and balcony for old-time's sake. If you're addicted to hot stuff—and consider no meal is fit to eat until it's doused with liquid fire—stop by **The Redneck Gourmet and Deli** (770-251-0092). Their array of hot sauces includes some so ferocious they come equipped with an eyedropper. At lunchtime downtown workers line up at the lunch counter for the Redneck's nonlethal hot and cold sandwiches, salads, and soups. You can pour your own "poison" from the selection on the counter.

If you're a fan of the late syndicated humor columnist Lewis Grizzard—a Coweta native son—you'll find all his books and tapes at **Scott's Books,** (770) 253–2960. Owner Earlene Scott was a close friend of Grizzard's, and she's always happy to share her memories. A Grizzard museum, described below, is in the small community of Moreland, south of Newnan.

Male Academy Museum, 30 Temple Avenue, Newnan, (770) 251–0207, is a must for Civil War enthusiasts. The historic school building displays a major collection of uniforms, weapons, artifacts, and soldiers' personal effects. Also clothing, furniture, and photographs from the mid-nineteenth to the early twentieth centuries and an 1890s classroom. Open Tuesday through Thursday 10:00 A.M. to 3:00 P.M. and Saturday and Sunday 2:00 to 5:00 P.M. Adults, $2.00; children 12 and under, free.

The late syndicated humor columnist Lewis Grizzard wrote fondly about growing up in tiny Moreland (population 450), on Highway 29 a few minutes south of Newnan. In appreciation, townsfolk have opened **The Lewis Grizzard Museum** (770-304-1490). In a turn-of-the-century doctor's office, the small museum displays his many books, photos, battered manual typewriters, and memorabilia. If you're a true fan, be here the first Saturday of April when thousands of his friends and fans come for the Annual Lewis Grizzard Storytelling and Barbecue. The museum is open Saturday and Sunday. Other times, Bill Myatt, who runs the gift shop next door, will let you in. Adults, $2.00; ages 6 to 12, $1.00.

Just across a small park, Coweta Countians have restored **"The Little Manse,"** birthplace of novelist Erskine Caldwell. The author of *God's Little Acre* and *Tobacco Road* was born in "The Manse" in 1903 when his father was a Presbyterian pastor here. The family left when Caldwell was five years old, and he never lived here as an adult. But the simple frame house is very much as he knew it. Biographical exhibits, personal items, copies of his books in several languages, and a video trace the career of the author, who died in 1987. The house is open 1:00 to 4:00 P.M. Saturday and Sunday and by appointment. Adults, $2.00, ages 6 to 12, $1.00. Call Winston Skinner at (770) 254–8657 for more information. You can go directly to Moreland from I–85 exit 8 and driving south on Highway 29.

Catalpa Plantation and Herb Farm, 2295 Old Poplar Road, Newnan 30263, is the closest antebellum plantation to Atlanta still on its original site. Built between 1835 and 1840, the Federal-Vernacular–style main house commanded 1,000 acres of cotton fields. Authentically restored by Rod and Renae Smith and furnished with period antiques, the mansion is open for tours by appointment. Renae's Herb Shop, adjacent to the house, sells dried aromatic herbs, fresh culinary herbs, seasonal wreaths, antiques, books, vinegars, and other gifts. Call (770) 253–3806 for mansion tours and Herb Shop hours.

Senoia, a drowsy little Coweta County town on Highway 85, 40 miles south of Atlanta, is like a delightful trip through Norman Rockwell–land. As you're strolling down Main Street, townsfolk smile and inquire politely about your family and your health.

The Buggy Shop Museum (770–599–1222), on Senoia's 1-block Main Street, was originally a collection of old-time memorabilia assembled by the late James Baggarly, Sr. Since "Mr. Jim's" death, his

I'll Have a Co-coler

F or millions of people around the world, Atlanta is synonymous with Coca-Cola. The soft drink was created in a Peachtree Street pharmacy in 1886. Dr. John S. Pemberton, originally from Columbus, Georgia, was seeking a nonalcoholic cure for the common headache. He blended coca leaves, African kola nuts, and other ingredients into an elixir he called Coca-Cola. It was first sold as a heavy syrup, diluted with water. But one day the clerk substituted soda water for tap water, and voila!, Coke was on its way around the world.

Headquartered in Atlanta, and sold in virtually every corner of the globe, its formula is a closely guarded secret. If you visit the World of Coca-Cola, a colorful three-story museum near the Georgia State Capitol, (404) 676–5151, you can see videos and films on Coke's history as well as hundreds of exhibits and souvenir items, and enjoy free samples of Coke and soft drinks the company makes for specialized markets around the world. It's open for self-guided tours Monday through Saturday 9:00 A.M. to 6:00 P.M., Sunday 11:00 A.M. to 6:00 P.M. Adults, $6.00; ages 55 and over, $5.00; ages 12 to college, $4.00; ages 6 to 11, $3.00.

son, Walter Baggarly, has refurbished an early 1900s Coca-Cola bottling plant and given it a new name. The eclectic horde includes nineteenth-century buggies and wagons, a 1925 Model A Ford James Baggarly drove on his rural postal route, a working Edison record player, Native American arrowheads, vintage farm implements, early Coca-Cola bottles and signs, a player piano, an early 1900s gasoline pump, and many, many other nostalgic treasures. It's open Saturday 10:00 A.M. to 6:00 P.M. and Sunday 1:00 to 6:00 P.M. Donations are welcome.

Also on Main Street, **Hutchinson Hardware** is another revered Senoia institution of long standing. Painted bright blue, with a parade of tall arched windows and doors, the building started out as a Ford dealership in the 1920s and became a hardware store early in World War II, when the Hutchinson's supply of Fords went dry. The aisles are stacked with anything you'd want for fishing, hunting, canning, serious farming and hobby gardening, or building a house or barn and keeping them in proper order. Owner Jimmy Hutchinson is used to hearing townspeople say: "I know what I need is in here somewhere" and "If Hutchinson ain't got it, I don't need it."

Senoia has two beguiling places to spend the night. The **Culpepper House** dates back to 1871, when it was built by Dr. John Addy, a returning Civil War veteran. Innkeepers Maggie Armstrong and Barbara Storm have three guest rooms with private baths and furnished with Victorian antiques. Public areas shine with gingerbread trim, stained glass, and pocket doors. A full Southern breakfast is included in the $85 rate for a double with private or shared bath. Write to 35 Broad Street, Senoia 30276, or call (770) 599–8182.

The **Veranda Inn** (770–599–3905), built as a hotel at the turn of the century, was one of the first places hereabouts to be electrified. Now operated by Bobby and Jan Boal, the Veranda sleeps up to sixteen guests in rooms blessedly free of televisions and telephones. For entertainment, guests step onto the spacious front veranda and avail themselves of rocking chairs and a porch swing. A double room with private bath is $99 to $150 and comes with a whopping big Southern breakfast. The mailing address is The Veranda, Box 177, Senoia 30276–0177.

Four miles north of Senoia, at the junction of Highways 85 and 74, stands **Starr's Mill,** one of Georgia's most photographed landmarks. One look at the 200-year-old red frame mill, by a pond and waterfall, and you'll be rushing for your camera, too. When you go, be sure to bring along a blanket and picnic.

Melear's (770–461–7180), on Highway 85 at Fayetteville's southern limits, has been serving delicious barbecue and Brunswick stew for more than thirty years. A big plateful costs under $6.00. During the short wait, amuse yourselves with the owner's collection of pig pottery and portraits. Open for lunch and dinner Monday through Saturday.

Sherman Meets the Suburbs

Since 1968 the picturesque rapids of Sweetwater Creek and the adjacent hardwood and piney woodlands have been the heart of *Sweetwater Creek Conservation Park,* a peaceful day-use state park. A short drive off I–20, 15 miles west of downtown Atlanta, the park serves the populace of rapidly growing Douglas County and many others who find it a delightful retreat from the hurly-burly of big-city life.

The ghostly ruins of the *New Manchester Manufacturing Company,* a Civil War–era enterprise torched by General William T. Sherman's troops, stands by the churning rapids, which provided the company with power to produce uniforms for the Confederate army. During the summer, kick off your shoes and join others wading in the swift, cool

Where Is Tara?

Visitors who come to Atlanta looking for Tara, the famous Gone With the Wind *plantation, look for it in vain. Author Margaret Mitchell drew her inspiration for the house from a number of antebellum homes she visited as a young woman. She placed it near Jonesboro, a now-modern Atlanta suburb, not far from Hartsfield International Airport. In her novel, Tara was much simpler than the movie's white-columned mansion. Miss Mitchell wrote the novel in the 1930s, while living in a Midtown apartment house she dubbed "The Dump." Recently restored and opened* to the public, Margaret Mitchell House & Visitors Center, 999 Peachtree Street, (404) 249–7015, includes a visit to her former basement apartment, with her battered typewriter, letters, and memorabilia; a video about her life and her book; and a gift shop. She was struck and killed by a taxi on her beloved Peachtree Street, 4 blocks north of the house, in 1949. Miss Mitchell is buried under a simple gravestone, with her married name "Marsh," in downtown Atlanta's historic Oakland Cemetery. Open daily 9:00 A.M. to 5:00 P.M. Adults, $6.00; seniors, $5.00; students, $4.00.

Judge Landis

In the wake of the Chicago "Black Sox" betting scandal during the 1919 World Series, Judge Kenesaw Mountain Landis was named major league baseball's first commissioner. He is credited with restoring the game's integrity and saving it from self-destruction. He was named for Marietta's Kennesaw Mountain, where his father was wounded during the Civil War. His father spelled the name with only one "n" instead of two.

waters. Be careful of the slick patches of moss covering the rocks.

Five miles of nature trails lead you through the woods beside the creek. A 250-acre reservoir is stocked with bass, catfish, and bream, which you can fry in a pan and serve on one of the park's picnic tables. The park is open daily from 8:00 A.M. to sundown. There is a $2.00 parking fee. Contact the superintendent, Lithia Springs 30057, (770) 732–5871.

With 550,000 residents, affluent Cobb is one of the nation's fastest growing counties and the northwest flagship of the Atlanta metropolitan area. Off the well-beaten paths of freeways and around the corner from high-rise hotels, glitzy shopping galleries, and trendy eateries, you'll find fascinating historic sites, charming town squares, and outdoor recreation.

After the fall of Chattanooga in late 1863, the Confederates grudgingly fell back to Kennesaw Mountain, 25 miles north of Atlanta and the site of **Kennesaw Mountain National Battlefield Park.** For two weeks in June 1864, 60,000 soldiers dug into the wooded flanks of the 1,808-foot mountain. When a series of assaults failed to dislodge the Southerners, Union commander General William T. Sherman executed a flanking strategy, which forced the Confederates to leave the mountain and retreat to Atlanta.

Stop first at the National Park Service Visitors Center and view the slide presentation and exhibits. Outside are some of the cannons that took part in the battle. From Monday through Friday you may drive your car up a paved road to a parking area 200 yards below the summit. From there take an easy walk through the woods studded with cannons, earthworks, and markers telling the story of the battle. On Saturday and Sunday the mountain road is open only to a free shuttle bus that makes the trip every half hour. In fair weather many visitors hike at least one way on an easy 1-mile trail. If you've the stamina, you can extend your hike from the Kennesaw summit 4 miles to **Cheatham Hill** and 7 miles to **Kolb's Farm,** other principal battlegrounds in the Kennesaw theater. The two areas are also accessible by car.

Picnic tables, grills, and rest rooms are in a grove of trees near the visitors center parking area. The park, about 4½ miles west of I–75 exit 116, is open Monday through Friday 8:30 A.M. to 5:00 P.M.; Saturday and

Sunday to 6:00 P.M. Contact the superintendent, P.O. Box 1167, Marietta 30061, (770) 427–4686.

The *locomotive General* is another tangible souvenir of the Civil War. On April 12, 1862, Union raiders stole the locomotive as it sat in the Kennesaw depot. Their plan to decimate Confederate rail lines as they drove north to Chattanooga was foiled after a 100-mile chase. Eight of the raiders were hanged; the adventure was dramatized in the Disney movie *The Great Locomotive Chase*. The General is now permanently parked in the *Big Shanty Museum* in the small town of Kennesaw, 3½ miles from Kennesaw Mountain. You may also see a twelve-minute slide show and Civil War weapons and artifacts. It's open daily. Admission for adults is $2.50; children, $1.00.

Marietta Town Square, officially called Glover Park, is a charming nineteenth-century microcosm of mellow brick buildings, shady streets, and gingerbread Victorian homes. The grassy park in the center of the square has been landscaped as a restful Victorian green, with a gazebo, playground, a fountain, and plenty of benches for quiet relaxation. Shops around the square are stocked with antiques, art and handicrafts, jewelry, and apparel. The square also boasts several good restaurants. *Schillings on the Square* (770–428–9520) has a downstairs pub with sandwiches and light fare and a white-tablecloth upstairs dining room featuring lamb, veal, steaks, and seafood.

Stop first at the Marietta Welcome Center, in the restored Western & Atlantic Railway Depot just off the square, (404) 429–1115, for information and directions for a walking tour of the city's lovely antebellum and Victorian neighborhoods. To get to the Marietta square from Highway 41, go west on Roswell Street about 1 mile from the Big Chicken, a local landmark.

Theatre in the Square, 11 Whitlock Avenue, Marietta, (770) 422–8369, is one of the Metro area's most outstanding live theater companies. The year-round repertoire includes new, cutting-edge (sometimes controversial) productions, standard works, and seasonal specials.

When Georgia's summer heat and humidity get you down, take a refreshing plunge into the Atlanta Ocean, a big, boisterous wave pool at *White Water Park* (770–424–9283), on Highway 41 at Marietta. Open daily from May through August, the park has more than thirty attractions: the Ocean, a 750,000-gallon pool that whips up 4-foot waves; a variety of water slides; and special areas for the small fry. All inclusive, $22 for adults and $13 for age 3 to 4 feet tall.

For other water-oriented recreation, try *Lake Allatoona,* which borders Cobb County on the north, and the *Chattahoochee River,* which Cobb shares on the south with Fulton County and Atlanta.

Pickett's Mill Battlefield, 5 miles northeast of Dallas, should be high on Civil War buffs' "must-do" list. The battlefield is much as it was when blue and gray troops fought here during the Battle of Atlanta campaign. Living-history programs demonstrate cooking, weapons firing, and military drills of the Civil War era. Artifacts and exhibits are in the interpretive center/visitors center. The battlefield is at Mt. Tabor Road, Dallas 30132, (770) 433–7850. Admission is $2.00 for adults and $1.00 for students. Open Tuesday through Sunday.

PLACE TO STAY IN METRO ATLANTA

MIDTOWN/VIRGINIA/ HIGHLAND/LITTLE FIVE POINTS AREA
Ansley Inn,
253 Fifteenth Street,
(404) 872–9000,
(800) 446–5416,
fax (404) 892–2318.

Twenty-two guest rooms in an Ansley Park Tudor mansion have cable TV, direct-dial phone, individual heat and AC controls, and whirlpool baths. Close to Woodruff Art Center/High Museum of Art, restaurants, shops; $95 to $145.

Gaslight Inn,
1001 Saint Charles Avenue,
(404) 875–1001,
fax (404) 876–1001,
www.gaslightinn.com.

Six rooms with private bath are in this delightful bed and breakfast within walking distance of the Virginia-Highland action. Guests can relax in the Southern-style walled garden; $85 to $195.

King-Keith House Bed & Breakfast,
889 Edgewood Avenue,
(404) 688–7330,
(800) 728–3879,
fax (404) 584–0730,
http:/travelbase.com/destinations/atlanta/king-keith/

The spectacular Queen Anne–style "painted lady" mansion is on a tree-shaded street in Inman Park, a regentrified Victorian neighborhood 2 miles east of downtown. Jan and Windell Keith have five guest rooms with antiques and modern amenities. Close to shops, restaurants, live theater, entertainment, and the Inman Park MARTA rapid rail station. Rates of $65 to $125 include full breakfast.

If you'd like to stay at a homey bed-and-breakfast inn and meet some engaging Atlantans, contact Bed-and-Breakfast Atlanta, 1801 Piedmont Avenue, Atlanta 30324, (404) 875–0525, fax (404) 875–9672.

Accommodations are in beautiful private homes, and rates usually include a full breakfast and the opportunity to meet Atlantans on an informal basis.

BUFORD
Bona Allen Mansion,
395 East Main Street,
(770) 271–7637,
fax (770) 271–0324.

A regal Italianate mansion built in 1911 by owners of the town's tannery. Leslie and Doug Turner, who also run Main Street Gourmet, have three exquisite guest rooms furnished with antiques and family keepsakes. Guests can stroll the six acres of grounds and swim in the outdoor pool.

Rates of $135 for a double include a large breakfast. Because the mansion hosts many weekend wedding receptions, corporate galas, and other special events, individual guests are limited to weekdays.

DECATUR
The Atlanta Dream Hostel, 222 East Howard Avenue, (404) 370–0380.

The metro area's only hostel. An adventurous international clientele park their backpacks and bunk in 300 mostly dormitory beds for $14.60 a night. Private rooms are $25 single, $36 double. Guests have the run of the Dream's large garden and Elvis shrine and can stop in for afternoon tea at the full-size Native American tepee.

Sycamore House,
624 Sycamore Street,
(404) 378–0685,
fax (404) 373–6631.

Judy and Ren Manning's beautiful home, in one of Decatur's historic neighborhoods, is within walking distance of shops and restaurants and the MARTA rail station. A first-floor suite has a queen bed and bath ($90). Two upstairs rooms have a queen bed and twins and their own baths ($70). You can unwind in the heated pool and hot tub in their secluded garden. Full breakfast included.

STONE MOUNTAIN VILLAGE
Stone Mountain Village Bed & Breakfast,
5470 East Mountain Street, phone and
fax (770) 413–0611.

Has three bedrooms with private bath and cable TV close to shops and restaurants and MARTA bus line. Full breakfast in $95 rate. Take the Memorial Drive/Village of Stone Mountain exit off Highway 78/Stone Mountain Freeway, 10 miles east of Decatur.

The Village Inn Bed & Breakfast,
992 Ridge Avenue,
(770) 469–3459,
(800) 214–8385,
fax (770) 469–1051.

Has six guest rooms wih private bath and antiques. Some have two-person whirlpool baths and fireplaces. Just outside the park, within walking distance of Village shops and restaurants. Full breakfast in $85 to $125 rates.

NEWNAN
Bonnie Castle Bed & Breakfast,
2 Post Street, Grantville 30220, (770) 583–3090 and (800) 261–3090.

This brick Romanesque-Revival Victorian is a startling contrast to Newnan's white columns. Built in 1896 by a wealthy Coweta County family, the turreted mansion, with a

slate roof and wraparound porch, has been transformed into a gracious historic inn by Darwin and Patti Palmer, who invite guests to relax in the romantic ambience of antique furnishings, regional art collections, hardwood floors, gilded ceilings, and stained glass. Off I–85, 15 minutes south of Newnan. Includes full Southern breakfast and evening refreshments for $70 to $90.

The Old Garden Inn, at 51 Temple Avenue, (770) 304–0594 and (800) 731–5011.

Has three cheerful guest rooms in a white-columned Greek Revival mansion. Each has a different decorative theme. One has a private entrance popular with smokers who can step outside and puff away. Breakfast, included in rates of $75 to $89, features owner Patti Girondi's sweet potato biscuits and cheese grits souffle.

The Parrot Camp Soucy Home and Gardens,
155 Greenville Street, (770) 502–0676.

Literally stops traffic in its tracks. The stunning Second Empire–style mansion, built in 1842 and redesigned in 1884, with a wealth of gables, a wide veranda, and intricate exterior millwork, is straight out of the Gilded

Age. The fantasy is carried out inside, where former Californians Helen and Rick Cousin have created a sumptuous bed and breakfast. Four guest rooms are furnished with Victorian antiques, canopy and half-tester beds, fireplaces, and modern private baths. Guests enjoy four acres of formal gardens, a heated spa and outdoor pool, and a full gourmet breakfast. Doubles run $105 to $165.

Southern Comfort Bed & Breakfast Inn,
66 La Grange Street, (770) 254–9266.

The Greek Revival mansion is the quintessential Old South, although it wasn't built until after The Late Unpleasantness was concluded. With 30-foot Corinthian columns, wide verandahs, and antique furnishings, it's a perfect complement to your antebellum Newnan visit. Four guest rooms, two with private bath, two with shared bath. Continental breakfast in double rates of $75 to $90.

MARIETTA
Sixty Polk Street, A Bed & Breakfast,
60 Polk Street, (770) 419–1688, (800) 845–7266.

Four guest rooms in Joe and Glenda Mertes's 1872-era French Regency

showplace are furnished with antiques and private baths. Full Southern breakfast is served in the grand dining room. Take a short walk to the antiques shops, restaurants, and other attractions around the square. Doubles go for $85 to $125.

Whitlock Inn Bed & Breakfast,
57 Whitlock Avenue, (770) 428–1495, fax (770) 919–9620.

Innkeeper Alexis Edwards has five guest rooms with private baths in her Victorian mansion a block from the square. The spacious public rooms are popular for weddings, corporate gatherings, and other special events. Rates of $100 to $125 include continental breakfast.

PLACE TO EAT IN METRO ATLANTA

MIDTOWN/VIRGINIA/ HIGHLAND/LITTLE FIVE POINTS AREA
American Roadhouse,
892 North Highland Avenue, (404) 872–2822.

Busy family-friendly neighborhood eatery. Terrific breakfasts, also great for lunch and dinner sandwiches, salads, fresh vegetables, chicken, fish,

meatloaf and pasta plates. Breakfast, lunch, dinner daily.

Blind Willie's,
828 North Highland Avenue, (404) 873–2583.

Some of the country's best known blues rockers come close to blowing the roof off this popular storefront club, which packs in the crowds every night of the week.

Doc Chey's Noodle House,
1424 North Highland Avenue, (404) 888–0777.

Pan-Asian noodle house is a beehive-busy place to enjoy huge, cheap helpings of Vietnamese soup and other noodle- and rice-based dishes. Lunch, dinner daily.

Eats,
600 Ponce de Leon Avenue, (404) 888–9149.

Another perpetually packed "filling station." Students, families, and business types stand in usually long cafeteria lines for pasta, jerk chicken, and fresh veggies at rock-bottom prices. Lunch, dinner daily.

George's Restaurant,
1041-A North Highland Avenue, (404) 892–3648.

Longtime neighborhood tavern hasn't changed in more than forty years. Some of the best hamburgers in town. Open daily.

Indigo Coastal Grill,
1397 North Highland
Avenue, (404) 876–0676.

Like a fantasy trip to a
tropical island, this casual
but extremely accomplished
seafood eatery specializes
in coastal cuisines from the
Keys to Cape Cod. Dinner
nightly, Sunday brunch.

Limerick Junction,
824 North Highland
Avenue, (404) 874–7147.

Rollicking Irish pub has
Guinness and Harp on tap,
musicians from Dublin and
Belfast (and Limerick), and
plenty of hearty pub-style
eats. Dinner and
entertainment nightly.

Mambo,
1402 North Highland
Avenue, (404) 876–2626.

Ropa Vieja, black beans
and rice, a nightly "Chino-
Latino" special, and other
peppy Cuban dishes keep
this lively ristorante
jumping every night.

Manuel's Tavern,
602 North Highland
Avenue, (404) 525–3447.

Atlanta's best neighborhood
saloon. Generations of jour-
nalists, politicians, and and
just-plain folks have whiled
away their days and nights
at the worn wooden booths
and long bar festooned with
photos of JFK, Hubert
Humphrey, and other
Democratic icons. Put away
chili dogs, burgers, BLTs,
onion rings, and steak fries

while you sip beer and spirits and watch sports on big-
screen TVs. Like Cheers,
after a couple of visits,
they'll know your name and
your poison. Open daily.

Mary Mac's Tea Room,
224 Ponce de Leon Avenue,
(404) 876–1800.

Two blocks east of
Peachtree Street, this maze
of a cheerful dining room
has served celestial fried
chicken, turnip greens,
squash soufflé, biscuits and
cornbread to several
generations of Atlantans
and out-of-towners seeking
the truth in Southern home
cooking. Lunch, dinner
Monday through Saturday.

Son's Place,
100 Hurt Street at DeKalb
Avenue, across from the
Inman Park MARTA rail
station, (404) 581–0503.

The answers to all your
soul food needs are on the
cafeteria line of this plain
but friendly diner, where
the spectrum of society
comes to fill up on top-
grade fried chicken and
fish, chitterlings, cornbread,
vegetables, and homemade
pies and cakes. Breakfast
and lunch weekdays.

Helpful Web Sites

Georgia Tourist Division,
www.gomm.com and www.itt.state.ga.us
(Both sites have information on all the state's regions.)

Atlanta Convention & Visitors Bureau,
www.acvb.com

Atlanta Braves baseball,
www.atlantabraves.com

High Museum of Art,
www.woodruff.arts.org

DeKalb County Convention & Visitors Bureau,
www.dcvb.org

Southern Off-Road Bicycle Association,
www.sorba.org

Historic Roswell Convention & Visitors Bureau,
www.ci.roswell.ga.us/

Georgia State Parks,
www.gastateparks.org

Surin of Thailand,
810 North Highland
Avenue, (404) 892–7789.

Spicy Thai curry, noodle, rice, seafood, meat, and chicken dishes make this spacious restaurant one of Viriginia-Highland's main-stays. Lunch, dinner daily.

The Vortex,
438 Moreland Avenue,
(404) 688–1828
and 878 Peachtree Street,
(404) 875–1667.

Don't let the laughing-skull front door scare you away from some of the best burgers and zaniest surroundings in town. Top your whopper with blue cheese, pimiento cheese, bacon, or jerk sauce, and sit back and enjoy the experience and big-time attitude. Lunch, dinner daily.

DeKalb County's Little Asia
Ben Thuy,
Northwoods Shopping Center, 5095 Buford Highway, (770) 454–9046.

The local critic's choice for the best Vietnamese cooking. Lunch and dinner daily.

Machu Picchu,
Northeast Plaza Shopping Center, 3375 Buford Highway, (404) 320–3326.

A delightful little Peruvian entry into Buford Highway's ethnic stewpot. Decorated with colorful woven tapestries, with weekend music by an Andean flute and guitar combo, the restaurant's specialties include several varieties of *ceviche* (slices of raw fish "cooked" in lime juice acid, with cilantro) and large plates of seafood, chicken, and pork mixed with rice and potatoes. Lunch and dinner daily.

Pung Mie,
5145 Buford Highway,
(770) 455–0370.

A large, bright, and shiny Chinese restaurant with a distinctly Korean spin. Complimentary bowls of kimchee, mung beans, pickled and dried fish, and other appetizers precede your lunch and dinner. Don't miss the steamed dumplings! Lunch and dinner are served daily.

Seoul Garden,
5938 Buford Highway,
(770) 452–0123.

A large, friendly restaurant in a former chain steak house is one of the best of numerous Korean eateries. Kimchee, seafood pancake, barbecued meats, and rice and noodle dishes are excellent. There's also a sushi bar. Lunch and dinner daily.

Decatur
The Brick Store Pub,
125 East Court Square,
(404) 687–0990.

A cleverly revamped brick-walled former mercantile store that now dispenses a global variety of bottled and draft beers and ales, over a dozen single-malt scotches, and other spirits. The pub fare menu includes fish and chips, burgers, sandwiches, and salads. You can toss darts in the upstairs den. Families are welcome. Lunch and dinner daily.

Cafe Alsace,
121 East Ponce de Leon
Avenue, (404) 373–5622.

A cozy, charming bistro with quiches, seafood, salads, sandwiches, and soups. Lunch Monday through Friday, dinner nightly.

Eddie's Attic,
a second-floor walkup around the corner at 515 North McDonough Street, (404) 377–4976.

One of the best places in town to hear local acoustic groups and pop and folk singers. Bar food, beer, wine, and cocktails are available.

The Food Business,
115 Sycamore Street,
(404) 371–9121.

A lively three-story restaurant with a cutting-edge menu of seafood, pastas, chicken, and beef dishes; salads; and sandwiches. Crab cakes are the house specialty. The best seats are by big windows on the third floor, where you can scan the activities around the square. Lunch and dinner daily.

Our Way Cafe,
across the train tracks next to Agnes Scott College, 303 East College Avenue, (404) 373–6665.

Serves big plates of inexpensive, very good Southern homecooking at weekday lunch. Squash souffle, broccoli casserole, real mashed potatoes, meatloaf, and barbecued pork are big favorites of the hungry hordes that queue up in the cafeteria line Monday though Friday.

The Purple Cactus,
123 East Court Square, (404) 377–1399.

Serves spicy Southwestern fare and major margaritas. Lunch and dinner daily.

The St. Agnes Tea Garden,
222 East Howard Avenue, (404) 370–1995, about 3 blocks from the square.

A cheerfully offbeat indoor/outdoor restaurant adjoining the Atlanta Dream Hostel. With its rustic wood-beamed ceiling and walls, comfy couches and chairs, vintage signs and international newspapers, it has the whimsical ambience of the sixties and seventies. The Tea Garden serves a variety of teas, but the cuisine includes hearty Alsatian meatloaf, seafood, pastas, fish, and vegetarian dishes.

Ya Ya's Cajun Cuisine,
3 blocks west of the square, 426 West Ponce de Leon Avenue, (404) 373–9292.

Has been doing SRO business since David and Leslie Lester opened in early 1998. Lunch is highlighted by the best po-boy sandwiches in town. At dinner, the menu sparkles with gumbo, fried crawfish, crawfish etouffe, jambalaya, fried catfish, red beans and rice, and blackened chicken and fish. Cajun bands rock the place on Friday and Saturday nights. The good times roll at lunch Monday through Friday; dinner nightly.

NEWNAN
10 East Washington Street, (770) 502–9100.

Czech native George Ravosky and his wife Carmela oversee Newnan's most stylish restaurant. Their urbane dining room delights lunch and dinner guests with everything from hamburgers and Reubens to pastas, crab cakes, steaks, lamb tenderloin, seafood, and European-style desserts. Excellent wine list. Lunch is served Tuesday through Friday; dinner Tuesday through Saturday.

NORCROSS
Dominick's,
95 South Peachtree Street, (770) 449–1611.

Proclaims, "Little Italy, Lotta Food," and they're not kidding. The handsomely redone nineteenth-century mercantile building, with redbrick walls, wooden floors, and original tin ceilings, serves platters of every kind of pasta, seafood, chicken, and veal dishes ample enough for two or three major appetites. It's fun to come with a large group and pass the platters Italian-family style. You can also get half-portions, which are still big enough to share. Open for lunch Monday through Saturday, dinner daily.

Norcross Station Cafe, in the refashioned depot, 40 South Peachtree Street, (770) 409–9889.

The eclectic menu includes shrimp, steak, baby-back ribs, pastas and other Italian dishes, quesadillas, quiches, sandwiches, soups, salads, and kids' plates. Open for lunch and dinner Monday through Saturday.

Chattahoochee Trace

La Grange, a pretty town of 30,000 near the Georgia-Alabama border, was named in honor of the Marquis de Lafayette's French estate, which accounts for the bronze likeness of the Marquis in the center of downtown Lafayette Square. Away from the square, regal white-columned mansions preside over well-tended lawns, gardens, and tree-shaded streets.

Bellevue Mansion, 204 Ben Hill Street, (706) 884–1832, was the stately Greek Revival home of U.S. Senator and acclaimed orator Benjamin Harvey Hill. Built in the early 1850s, the home is an architectural treasure inside and out, filled with magnificent furnishings and artworks. It's the La Grange area's favorite wedding venue. Open Tuesday through Saturday 10:00 A.M. to noon and 2:00 to 5:00 P.M., Bellevue charges an admission fee of $1.50.

Lamar Dodd Art Center (706–882–2911), on the neighboring La Grange College campus, is a strikingly modern museum displaying changing regional and national exhibitions and a permanent collection of American Indian art. It is open Monday through Friday 10:00 A.M. to 4:00 P.M.; Saturday and Sunday, 1:00 to 4:00 P.M.

The *Chattahoochee Valley Art Museum* (706–882–3267), near Lafayette Square at 112 Hines Street, displays paintings, sculpture, and decorative arts in a restored 1890s jail building. It's open Monday through Friday 9:00 A.M. to 5:00 P.M., Saturday until 1:00 P.M.

West Point Lake, a mammoth 26,000-acre inland sea a few minutes from downtown La Grange, offers plenty of opportunities for fishing, boating, swimming, waterskiing, and sunbathing. Contact the West Point Lake Resource Manager, P.O. Box 574, West Point 31833, (706) 645–2937. The lake's commercial outlets include Highland Marina, P.O. Box 1644, La Grange 30241, (706) 882–3437, where you can rent fishing boats and go after the lake's channel catfish and white and largemouth bass. Also at the marina, you can rent a houseboat or stay

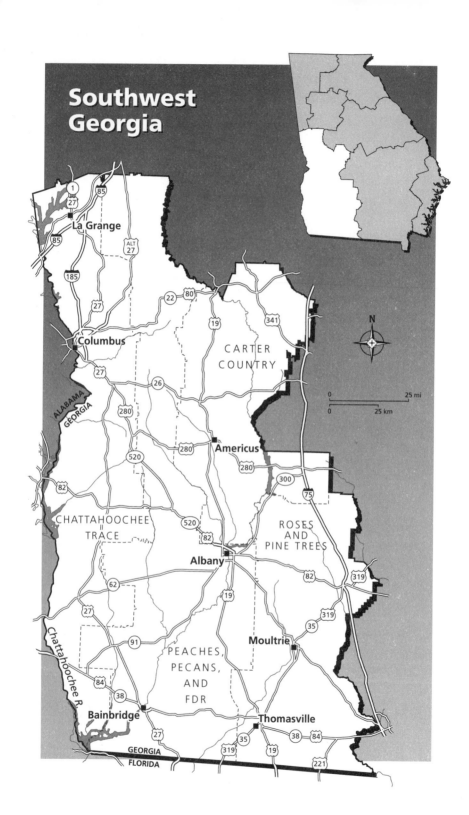

in a campground or furnished cottage. The lake is a U.S. Army Corps of Engineers impoundment of the Chattahoochee River, which forms most of the Georgia-Alabama border.

In the mood for a hot dog? **Charlie Joseph's** has been serving them up, and Troup Countians have been gobbling them up since 1920, when Charlie's opened as a fruit stand in downtown La Grange. They've been at 128 Bull Street (706–884–5416) since 1946. You can have your dog with just plain mustard and onions, or dressed up with slaw, chili, cheese, relish, and other fixin's. They also have hamburgers and sandwiches and breakfast-time egg and cheese sandwiches. Charlie's second location, 2238 West Point Road (706–884–0379), serves breakfast, lunch, and early dinner. Both Charlies are open Monday to Saturday.

As you drive Highway 29 from La Grange to Hogansville and pass a humble-looking cinder-block restaurant called **Hogan's Heroes** (706–637–4953), don't think your nose is deceiving you. Instead of the aromas of barbecue and fried chicken you'd expect in a small west-Georgia textile town, what assails you are the intoxicating fragrances of oregano, thyme, garlic, rosemary, calamari, and veal scallopini.

Hogan's Heroes owner/chef Jeff Spader learned Italian cooking in his native New Jersey. He brought his skills to Hogansville in the late 1980s and has been doing land office building ever since. Regulars flock from across west Georgia and east Alabama to sample his pasta, veal, chicken, and seafood dishes draped in rich, hearty sauces. You can usually find a table during weekday lunchtime, but savvy regulars make dinner reservations at least two weeks ahead. The restaurant has a good selection of wines by the bottle and glass. Prices are moderate.

If you fancy antiques and collectibles, you'll find some good browsing places on *Hogansville's Main Street.* Several old mercantile buildings now sport Depression glass, vintage china and silver, old toys, antique farm implements, and other treasures.

Ken Hammock's original *Fair Oaks Inn,* 703 East Main Street, Hogansville 30230, (706) 637–8828, is a stunning 1901 Queen Anne Victorian loaded with antiques, fireplaces, pocket doors, woodwork, and mantels. Six guest rooms (two sharing a bath) and a large suite with a whirlpool are in the main house. The Carriage House is popular with honeymooners and others seeking seclusion. Guests enjoy formal gardens and an outdoor swimming pool and hot tub. Weekday rates of $50 to $85, $65 to $110 on weekends, include gourmet breakfast and poolside wine and cheese. With all these fragile antiques, no children under 14 are allowed.

Butterflies—thousands of them, in all sizes and colors, from exotic places around the world—are free and on the wing at the *Day Butterfly Center* at Callaway Gardens in Pine Mountain. Opened to visitors in September 1988, America's first such natural attraction was inspired by similar preserves in Europe and the Orient, with some distinctive Georgia touches. It was named in honor of Cecil Day, late founder of the Days Inns of America motel corporation, and is a year-round, indoor-outdoor experience.

As you walk into an 8,000-square-foot, glass-enclosed "rain forest," you're suddenly caught in clouds of feathery giant swallowtails (*Papilio cresphontes*), Paris peacock swallowtails (*P. paris*), green-banded swallowtails (*P. palinurus*), owl butterflies (*Caligo sp.*), passion flower butterflies (*Helinconius sp.*), and a rainbow of other iridescent beauties from the Orient, the Andes, and the South Pacific. Butterflies and tropical birds perch side by side on exotic plants. A waterfall gently spatters. Bleeding-heart doves hide in the thick tropical foliage. Indoors, you'll find educational displays and a theater with a film all about the remarkable lives of butterflies.

Outside, the native butterfly garden is cunningly designed to lure homegrown butterflies to *Callaway Gardens*. If you'd like to have your own butterfly center, Callaway's horticulturists will show you how to plant a "tender trap" in your backyard.

While you're at Callaway Gardens, you can also take a driving tour of the 2,500 acres of gardens planted with 700 varieties of azaleas and more than 450 types of holly, mums, mountain laurel, rhododendron, dogwood, and wildflowers. These may be viewed in their natural habitat along 13 miles of roads and walking trails, and inside the *John A. Sibley Horticultural Center,* a stunning indoor-outdoor conservatory with pools, cascades, and scores of floral displays that change with the seasons.

Callaway's 14,300 rolling, wooded acres also embrace thirteen lakes for swimming, fishing, boating, and waterskiing. Golfers may play sixty-three picturesque holes and sample from a recreational smorgasbord that includes tennis, skeet shooting, biking, and a summertime big-top circus. A half-dozen restaurants range from candlelight to casual.

Lodgings range from rooms at the Inn to deluxe villas and cottages. Callaway Gardens lies 12 scenic miles from Warm Springs and Franklin D. Roosevelt's Little White House. Contact Callaway Gardens, Pine Mountain 31822, toll-free (800) 225-5292. The Day Butterfly Center is open daily year-round. Admission is $10.00 for adults; $5.00 for ages 6 to 12; ages 5 and under, free. It includes all Callaway Gardens nonresort areas.

At *Pine Mountain Wild Animal Safari* (706–663–8744), you can drive your own car, or take the Safari Bus, through a 500-acre preserve populated by zebras, giraffes, camels, axis deer, gnus, antelopes, water buffalo, and other wild, nonpredatory creatures. Also visit the petting zoo, monkey house, and serpentarium, all 2 miles north of the town of Pine Mountain. Open Monday through Friday 10:00 A.M. to 5:30 P.M. and Saturday and Sunday 10:00 A.M. to 6:30 P.M. Adults, $10.95; ages 10 to 16 and senior citizens 55 and over, $9.95; ages 3 to 9, $7.75.

Thomasville Antiques Show and Sale, early March, Exchange Club Fairgrounds, (912) 225-3919

Thomasville Rose Festival, late April, (800) 704-2350

Callaway Gardens Spring Celebration, mid-April, (800) 282-8181

Riverfest Weekend, late April, Columbus Riverwalk, (706) 322-0756

Cotton Pickin' Country Fair, early May, Gay, (706) 924-2558

Andersonville Spring Fair, late May, (912) 924-2558

Indian Battle Reenactment, late May, Westville, (888) SEE-1850

Watermelon Festival, first week July, Cordele, (912) 273-1668

Christmas in Thomasville, early December, (912) 226-2344

Voices of Christmas, early December, Albany, (912) 787-1008

Christmas Festival of Lights, Callaway Gardens, (800) 282-8181

Callaway Gardens

Blanton Creek Park, I– 185 exit 11, is a nicely kept Georgia Power Company recreation area on 5,800-acre Lake Harding. The park features fifty-one RV and tent camping sites ($10 a night), which have electrical and water hook-ups. The park also has boat ramps, picnic pavilions, and playgrounds. Call (706) 643-7737.

A number of moderately priced motels, bed and breakfasts, cottages, and chalets are around Pine Mountain, Hamilton, and Warm Springs. Contact the Pine Mountain Tourism Association, P.O. Box 177, Pine Mountain 31822, (800) 441–3502.

To really get away from everything and everybody, or hang out with a gang of close friends, **Annie's Log Cabin** (706–628–5729) could be your place. Tucked among twenty wooded acres 4 miles south of Callaway Gardens, the six-room 1854 "dogtrot" log cabin sleeps as many as twelve. You'll have the entire place to yourselves, with a complete kitchen, TV, phone, a working fireplace, and a big front porch for sittin' and rockin'. Rates are $75 to $95 for two persons, $10 for each additional person.

Magnolia Hall (706–628–4566), a rejuvenated Victorian cottage in the little Harris County seat of Hamilton, invites guests to stay overnight in two bedrooms and two suites furnished with antiques. A big Southern breakfast comes with the $80 to $90 tariff.

Bon Cuisine Restaurant (706–663–2019), in the town of Pine Mountain north of Callaway Gardens, promises "An Adventure in Dining." It lives up to its word with a "Wild Game of the Day," which may be alligator, wild boar, antelope, snapping turtle, or white-tailed deer. Tamer tastes can enjoy soft-shell crab, sauteed orange roughy, filet mignon, rib-eye steak, red snapper, and flame-baked shrimp. Dinner is served Monday to Saturday.

Columbus is Georgia's third largest city. To get your bearings in the city of 300,000, stop by the **Columbus Visitor Center** (706–322–1613 and 800–999–1613) at Tenth Street and Bay Avenue, facing the new Chattahoochee Riverwalk.

The **Columbus Riverwalk,** a wide brick pathway with trees, benches, and attractive lighting, meanders a quarter-mile along the Chattahoochee in the downtown historic district. It's adorned with lots of ornamental brick and ironwork, flowers and landscaping, and steps that lead right to the river's edge. You can get out on the river, which divides Georgia from Alabama, on the **Chattahoochee Princess,** an 1850s-looking paddleboat that offers seventy-five-minute daytime cruises, romantic moonlight cruises, and evening dinner cruises. Phone (706) 324–4499 for more information.

Close to the Riverwalk, **Heritage Corner Tours,** sponsored by the Historic Columbus Foundation, takes you through four homes at the corner of Broadway and Seventh Street. They include an early 1800 pioneer log cabin; an 1828 Federal-style cottage; the Victorian cottage home of Dr. John Stith Pemberton, a Columbus pharmacist who left here for Atlanta, where he invented Coca-Cola in 1886; a mid-nineteenth-century farmhouse that now houses the Period Pieces Gift Shop; and the Victorian townhouse at 700 Broadway that serves as the Historic Foundation's

Peanut Soup with Pepper Jelly

*H*ere's a delectable way to prepare one of Georgia's favorite "fruits":

PEANUT SOUP WITH PEPPER JELLY

2 tablespoons butter

2 tablespoons grated onion

1 stalk celery, thinly sliced

2 tablespoons flour

3 cups chicken broth

½ cup creamy peanut butter

½ teaspoon salt

1 cup light cream

2 tablespoons chopped roasted peanuts

½ cup hot-pepper jelly

Melt butter in a saucepan over low heat. Add onion and celery. Saute for about 5 minutes. Add flour and mix until well blended. Stir in chicken broth and simmer for about a half-hour. Remove from heat, strain broth. Stir peanut butter, salt, and cream into the strained broth until well mixed.

Garnish each serving with a teaspoon of chopped peanuts and a dollop of hot-pepper jelly. Serve hot. Makes 4 servings.

headquarters. Tours begin at the headquarters for an all-inclusive $3.00. Phone (706) 322–0756 for information.

If it's open—or holding one of its many regular stage productions—don't miss a chance to see the restored *Springer Opera House,* built in 1871, which has hosted such illuminati as Oscar Wilde, Will Rogers, and Edwin Booth.

You can also take a walking/driving tour of numerous historic homes, churches, and public buildings with an illustrated brochure called *"Original City Tours,"* available at the Historic Columbus Foundation.

The *Coca-Cola Space Science Center,* 701 Front Avenue, (706) 649–1470, is the Riverwalk's most exciting new attraction. Developed in conjunction with Columbus State University, its components include the Mead Observatory, which captures high-detail images of far-flung celestial bodies (you can take a space flight and land on the moon); the Challenger Learning Center, an interactive, hands-on experience that helps sharpen science, math, team-building, and communications skills for schoolchildren and other groups; and the Omnisphere Theater, which projects laser shows, science and science fiction movies, concerts, and theatrical performances onto a giant domed ceiling. An accurate replica of the Apollo Space Capsule is one of the many permanent exhbits. Special events include "Night Out Under the Stars," an overnight campout at the Space Center that includes a Challenger Center Mission, the Omnisphere Theater, construction and launch of a model rocket, a laser concert, and a science fiction movie. Open Tuesday through Friday, 10:00 A.M. to 4:00 P.M., Saturday 1:30 to 9:00 P.M., Sunday 1:30 to 4:00 P.M. Call, or fax (760) 649–1478, or access www.ccssc.org for group and special events rates.

The *Columbus Black Heritage Tour* is a self-guided tour of more than two dozen sites that played vital parts in the city's rich African-American culture. The tour begins with the last home of legendary blues singer Gertrude "Ma" Rainey (1886–1939) and includes churches, schools, theaters, businesses, and landmarks that showcase achievements of the city's black community. Pick up the free brochure at the Columbus Welcome Center, 1000 Bay Avenue, (800) 999–1613.

Oxbow Meadows Environmental Learning Center, South Lumpkin Road, north of the Ft. Benning Military Reservation, (706) 687–4090, is a fun and fascinating place to get out in the countryside and learn something about the world around you. Start your visit to the 1,600-acre site in the Chattahoochee River flood plain in a 2,000-square-foot building where you can observe live, mounted, and re-created plant and animal life. Two nature trails will let you stretch your legs in the wetlands and woodlands and come face-to-face with the creatures that live there. Open Tuesday through Friday 10:00 A.M. to 5:00 P.M. and Saturday and Sunday noon to 4:00 P.M. Free admission.

Even if you're staunchly antiwar, don't miss the *National Infantry Museum,* 101 Fourth Avenue, (706) 327–9798, on the mammoth Fort Benning Army compound. The museum's three floors and twelve spacious galleries exhibit more than 6,000 items from the French and Indian War and the Revolution, through the World Wars, and all the way to Vietnam and the Persian Gulf conflict. You'll see a porthole from the battleship Maine, sixteenth-century English armor, the wing of a WWII Japanese Zero, ancient Korean and Chinese weapons and armor, gas masks worn by WWI horses, and wartime documents signed by twenty U.S. presidents. It's open daily except for major national holidays. Free admission.

Also of military interest, the *Civil War Museum of Naval History* displays the salvaged remains of the Confederate gunboats *Jackson* and *Chattahoochee.* It's open every day except Monday. Free admission.

The *Columbus Museum* is a peaceful place to spend a few hours browsing. Permanent exhibits include a hands-on discovery gallery for youngsters and adults, a fine arts decorative gallery, a regional history gallery, and changing exhibits of regional art. Located at 1251 Wynnton Road, (706) 649–0713, the museum is open daily except Monday. Donations are invited.

Providence Canyon State Park preserves the scenic beauty of an area often referred to as "Georgia's Little Grand Canyon." More than a dozen canyons in the 1,108-acre park have been chiseled out over the past 150 years by the slow, relentless process of soil erosion. As deep as 150 feet, the canyons offer a geological primer and a stunning visual display of stratified soil layers. Many fascinating formations stand alone in the midst of the canyons.

During spring and fall, those making the easy hike to the canyon floor are rewarded by multicolored wildflowers, which complement the pinks, purples, and whites of the Providence soils. From July to September, the rare plumleaf azalea blooms in shades from light orange to salmon and various tones of red and scarlet.

Stop first at the park's interpretive center (912–838–6202) for an overview. A day-use park, Providence has picnic tables, shelters, and rest rooms. It's on Highway 39C, 7 miles west of Lumpkin, and is open daily from 7:00 A.M. to dark. There is a $2.00 per visit parking fee.

You may stay overnight and fish and boat in the Chattahoochee River at *Florence Marina State Park,* Route 1, Box 36, Omaha 31821, (912) 838–6870. Campgrounds have electricity, water, rest rooms, and showers. Furnished efficiency apartments, sleeping up to five, with kitchenettes are available. Six new two-bedroom cabins are completely furnished and have fully equipped kitchens. Call (800) 864–PARK for rates and reservations. The park also has a swimming pool, tennis courts, a playground, and a small grocery store. The park is on Highway 39C, 10 miles west of Providence Canyon. There is a $2.00 per visit parking fee.

If *Westville* were near an interstate highway, more than a million visitors a year would enjoy it. As it is, far from major thoroughfares at the tiny Stewart County seat of Lumpkin, Georgia's "Village of the 1850s" is appreciated by only a fortunate 50,000 or so. Forty miles southeast of Columbus, 25 miles west of Jimmy Carter's Plains, this Williamsburg-style re-creation includes more than two dozen authentic nineteenth-century homes, public buildings, and craftsmen's shops lining the hard-packed clay streets.

As you walk about the town, you'll be treated to a symphony of workaday sounds: the blacksmith hammering nails, horseshoes, farm implements, and household utensils; the cobbler tapping together a pair of fine riding boots; the schoolmarm calling her charges to class. Elsewhere, townsfolk make their own soap, furniture, and candles; hand-stitch quilts; and cook corn breads, stews, and gingerbread over an open hearth. A mule plods in stoic circles, turning an enormous round stone that grinds sugar cane into thick, amber syrup.

Lifestyles range from the rich and famous at the Greek Revival McDonald House to the cottages of the working folk. Every season has its special events: the Spring Festival in early April; May Pole Dances, May 1; Early American, July 4; the Fair of the 1850s, late October–early November; and, at Christmas, strolling carolers and yule log lighting.

Westville, P.O. Box 1850, Lumpkin 31815, (888) 733–1850, is open Tuesday through Saturday 10:00 A.M. to 5:00 P.M.; Sunday 1:00 to 5:00 P.M. Admission for adults is $8.00; ages 65 and over, $7.00; college students and military personnel, $6.00; other students, $4.00; and ages 6 to 12, $3.00.

With its redbrick courthouse, granite Confederate soldier, and one-story buildings flanking the quiet square, Lumpkin could be moved, intact, into a museum as an exhibit of nineteenth-century Americana. The *Bedingfield Inn,* (912) 838–4201, was built in 1836 as a doctor's residence and stagecoach inn. It's open 1:00 to 5:00 P.M. daily.

Bill's Favorites

*Lamar Dodd Art Center
and Chattahoochee
Valley Art Museum*

*Day Butterfly Center,
Callaway Gardens,
Pine Mountain*

Columbus Riverwalk

National Infantry Museum

*Providence Canyon State
Park and Westville
1850s Village*

FDR's Little White House

Chehaw Wild Animal Park

*Jimmy Carter National
Historic Site*

*National Prisoner of War
Museum, Andersonville
National Cemetery*

Georgia Agrirama

Pebble Hill Plantation

George T. Bagby State Park, fronting the Chattahoochee River's 48,000-acre Lake Walter F. George, is a resort-style getaway. The thirty-room Walter F. George Lodge has all the modern comforts and a full-service restaurant. Call (800) 864–PARK for lodge and cottage rates and reservations. Around it you'll find boat ramps and marinas, swimming pools, tennis courts, an 18-hole golf course, and hiking and picnic areas. You can also stay in furnished cottages. There's a $2.00 per visit parking fee. Contact Box 201, Ft. Gaines 31751, (912) 768–2571.

At *Frontier Village* in neighboring Ft. Gaines, a one-third-scale replica of the original fort, built in 1814, has Civil War cannons and authentic log cabins that reflect the area's frontier heritage.

Kolomoki Mounds State Historic Park, Route 1, Blakely 31723, (912) 723–5296, is an important archaeological site, as well as a recreation area. Within the 1,293-acre park you may climb some of the seven burial mounds and temple mounds built by Creek Indians in the twelfth and thirteenth centuries. The small museum has artifacts unearthed from the mounds and the excavated burial mound of a tribal chief. Also in the park, you're invited to swim in two pools, fish and boat in a pair of lakes, have a picnic, and play miniature golf.

The park's thirty-five camping sites have water and electricity, hot showers, and rest rooms.

Driving around the *Early County Courthouse* in Blakely, look for the monument to the peanut.

If ever a body of water were created with fishermen in mind, it's got to be *Lake Seminole.* And if ever a man were created for a fisherman's lake, it must be Jack Wingate. Formed by an impoundment of the Chattahoochee and Flint Rivers, the 37,500-acre lake, with a 250-mile shoreline, is especially bountiful grounds for bass fishing. Largemouth routinely weigh in at upwards of fifteen pounds. Anglers also snare a wealth of bodacious black bass, white bass, hybrid bass, and stripers, as well as bream, chain pickerel, catfish, yellow perch, and many other varieties.

Yet the marshy, reedy lake—afloat with thousands of acres of grass beds and lily pads and spiked with the ghostly trunks of cypress and live oak trees—is so far off the beaten path, down where Georgia's southwest corner bumps against Alabama and Florida, that when more than fifty boats appear on a single day, old-timers grumble that "Ol' Sem" is turning into a waterbound I–75.

One of the first persons you'll meet around the lake is Jack Wingate. His **Bass Island Campground and Lodge,** Route 1, Box 3311/139 Wingate Road, Bainbridge 31717, (912) 246–0658, is the oldest commercial fishing camp on this whole vast waterway. Character supreme, raconteur, humorist, tall-tale teller, sometime newspaper columnist, and walking encyclopedia of anything that has to do with fishing, Wingate grew up in these parts well before the Jim Woodruff Reservoir flooded the landscape in 1957. He can point to a place, now underwater, where Spanish friars from Cuba established missions in the 1650s and another where Generals Andrew Jackson, Zachary Taylor, and Winfield Scott built a fort in 1816 to attack Seminole and Creek Indians.

With an average depth of 9 to 12 feet and in many areas shallow enough for you to stand on the bottom and flycast, these stump-studded waters can rip open an inexperienced boat like an aluminum can. Hence, you'll need the services of Wingate or one of his fellow guides ($150 to $175 for two persons a day, including fuel, boat, and motor). Some do double-duty as guides for duck hunting, for which Seminole is also renowned. You can engage them at the Lunker Lodge, off Highway 97 south, between Bainbridge and Chattahoochee, Florida.

The lodge carries complete lines of fishing gear, ice, groceries, and rental boats. The restaurant is worth the trip, even if you're not intending to fish. Festooned with stuffed trophies, Indian arrowheads, World War I helmets, and other odds and ends, the rustic dining room specializes in absolutely first-class fried and broiled fish, shrimp, oysters, barbecue, chicken, and hearty Southern breakfasts, at very modest prices.

The adjacent Bass Island Campground and Lodge has forty-eight campsites going for $12 a night (for full hookup, electricity, water, sump pump, and cable TV) and sixteen motel rooms with kitchenettes ($32 a double). The Stag Lodge sleeps groups as large as eighteen for $160. Aspiring young fishermen between ages 8 and 14 may want to sign up for Jack Wingate's Boys Camp, a week of fishing, fun, and water sports during the summer.

The lake's other recreational area is **Seminole State Park,** off Highway 39, 16 miles south of Donalsonville (912–861–3137). Facilities include fishing, boating, swimming, waterskiing, picnicking, camping, and furnished cottages. Call (800) 864–PARK for camping and cottage rates and reservations. There is a $2.00 per visit parking fee.

Peaches, Pecans, and FDR

President Franklin Delano Roosevelt left his everlasting imprint on the hills and piney woodlands of Meriwether County. The future president first came to this isolated rural county, 85 miles southwest of Atlanta, in 1924 to immerse his polio-afflicted limbs in the mineral waters of Warm Springs. His **Little White House,** secluded in a wooded grove, became his sanctuary from the monumental pressures of World War II. Now maintained by the Georgia Department of Natural Resources, the comfortable little house remains as he left it when he died there on April 12, 1945.

In the kitchen, simple dishes, pots and pans, a hand-cranked ice-cream maker, and other utensils are neatly stacked. In the woodwork, FDR's

FDR's Favorite

*M*s. Bonner left another legacy. Her recipe for Chicken Country Captain was one of FDR's favorites. It's still served in middle and southwest Georgia restaurants and homes.

DAISY'S CHICKEN COUNTRY CAPTAIN

1 hen or 2 fryers

2 or 3 chopped green peppers

2 or 3 cloves garlic

2 chopped onions

1 can whole tomatoes

1 teaspoon curry powder, or more to taste

2 cups rice, boiled until dry

1 teaspoon thyme

¼ cup raisins to garnish top

¼ cup almonds or other nuts for sauce

¼ cup almonds or other nuts for garnish

¼ can sliced mushrooms, or equivalent fresh sliced mushrooms

Salt and pepper to taste

Boil chicken until done, then debone. Make the sauce of cut green peppers, onions, tomatoes, mushrooms, almonds, raisins, thyme, salt, pepper, garlic, and curry powder. Add chicken, let simmer on top of stove or in a casserole for one hour, until sauce is thin. Serve over rice. Garnish with cut green peppers, raisins, and nuts.

Daisy usually accompanied her Country Captain with baked grapefruit, French-cut green beans, salads, rolls, and chocolate souffle.

cook penciled this touching message: "Daisy Bonner cooked the first meal and the last one in this cottage for the President Roosevelt." The four-term president was seated in a living room chair, posing for a portrait, when he was fatally stricken. The unfinished portrait remains on its stand.

From the house, the "Walk of States" leads to the *Roosevelt Museum.* A twelve-minute film includes segments of home movies showing the president swimming, playing with his Scottie dog Fala, carving the Thanksgiving turkey, and driving about the countryside in his 1938 Ford convertible, equipped with hand controls. (The car, all polished, sits in the garage next to the house.) Also displayed in the museum are glass cases filled with gifts and memorabilia: his wheelchair and cigarette holder, hundreds of walking canes, and a sweater knitted by First Lady Eleanor Roosevelt.

The Little White House and Roosevelt Museum (706–655–5870) are open daily, except Thanksgiving and Christmas, 9:00 A.M. to 5:00 P.M. Admission for adults is $4.00; ages 6 to 18, $2.00; and ages 5 and under, free. Special observances on April 12 commemorate FDR's extraordinary presidency.

The adjacent village of Warm Springs (population 450) has been revived with visitors in mind. More than sixty stores along the main street are stocked with antiques, collectibles, and Georgia-made arts and crafts.

The *Warm Springs Welcome Center* (800–FDR–1927), in the depot-looking building on the village's main street, is open every day for information and brochures.

The Hotel Warm Springs, 47 Broad Street, Warm Springs 31830, (800) 366–7616, fax (706) 655–2771, once housed the press, Secret Service, and visitors to FDR's Little White House. Now, the three-story, 1907 hotel receives bed and breakfast guests who come here to see the FDR shrines and shop at Warm Springs' dozens of handicraft stores. Fourteen guest rooms with two full beds are furnished with original oak Val-Kill Furniture. The Presidential Suite has two separate rooms with a connecting bath. The lobby has original ceramic tile floors, a vintage Stromberg-Carlson cord switchboard, stenciled walls, and 16-foot ceilings. The hotel has a restaurant and an old-fashioned soda shop with ice cream (home-made Georgia peach is innkeeper Lee Thompson's special treat). A bountiful Southern "Breakfast Feast" is included in rates of $60 to $135.

Franklin D. Roosevelt State Park, about 5 miles west of Warm Springs, on Highway 190, is ideal for a minivacation. On the wooded crest of Pine Mountain, the 9,480-acre park has a lake for swimming, fishing, and boating; hiking trails; horseback riding; and picturesque picnic spots. Roosevelt's favorite was Dowdell's Knob, with sweeping views of the Pine Mountain Valley. Many of the fieldstone buildings in the park were the product of the Depression-era Civilian Conservation Corps. Campsites ($10 a night) have water, electricity, hot showers, and rest rooms. Cottages have fireplaces and fully equipped kitchens for standard state fees. Call (800) 864–PARK for rates and reservations. There is a $2.00 per visit parking fee. The park office, Box 749, Pine Mountain 31822, (706) 663–4858, is open daily 8:00 A.M. to 5:00 P.M.

Hikers in your crowd can lace up their boots and hit the scenic 23-mile **Pine Mountain Trail.** Starting at the Callaway Gardens Country Store on Highway 27, the trail winds past rock formations, waterfalls, big stands of trees, and lush vegetation on its way to its terminus at the TV tower on Highway 85W near Warm Springs. One of the country's southernmost mountain trails, it has twelve access points, so you can get on and off with ease. Pick up a trail map at the FDR Park office.

If you'd like to spend some time canoeing on a scenic, unspoiled river, get in touch with **Flint River Outdoor Center,** 4429 Woodland Road, Thomaston 30286, (706) 647–2633. Guided and self-guided trips on the river begin at Highway 36, 15 miles south of Warm Springs. You pass through mostly mild rapids, waterfalls, hills and valleys, wildflowers, ferns, and animal habitats. You can overnight at a seven-room lodge and five RV hookups.

The **Pasaquan Folk Art Compound** would probably seem extraordinary even in India or the Land of Oz. In rural Marion County, near the tiny county seat of Buena Vista, this outdoor ensemble of toothy totem faces, smiling snakes, whirling pinwheels, suns, moons, and stars—all painted in brilliant primary colors—is positively otherworldly. It was the product of the late Eddie Owens Martin, who was born here in 1908, traveled to New York and abroad, and returned in 1950 to create this fabulous legacy. To finance his creativity Martin came to town in a turban and robes and told fortunes and sold jewelry around the courthouse.

Since Martin's death in 1986, his "Land of Pasaquan" has been meticulously restored and opened to the public on weekends and by appointment. For information call (912) 649–9444.

You'll find comfortable bed-and-breakfast accommodations at **Yesteryear,** a restored 1886 mansion at 229 Broad Street, Buena Vista 31803, (912) 649–7307.

Albany's Ray Charles

American music icon Ray Charles was born Ray Charles Robinson in Albany. Blind at age 7 and orphaned at 15, he forged an incredible career as a pianist, singer, songwriter, and band leader. He has won gold and platinum records for such worldwide hits as "What'd I Say," "I Can't Stop Loving You," "Hallelujah, I Love Her So," and "Georgia on My Mind," Georgia's official state song.

Approaching Albany from any direction, you'll pass symmetrical groves of papershell pecan trees. Pecans are available year-round, still in the paper-thin shell or roasted and boxed. Some groves invite you to come in and pick your own. The attractive city of 75,000 has other pleasant surprises as well.

At *Chehaw Wild Animal Park,* on Highway 91, 2½ miles northeast of the city, (912) 430–5275, African elephants and giraffes, Andean llamas, North American black bears, bobcats, elk, bison, and deer roam in natural habitats designed by Jim Fowler, former naturalist with TV's *Wild Kingdom.* You view the animals from protected elevated walkways. Wild Animal Park admission is $2.00 for adults; senior citizens, ages 3–11, and military personnel, $1.00. An additional $2.00 a carload lets you in the companion recreational park with play areas, jogging, hiking and biking trails, a re-created Creek Indian village, miniature train rides, a boat dock, and picnic areas. The *Chehaw National Indian Festival,* held in the park the third weekend of May, is one of the Southeast Tourism Society's top twenty yearly events. The park is open 9:00 A.M. to 6:00 P.M. daily

Thronateeska Heritage Foundation, 100 Roosevelt Avenue, (912) 432–6955, is a delightful time-trip through the nineteenth and early twentieth centuries. The complex includes an early 1900s "prairie style" train depot, a 1910 steam locomotive, an 1840s house, and a planetarium and science center in a vintage Railway Express Co. office. It's open Monday to Friday from noon to 5:00 P.M., Sunday from 2:00 to 5:00 P.M.

The *Albany Museum of Art,* 311 Meadowlark Drive, (912) 439–8400, has permanent and changing displays of regional and national artists. Open Tuesday to Saturday from 10:00 A.M. to 5:00 P.M. Admission for adults is $2.00; students, $1.00; under 12, no charge.

Contact the Albany Chamber of Commerce, Box 308, Albany 31702, (912) 883–6900.

Every spring in the swamps and bogs of southwest Georgia, a throny, scrubby, rather homely tree called the mayhaw produces an applelike fruit prized by gourmets and homemakers. The small, coral-hued fruit is gathered in fishing nets and by hand, and then turned into a delectable sweet-tart jelly that's sold in stores around the small Miller

County seat of Colquitt. The fruit is the star of Colquitt's early April Mayhaw Festival.

While you're in the Colquitt area, try to catch a performance of *"Swamp Gravy,"* an entertaining folklife play about the comedies and tragedies, tall tales, music, dance, and songs of Miller County and rural Georgia. Sponsored by the Colquitt/Miller Arts Council, it's performed in March, April, October, and November. Call (912) 758-5450 for more information.

The Tarrer Inn, 155 South Cuthbert Street, Colquitt 31737, (912) 758-2888, is another welcome newcomer to downtown Colquitt. Built in 1861 as a boardinghouse, the inn has recently been refurbished as a comfortable small hotel. Twelve guest rooms are decorated with antiques and modern amenities. Your continental breakfast comes with biscuits and homemade mayhaw jelly. At lunch and dinner the restaurant is renowned for its yeast rolls, seafood, quail, and lobster bisque. Sunday brunch is highlighted by omelets and other dishes prepared to order. Rates are $66 to $95.

You can hardly miss *The John Dill House,* 102 South Washington Street, Fort Gaines 31751, (912) 768-2338, as you drive through tiny Fort Gaines. The two-story house is painted brilliant pink, which innkeepers Ramona and Philip Kurland say was the original shade when the house was built in the late 1820s. The Kurlands have nine guest bedrooms, with many pieces of Victoriana. Each room has a private bath, and the Kurlands will send you off with a hearty breakfast. Rates are $65 for a double. You may also enjoy browsing the gift shop.

If you're a fan of country fairs and enjoy good, old-fashioned fun, put *Climax Swine Time* (912-246-0910) on your post-Thanksgiving calendar. Held the Friday and Saturday after Thanksgiving in the Decatur County community of Climax, many of the activities are pig-related: a hog-calling contest, best-dressed pig competition, a greased-pig chase, and a "chitlin" (chitterling) eating contest. Also on the agenda are country and gospel music, a 10-K race, cane grinding and syrup making, and barbecue and fried chicken for those who care not for "chitlins."

The *Rattlesnake Roundup* (912-762-4243), the last weekend of January, is the social event of the year at the small Grady County town of Whigham, 6 miles east of Climax. The event began a couple of decades ago when Whigham residents, tired of being accosted by the hissing reptiles every time they walked through their fields and farms, decided to do something about it and have some sport at the same time. On the big day, visitors pack tiny downtown Whigham as snakes by the hundreds are brought in and displayed.

Carter Country

Peach County leaves little doubt that it's the heart of Georgia's most luscious industry. Traveling on I–75 at night, you can't miss "The Big Peach," an enormous illuminated rendition of the fruit on a hundred-foot-pole at the Byron/Fort Valley exit. During the summer, visitors have plenty of opportunities to go into the orchards and pick their own or to buy fresh peaches at packing houses and roadside stands. The Byron/Fort Valley exit 49 is the northern end of the Andersonville Trail, which leads through Fort Valley to Plains on Highways 49 and 280.

In mid-June you're invited to the *Georgia Peach Festival* in Byron and Fort Valley. This weeklong event includes parades, street dances, peach pie cookoffs, peach-eating contests, and a king-and-queen coronation.

Six miles south of Fort Valley, at the Peach/Macon County line, look for a left turn off Highway 49 into Massee Lane Gardens, home of the *American Camellia Society.* Between November and March, pink and white blossoms in every known variety bloom in the Society's nine-acre gardens. All year round, you're invited into the Society's Williamsburg-style headquarters to admire the 170 porcelain birds and flowers created in the studios of the late American artist, Edward Marshall Boehm. The pieces are so lifelike they appear to be on the verge of flight. Some were created as gifts-of-state from presidents and kings.

The American Camellia Society, P.O. Box 1217, Fort Valley 31030, (912)

Peaches, Peaches Everywhere

Georgia has a peach fixation. Although it's called "The Peach State," the succulent fruit is no longer the state's most important agricultural commodity. It yielded eminence some years ago to soybeans, peanuts, broiler chickens, and other products. Nonetheless, it's hard to escape the spectre of peaches. It's on the license plates. There's a Peach County in middle Georgia, where the peach industry is concentrated, and the planned community of Peachtree City in Fayette County near Atlanta. More than three dozen streets in Metro Atlanta have "Peachtree" in their names, from Peachtree Street to Peachtree Battle Avenue and Peachtree Industrial Boulevard. The Peach Bowl is a postseason college football game played in Atlanta's Georgia Dome. One of the state's most famous athletes was Tyrus Raymond Ty Cobb, "The Georgia Peach," who won twelve batting titles and terrorized opposing players and his own Detroit Tiger teammates on and off the playing field.

967–2358, has open grounds daily from dawn to dusk; the headquarters building and Boehm collection are open Monday through Friday 8:30 A.M. to 4:00 P.M.

Part of the Andersonville Trail, Macon County is the home of Georgia's largest Mennonite community. You may admire antebellum white columns in the small towns of Marshallville and Montezuma.

The Macon County seat and a thriving Mennonite community, **Montezuma** was named by returning Mexican War veterans. The area has made a remarkable recovery from the devastating Flint River floods that occurred in 1994. Nearly one hundred Mennonite families give the little town some of the appearance of the Pennsylvania Dutch country. Drive east of Montezuma on Highway 26 past the neat barns and silos and the contented herds of the Mennonite dairy farms. Three miles from Montezuma—and 14 miles west of I–75 exit 41—look for a black buggy parked in front of **Yoder's Deitsch Haus** (912–472–2024), a sparkling clean cafeteria where Mennonites in traditional dress prepare truly admirable Southern cooking, spiced with such Pennsylvania Dutch specialties as shoofly pie and pot roast. Before leaving, stop by the bakery for a sackful of cakes, cookies, breads, and strudel. It's open for breakfast, lunch, and dinner Tuesday through Saturday. Handmade Mennonite dolls, afghans, coverlets, garden ornaments, and other items are on sale in the adjacent gift shop.

You may pick up a driving tour map from the Macon County Chamber of Commerce, P.O. Box 308, Montezuma 31063, (912) 472–2391.

Sumter County, the epicenter of Georgia's peanut industry, is home of the world's most famous peanut farmer, our thirty-ninth president. The southern anchor of the Andersonville Trail, Sumter is also the site of the Civil War's most notorious prisoner-of-war camp.

These days, all is green and peaceful at the **Andersonville National Cemetery and Historic Site.** Stop first at the National Park Service Visitors Center to view the film and exhibits, then take the self-guided driving tour.

Built in 1864 as confinement for 10,000 Union prisoners of war, the 26½-acre stockade soon became a charnel house for upwards of 33,000 captives. With the Confederacy barely able to feed and clothe its own forces, about 12,000 of the Andersonville inmates perished of disease and starvation. As park rangers point out, however, Southern prisoners in the more well-off North often fared no better than the Union prisoners at Andersonville.

After the war, the camp commander, Swiss-born Captain Henry Wirz, was found guilty of war crimes and hanged. The self-guided tour leads you past thousands of graves and impressive memorials erected by states whose sons died here. Tunnels testify to the prisoners' usually failed attempts to escape the horrors.

The *National Prisoner of War Museum,* opened in spring 1998, honors the 800,000 American solidiers, sailors, and airmen who've endured the horrors of capture and imprisonment from the Revolution to the Persian Gulf War. The 10,000-square-foot museum was built in partnership between the American Ex-Prisoners of War (AXPW), a national organization of 20,000 former POWs, and Friends of the Park, local citizens who support the National Park Service at Andersonvillle. Funds were raised by the sale of 270,000 commemorative coins created by the U.S. Mint. More than 10,000 donors and corporations gave about $700,000 and the Georgia Department of Transportation built a new entrance road and parking areas. Andersonville was chosen for the museum in recognition of the site's tragic history as the nation's most infamous POW camp. During the tour, you "experience" the terror of being captured by enemy troops and taken to prison. One room highlights the horrors of WWII's Bataan Death March and the forced marches to North Korean POW camps. Another room displays drawings, poetry, carvings, and clandestine radios POWs created to help them keep their sanity. The tour ends with a full-scale replica of POWs digging an escape tunnel under a Nazi prison camp.The museum's courtyard opens onto the remains of the Civil War Andersonville stockade. A fountain gushing water into a stream symbolizes the lack of fresh water prevalent in most POW camps.

A granite springhouse marks the site of *Providence Spring,* which legends says flowed from barren ground in answer to prisoners' prayers.

Across Highway 49, the village of *Andersonville* (population 250) has been returned to its 1860s appearance. At the Train Depot–Welcome Center, you'll be greeted by Peggy Sheppard, a live wire transplanted from Yonkers, New York. She'll direct you to the village's antiques and crafts shops, picnic groves, and antebellum churches and homes. The *Drummer Boy Museum* houses an extensive collection of guns, swords, battle flags, and documents signed by Jefferson Davis and Abraham Lincoln. The village's major yearly happenings are *The Great Southern Carriage and Wagon Auction* in early April, the *Andersonville Antiques and Civil War Artifacts Fair* Memorial Day weekend, and the *Andersonville Historic Fair* in early October, which features battle reenactments and scores of craftsmen and musicians.

Andersonville National Historic Site (912–924–0343), Andersonville 31711, is open daily 8:00 A.M. to 5:00 P.M. Also contact Andersonville Town Council (912–924–2558) at the same address.

Peggy Sheppard runs a charming country bed and breakfast called *"A Place Away."* The two bedrooms in the comfortable, rustic-looking cottage have private baths, refrigerators, and coffeemakers. Guest rooms and a sitting room are decorated in kick-off-your-shoes casual country style. Rates of $50 a double come with a bountiful Southern breakfast. Contact Andersonville Welcome Center, Andersonville 31711, (912) 924–2558.

At nearby *Americus,* stop at the Americus/Sumter County Tourism Council Welcome Center at the Windsor Hotel, (912) 924–2646, for a driving guide to the historic showplaces around the pleasant city of 20,000. Memorabilia of our thirty-ninth president are displayed at the *James Earl Carter Library* of Georgia Southwestern University.

For contemporary comforts wrapped in a splendid turn-of-the-century package, check into the *Windsor Hotel* in downtown Americus. Built in 1896, the redbrick, turreted-and-towered Italianate landmark reopened in 1991 to rave reviews. The fifty-three large guest rooms ($68 single, $78 double) are beautifully furnished and decorated. The Grand Dining Room serves high-Southern and continental cuisine, and there's a full bar and an open veranda with wicker rockers. The private Lindbergh Dining Room was named for "Lucky Lindy," who purchased his first plane and made his first solo flight from nearby Souther Field. Some old-timers remember him playing pool across the street from the hotel. The Windsor is at 125 West Lamar Street, Americus 31709. Call (912) 924–1555 or toll-free (800) 252–7466.

At the *DeSoto Confectionery & Nut Co.,* 13 miles east of Americus on Highway 280, the area's renowned product is sold in and out of the shell; wrapped in vanilla, chocolate, and peanut butter fudge; and peanut brittled, caramelized with corn, and otherwise glorified. The "Nut House" is open Monday through Saturday. They also do a booming mail-order business. Write P.O. Box 72, DeSoto 31743, or call (912) 874–1200.

More than a dozen years after leaving the White House, Jimmy Carter is still a magnet for visitors to his little hometown of *Plains.* Stop first at the Plains Visitors Center, on Highway 280 between Plains and Americus, to pick up information on attractions all over the area. The center also has its own stocked fishing pond. In town go first to the National Park Service Visitors Center in the former train depot/presidential campaign headquarters to see displays and hundreds of photos of the Carters.

Pea-Nuts! Fresh Roasted Pea-Nuts!

Jimmy Carter, Georgia's peanut farmer–president, drew the world's attention to the state's most bountiful crop. His native Southwest Georgia is the heart of this tasty industry, and it produces most of the more than two billion pounds of goobers grown in the state every year.

Breaking it down, there are about 200 peanut pods to a pound, and usually two peanuts per pod. They would make a mountain of about 800 billion peanuts. Laid end to end, they'd extend for more than six million miles, about twenty-five times the distance from the earth to the moon. "Goober" is believed to come from the African word, nguba, which, of course, means "peanut."

Most of the landmarks associated with Carter's before-during-and-after presidency are included in the *Jimmy Carter National Historic Site.* One of the best ways to see them is on a guided tour. *B.J.'s Tours,* which depart from Plains Peanuts on Main Street, take you by the Plains High School, Welcome Center and Museum, Carter's family farm and boyhood home, and when the Secret Service permits, the ranch-style home where he now lives. The cost is modest, and tours are laced with plenty of humorous anecdotes. When the past president is in town, he often appears at local social functions. On Sundays he teaches a class at Maran-atha Baptist Church.

Shops on the 1-block Main Street are stocked with Carter paraphernalia and, naturally, peanuts in many different guises.

Plains Bed and Breakfast, in the Victorian house where Carter's parents spent their early married years, has antique furnishings and modern comforts, but no souvenirs of the famous parents' boarding days. Doubles with private bath and full breakfast cost $65. Write Plains Bed and Breakfast, P.O. Box 217, Plains 31780, or call (912) 824–7252. Also contact Jimmy Carter National Historic Site, Plains 31780, (912) 824–3413.

Hello, Central! The *Georgia Rural Telephone Museum* in the small Sumter County town of Leslie recalls the bygone era when the telephone was a friend, not an impersonal convenience and telemarketing nuisance. Tommy Smith, who owns the local Citizen's Telephone Company, opened the museum in 1995 in a 1911 cotton warehouse he saved from destruction. His 2,000 pieces of telephonia include hand-cranked wooden voice boxes, early telephones of every size and description, and lifesize disoramas of switchboard operators in period dress. You'll also see a re-creation of Alexander Graham Bell's workshop, phone booths, and an early 1900s Model A Ford service truck. The museum is located on Highway 280 west, 22 miles off I–75, exit 33 (Cordele). Open Monday through Friday 9:00 A.M. to 3:00 P.M. Free admission. Phone (912) 874–4786.

Georgia Veterans Memorial State Park is a tranquil haven 9 miles west of Cordele and the racetrack lanes of I–75. A museum and vintage aircraft honor the state's military veterans. The park sits on Lake Black-shear, an 18-mile-long waterway renowned for catfish, black bass, bream, pickerel, and other delicious catches. Visitors may also enjoy boating, an 18-hole golf course, swimming in a freshwater pool, and a nature interpretive center and playground. The one hundred camping and trailer sites have electricity, water, rest rooms, and hot showers. Ten two- and three-bedroom cottages, with fireplaces and fully equipped kitchens, are available. For rates and reservations call (800) 864–PARK. There is a $2.00 per visit parking fee. The park office, on Highway 280, Cordele 31015, (912) 273–2190, is open daily 8:00 A.M. to 5:00 P.M.

Daphne Lodge, on Highway 280 near the park entrance, (912) 273–2596, is a pleasantly rustic, family-owned restaurant famous for its fried catfish and hush puppies. They also serve shrimp, steaks, and fried chicken at dinner Tuesday through Saturday.

If you're down this way the first week of July, join in the fun of Cordele's annual *Watermelon Festival.*

Roses and Pine Trees

The *Georgia Agrirama* is an off-the-beaten-path experience less than a quarter-mile off the well-beaten path of I–75. About three dozen vintage farm buildings make up the state's agricultural heritage center. Inside the gates of this nineteenth-century time warp, youngsters may go nose-to-nose with friendly farmyard animals and take a trip on a steam-powered logging train. Cotton is planted in the old-fashioned way by a farmer in bib overalls commanding a mule and a plow. The village blacksmith hammers out nails and utensils over a white-hot forge. Sugar cane is harvested by hand and ground into syrup and corn into grits and meal at a picture-postcard gristmill. A country store sells handmade quilts, preserves, cookbooks, toys, and corn shuck dolls.

The Agrirama, P.O. Box Q, Tifton 31793, (912) 386–3344, is open from Labor Day through May 31, Monday through Saturday 9:00 A.M. to 5:00 P.M. and Sunday 12:30 to 5:00 P.M.; June 1 to Labor Day, daily, 9:00 A.M. to 6:00 P.M. All-inclusive admission is $8.00, adults; $6.00, ages 55 and over; $4.00, ages 4 to 18; no charge, under 4.

Downtown Tifton has been revitalized thanks to the Georgia Main Street Program. About thirty shops and eateries are now attracting visitors to a complex of restored nineteenth and early twentieth century buildings. The 1906 Myon Hotel now houses City Hall, a permanent collection of regional art, shops, offices, and a restaurant. Contact the Tifton/Tift County Tourism Association, 115 West Second Street, Tifton 31793, (912) 386–0216.

From 1870 to the turn of the new century, **Thomasville** was a Southern Newport, the forefather of Palm Beach and Miami. Encouraged by reports of the area's healthy climate, wealthy Northerners came by private train to spend the winter at grand hotels, which brought chefs and orchestras all the way from New York and Europe. Many regular visitors built their own lavish homes and purchased surrounding plantations for grouse and quail hunting. In the early 1900s, the rich and famous discovered Florida, and Thomasville's "Golden Age" was over. Left behind was a remarkable heritage. Presidents, aristocrats, and "commoners" still flock to the city of 20,000 to hunt game birds and

Melhana Plantation's Stuffed Quail

*M*elhana dinner guests enjoy this variation on Thomasville's favorite game:

TURNIP-STUFFED QUAIL

Two 3-ounce quails per person stuffed with this mixture:

½ cup cooked wild rice

½ cup shredded turnip greens

2 tablespooons roasted pine nuts

1 teaspoon fresh chopped sage

1 tablespoon chopped cooked bacon

Brush quail with melted butter and season with salt and pepper. Bake 25 minutes at 275°. Baste frequently.

FRIED SWEET POTATO FRITTERS

2 cups grated sweet potatoes

3 whole eggs

1½ tablespoons flour

2 tablespoons grated onion

1¼ teaspoon salt

Combine and fry into 4-inch fritters until golden brown.

TOMATO-ROSEMARY GRAVY

3 cups veal stock

½ cup diced tomatoes

2 sprigs fresh rosemary

½ teaspoon salt

½ teaspoon fresh chopped garlic

Combine and cook slowly until reduced by one-third. Thicken with ½ teaspoon arrowroot.

antiques, tour homes and plantations, and participate in late April's Thomasville Rose Festival.

Stop first at the Destination Thomasville Tourism Authority Welcome Center, 109 South Broad Street, (912) 225–3919 and (800) 704–2350, where you can load up on maps, brochures, and self-guided walking and driving tour information. Guides can be arranged for tour groups. The Welcome Center is open Monday through Friday 9:00 A.M. to 5:00 P.M. and Saturday 10:00 A.M. to 3:00 P.M.

On your own, stop at the *Thomas County Historical Museum,* 725 North Dawson Street, where you'll see hundreds of photos and souvenirs of the "Golden Age." It's open daily 2:00 to 5:00 P.M. Admission for adults is $4.00; students, $1.00.

Nearby, the *Lapham-Patterson House,* 626 North Dawson Street, (912) 225–4004, is an outlandish Victorian mansion built for Chicago shoe manufacturer C. W. Lapham. Maintained as a state historical museum, the tri-winged, mustard-yellow mansion is highlighted by cantilevered interior balconies, double-flue chimneys, and fish-scale shingles. It's open Tuesday through Saturday 9:00 A.M. to 5:00 P.M.; Sunday 2:00 to 5:00 P.M. Admission is charged: adults, $3.00; ages 6 to 18, $1.00; under age 5, free.

Pebble Hill Plantation (912–226–2344) is a "must-see." The twenty-eight-room Georgian and Greek Revival main house and the gardens, stables, and kennels were left as a museum by the late Pansy Ireland Poe. Inside the house are thirty-three original John James Audubon bird prints and extensive collections of silver, crystal, and antique furnishings. Five miles southwest of Thomasville, on Highway 319, it's open Tuesday through Saturday 10:00 A.M. to 5:00 P.M. and Sunday 1:00 to 5:00 P.M. Adult admission fee is $2.00 to the grounds, $5.00 to the main house; under age 6 not permitted in main house.

Melhana Plantation Resort, 301 Showboat Lane, Thomasville 31792, (888) 920–3030, is a nineteenth-century hunting plantation Thomasville natives Charlie and Fran Lewis have transformed into a five-star quality country inn. Since 1996, the Lewises have restored the Pink House, the 1825 Greek Revival manor house, into eight guest rooms and suites tastefully furnished with antique reproductions, imported linens, fresh flowers, and private baths with whirlpool tubs for two. Other deluxe accommodations are in the former Williamsburg-style carriage house and dairy barns. The dining room serves three daily gourmet meals, and room service is available twenty-four hours. Guests can swim in the heated, enclosed, Olympic-size pool, play tennis, and enjoy horsedrawn carriage rides around the forty-acre grounds. Quail hunting and horseback riding can be arranged. Doubles are $150 to $400 a night.

Several of Thomasville's most beautiful old homes welcome bed-and-breakfast guests. All take pride in their antique furnishings and traditional south Georgia hospitality.

Some of the nicest homes include the *1884 Paxton House*, 445 Remington Avenue, (800) 278–0138; *Evans House*, 725 South Hansell Street, (800) 344–4717; *Grand Victoria Inn*, 817 South Hansell Street, (912) 226–7460; *Our Cottage on the Park*, 801 South Hansell Street, (912) 227–0404; and *Serendipity Cottage*, 339 East Jefferson Street, (912) 226–8111. Most are in the $65 to $100 price range and include breakfast. The zip code is 31792.

If you'd like to enjoy a bit of Thomasville's sporting life, shoot some skeet, and hunt birds and game, contact *Quail Hunting Thomasville*, P.O. Box 1540, Thomasville 31792, (912) 225–3919, and *Myrtlewood Plantation*, P.O. Box 32, Thomasville 31799, (912) 228–0987.

Apafia Farm, Route 2, Box 92–D, Hansell Chastain Road, Thomasville 31792, (912) 228–1682, offers Western-style horseback rides through plantation country.

Thomasville's really big annual event is the late April *Rose Festival*, a week of parades, pageantry, home tours, and rose judgings that attracts visitors from many countries. In the good-news-bad-news category, the renowned Thomasville Rose Test Garden has closed, but it's been replaced by the *Thomasville Rose Garden*, which displays scores of varieties of blooming plants around the shores of Cherokee Lake, at the corner of Covington and Smith Avenues. Admission is free.

For an up-to-date idea of what's happening, phone Destination Thomasville (800–704–2350).

PLACES TO STAY IN
SOUTHWEST GEORGIA

HOGANSVILLE-
LAGRANGE AREA
The House on Seventh,
311 East Seventh Street,
West Point,
(706) 645–2064.

The Queen Anne–style cottage was built at the turn of the century in the small textile town of West Point, on the Georgia-Alabama border. Ira and Emily Culpepper have three guest rooms with private baths and period antiques, and serve a generous country breakfast with their $80 tariff.

*Thyme Away Bed
and Breakfast,*
508 Greenville Street,
(706) 885–9625.

The imposing Greek Revival house in downtown La Grange has been returned to its 1840s elegance. Guest rooms are furnished with antiques, TV, phone, fridge, and private baths with whirlpool tubs and gas fireplaces. You can relax in the parlor, play the piano, and use the fax and modem services. Includes full breakfast, all for $75 to $80.

COLUMBUS
Columbus Hilton,
800 Front Avenue at the
Riverwalk, (800) 524–4020.

The city's best full-service lodgings. Built partially in a nineteenth-century ironworks, the 177-room hotel has an outdoor pool, restaurant, bar, and meeting rooms. Double occupancy rates are $85 to $125.

Gates House,
737 Broadway,
(800) 891–3187,
fax (706) 324–2070.

A short walk from Riverwalk, Carolyn and Tom Gates's 1880 Colonial Revival house is a time-trip to the elegance of Victorian America. Guest rooms have family antiques, private baths, queen or twin beds. You can have breakfast in the dining room, Victorian garden, or front porch. Double occupancy, $75 to $95.

Rothschild-Pound House,
201 Seventh Street,
(800) 585–4075,
fax (706) 322–3772.

Built in the 1870s, the Second Empire–style showplace has four guest suites with private bath, some with Jacuzzi hot tubs. Original art and antiques are throughout the house. Innkeepers Mamie and Garry Pound offer full breakfast and evening cocktails in their rates of $95 to $140.

*Woodruff House & The
Mansion Bed & Breakfast
Inns,*
1414 Second Avenue,
(888) 320–9309,
fax (706) 320–9304.

Companion houses invite you to step back into gracious, romantic eras. Woodruff House, a white-columned Victorian cottage built in 1885, was the birthplace of Robert W. Woodruff, whose leadership made Coca-Cola a worldwide refreshment. Thirteen suites have private bath, fireplace, cable TV, and phone. The adjacent Queen Anne–style mansion, also with guest rooms, was built in 1881 by businessman Joseph Garrett. Double occupancy, with breakfast, goes for $85 to $160.

BAINBRIDGE
*Gilded Cage
Bed & Breakfast,*
722 West Street,
(912) 243–2040,
fax (912) 243–7234.

Two rooms with private baths, two with shared baths, in an 1855 Victorian home in the downtown historic district. Amenities include TV, VCR, and billiard table. Rates are $55 to $85 for a double.

*The White House
Bed & Breakfast,*
320 Washington Street,
(912) 248–1703.

A gracious Georgian-style home built before the Civil War. One guest room with private bath, two share a bath. Swimming pool, in-room phones, continental breakfast. Rates are $50 to $60 for a double.

AMERICUS
The Pathway Inn,
501 South Lee Street, (912) 928–2078 and (800) 889–1466.

Sheila and David Judah's turn-of-the-century Victorian showplace is among the mansions and old trees in Americus's most beautiful residential neighborhood. Five guest rooms have private baths with whirlpools and king or queen beds. Full breakfast, wine, and refreshments with rates of $70 to $105.

Rees Park Garden Inn,
504 Rees Park, (912) 931–0122.

Built beween 1847 and 1848, Don and Jodi Miles's 5,000-square-foot home is set in an acre of walkways and gardens. Four guest rooms have plush antique furnishings, large private baths, phone, TV, and ceiling fan. Three have tubs large enough for two, 12-foot ceilings, and original fireplace mantels. "Scarlett's Room" has an optional adjoining room that makes a two-bedroom suite. Well-mannered pets are welcome. Rates are $62 for a double.

TIFTON
Hummingbird's Perch Bed & Breakfast,
I–75 exit 23, 5 miles north of Tifton, Rte. 1, Box 1870, Chula 31733, (912) 382–5431.

Gracious country living, with bird-watching and fishing around a small lake. Three guest rooms, with private or shared bath. Rates are $40 to $70.

PLACES TO EAT IN SOUTHWEST GEORGIA

COLUMBUS
Miriam's Cafe and Gallery, 1350 Thirteenth Street, (706) 327–0707.

Enjoy fine American and continental cuisine in a cozy cafe brightened by work of local artists. Specialties include seafood, filet mignon, pastas, and chicken dishes. Lunch Friday only, dinner Friday and Saturday, Sunday brunch.

The Olive Branch Cafe & The Loft,
1032 Broadway, (706) 596–8141.

Columbus's choice for continental and American fare, with some Greek flourishes to its lamb loin with spinach and olives, fried goat cheese, salad, and moussaka. Other house specialties include steaks, seafood, and pasta. Dinner Monday through Saturday. After dinner go upstairs to The Loft for jazz and other live entertainment.

WARM SPRINGS
The Bulloch House,
on Highway 27 just off Warm Springs's main street. (706–655–9057).

Really big appetites should check out the buffet line.

The Victorian Tea Room (706–655–2319).

A 1906 mercantile store has been turned into a cozy

dining room specializing in soups, salads, sandwiches, and Southern home cooking. It's open for lunch Tuesday through Sunday and for dinner Friday only.

PLAINS

Magnolia & Ivy Tea Parlor, Antiques, & Gifts,
109 Church Street,
across the train tracks
from Main Street,
(912) 824–4198.

In a part of the country better-known for heavy-hitting barbecue, fried chicken, and cornbread, sisters Kay Snipes and Terri Jackson have created genteel Victorian tearooms in Plains and three other small southwest Georgia towns. "Light Afternoon Tea," with a choice of fifteen varieties, is served with scones, finger sandwiches, fresh fruit, and pastries; "Full Afternoon Tea" puts additional delicacies on the table.

Other locations are in historic buildings in Parrott, (912) 623–4506; Cuthbert, (912) 732–5523; and Richland, (912) 887–2914.

THOMASVILLE

The Billiard Academy,
South Broad Street,
(912) 226–9981.

Thomasvillians can't seem to get through a day without chowing on Joe Kirkland's hot dogs, dressed in his special chili sauce. Out-of-towners drive miles for their daily fix. Folks in a hurry get 'em to go at the sidewalk window. If you've a little more time, step inside for a friendly game at the billiard tables and have a cool brew and a chat with the boys at the lunch counter/bar. Dogs and billiards are available from early morning to late at night, Monday through Saturday.

George & Louie's,
217 Remington Avenue,
(912) 226–1218.

Fresh seafood plates, channel catfish, snapper, broiled and fried shrimp and oysters, scallops, burgers and shish kabab, steaks, and sandwiches draw big crowds for dinner Monday through Saturday.

The Homecoming,
1164 Myrick Road,
(912) 226–1143.

A short drive out of town, this former country cabin with a big front porch is a nostalgic old-timey place for all-you-can-eat catfish and quail, and fried, boiled, and grilled shrimp, oysters,

scallops, fried chicken, and Delmonico steak. A kids-under-12 menu has smaller portions of catfish, shrimp, and chicken, as well as hot dogs, hamburgers, and PB&J sandwiches. Dinner Monday through Saturday.

Melissa's,
134 Madison Avenue,
(912) 228–9844.

Cleverly redone laundry warehouse does a great job with beer-battered shrimp, quesadillas, chicken tarragon, black bean cakes, pastas, grilled double-cut pork chops, and chicken tacos. Lunch and dinner Monday through Saturday.

Mom & Dad's Italian Restaurant,
1800 Smith Avenue,
(912) 226–6265.

Traditional Italian pastas, seafood, chicken, veal, steak, and other American fare. Dinner Tuesday through Saturday.

The Plaza,
217 South Broad Street,
(912) 226–5153.

An old, old favorite, The Plaza has served steaks, seafood, prime rib, and Greek dishes for nearly 80 years. Breakfast, lunch, and dinner Monday through Saturday.

Southeast Georgia

BBQ and Harness Horses

The *New Perry Hotel* has been a beacon for middle Georgia travelers since the 1920s, when it replaced a circa-1854 country inn. In bygone days, when Highway 41 funneled Florida-bound vacationers through the center of Perry, the New Perry's cheerful guest rooms—and especially its dining room—were a command performance. Even now, with most of the traffic a mile away on I–75, weary motorists still find their way to this surviving vestige of small-town hospitality.

Set among trees and gardens, across from the Houston (House-ton) County Courthouse, the New Perry has thirty-seven rooms in its main building and seventeen more in a modern motel-type addition by the swimming pool. They go for a modest $35 to $49 a night. They're nice, comfortable, and air-conditioned, but the dining room is the main attraction.

With its starched white tablecloths, fresh flowers, bird and floral prints, this is the genteel Southern dining room personified. The menu is the chapter-and-verse Sunday Southern dinner: fried chicken, broiled Spanish mackerel and perch, baked ham, turkey and dressing, stewed corn, turnip greens, yams, green beans, congealed salads, shrimp cocktail, pecan and peach pies. Breakfast is also the full Southern board of grits, hot biscuits, sausage, ham, and eggs.

Breakfast, lunch, and dinner are served daily, at prices that are inexpensive by any standard. Breakfast will be about $4.50, lunch around $6.00, and dinner with entree, three vegetables, and chilled relish tray, less than $10.00. No alcohol is served. Contact the New Perry at 800 Main Street, Perry 31069, (912) 987–1000 or (800) 877–3779.

The *Museum of Aviation* (912–926–6870), 2 miles south of Warner Robins Air Force Base, is a tribute to our winged military might. In two huge buildings you can admire more than seventy-five American and foreign military aircraft. You can also see a film on the history of the Air Force and numerous exhibits and displays. Take I–75 exit 45 (Centerville/Warner Robins) and follow the signs through the city of Warner Robins. Open daily 10:00 A.M. to 5:00 P.M. Free admission. Telephone (912) 926–6870.

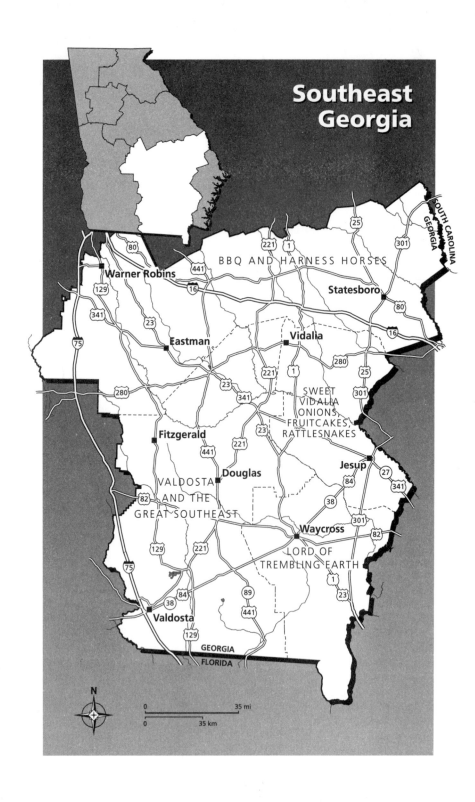

Southeast Georgia

BBQ AND HARNESS HORSES

SWEET VIDALIA ONIONS, FRUITCAKES, RATTLESNAKES

VALDOSTA AND THE GREAT SOUTHEAST

LORD OF TREMBLING EARTH

Warner Robins
Statesboro
Eastman
Vidalia
Fitzgerald
Douglas
Jesup
Waycross
Valdosta

SOUTH CAROLINA

GEORGIA
FLORIDA

N

0 35 mi
0 35 km

After touring the Aviation Museum, tuck into a hearty, perfectly cooked sirloin or T-bone with sauteed mushrooms, vegetables, and baked potato at **Montana's** (912–929–9555), 2212 Watson Boulevard, Warner Robins, and enjoy it with beer or wine. Dinner is served Monday through Saturday.

Barbecue is dear to Georgians' hearts, celebrated in song and story, and exalted at annual festivals such as the **Big Pig Jig** the second weekend of October at the little middle-Georgia town of Vienna (Vie-enna). Dubbed the "Cadillac of Barbecue Contests" and proclaimed the state of Georgia's official barbecue cooking contest by the state legislature, this is serious business indeed. The winning team takes home prize money, trophies, bragging rights, and the honor of representing Georgia at the annual International Pig Cook-off in Memphis, Tennessee— and just maybe coming back as world champion of the barbecuing arts.

Of course, there's a fun side to all this serious business. Judges sample the secret sauces, which, according to the rules, may include "any nonpoisonous substances" and the flavors and textures of ribs, shoulders, and other succulent portions of the porkers. Famished festivalgoers also get their chance to savor the entries and take part in a host of other activities. There's always plenty of bluegrass and country music, square dancing and clog dancing, arts and crafts, a 5-kilometer "Hog Jog," and a "Whole Hog Parade," featuring handsome porkers, still not ready for the grill, decked out in all manner of zany costumes.

For information contact Dooly County Chamber of Commerce, 204-A West Union Street, Vienna 31092, (912) 268-4500.

SOUTHEAST GEORGIA'S TOP HITS

New Perry Hotel

Museum of Aviation

Big Pig Jig

Harness Racing Festival

Georgia Cotton Museum

George L. Smith State Park

Magnolia Springs State Park

Statesboro/University Museum

Vidalia Sweet Onion

Wildlife/Raptor Center

Rattlesnake Roundup

Lake Grace

Edwin L. Hatch Nuclear Plant Visitors Center

Okefenokee Swamp Park/ Laura S. Walker State Park

Suwannee Canal Recreation Area

Stephen C. Foster State Park

Valdosta

The Crescent

Hahira Honeybee Festival

Reed Bingham State Park

Jefferson Davis Memorial Museum/Crystal Lake Water Park

General Coffee State Park

Douglas's public golf courses

Blue and Gray Museum

Statue of Liberty

Little Ocmulgee State Park

Cotton may no longer be king, but it's still important to the economy of Dooly and other southeast Georgia counties. At harvest time in September and October, the white bolls cover the ground like fresh-fallen snow.

The *Georgia Cotton Museum,* I–75 exit 36, Vienna, (912) 268–2045, created by farmers and other Dooly Countians, looks at "white gold's" past, present, and future with artifacts, displays, and tools that planted, plowed, and harvested the cotton in the days before mechanized farming. It also looks at the dark side, the slave labor that was vital to its production. Open Monday through Saturday 9:00 A.M. to 4:30 P.M. Admission is free.

Hawkinsville, the Pulaski County seat, is Georgia's harness racing capital. The *Harness Racing Festival,* the first weekend of April, celebrates this sport, which has been a part of Pulaski County's life since the late 1800s, when the county's mild climate made it a popular winter training grounds for harness horses from the Midwest, the Northeast, and Canada.

Nowadays, more than 350 of the sleek, high-stepping trotters and pacers come to the town of 4,000 between October and April. On the two-day festival weekend, more than 10,000 spectators crowd the grandstand at the festival grounds to watch the races and enjoy the country fair atmosphere that surrounds the red clay track. For those not familiar with the sport, the horses have two decidedly different gaits. Pacers wear plastic leg hoops (called hobbles) that cause the legs on each side of their body to move in tandem: left front and left rear, right front and right rear. Trotters navigate with a diagonal gait: left front and right rear legs move together, likewise right front and left rear. They seem to effortlessly pull the colorfully silked jockeys riding behind them in light two-wheeled sulkies.

After the festival the horses pack up and head for the big-money tracks up north. One thing missing from the event is parimutuel betting. Georgia law prohibits it, but that doesn't mean you can't find some friendly unofficial wagers around the track. For information call the Harness training facility at (912) 892–9463.

Away from the track, Hawkinsville's main attractions are its restored turn-of-the-century opera house and Georgia's only major kiwifruit farm. Built in early 1907 as a stop on the vaudeville circuit between New York and New Orleans, the *Old Opera House* was abandoned in the 1950s and was about to fall totally into ruins when a group of Pulaski County businesspeople came to its rescue a few years ago. Now it hosts touring concerts and local productions. If you're here when an event is scheduled, come and spend a nostalgic evening in the restored horseshoe-shaped auditorium. Call (912) 783–1717.

Double Q Farms (912–892–3794), 8 miles from town, is Janis and Charles Quimby's kiwi "ranch." There they raise the delicious green

Bill's Favorites

*New Perry Hotel
Dining Room*

Museum of Aviation

Big Pig Jig

Harness Racing Festival

Okefenokee Swamp Park

*Suwannee Canal
Recreation Area*

*Stephen C. Foster
State Park*

*Lamar Q. Ball Jr.
Raptor Center*

*Georgia Southern
University*

Blue and Gray Museum

fruit with the fuzzy brown skin that most of us associate with New Zealand. When the kiwis reach their peak in October, you can go out onto the seven-acre farm and pick your own. Janis Quimby's kiwi jams and jellies are sold at the farm store and shipped around the world. Kiwi jalapeño jelly is a big favorite.

The Black Swan Inn (912–783–4466), 411 Progress Avenue, Hawkinsville 31036, a white-columned early twentieth-century Southern Colonial mansion, is Hawkinsville's premier lodging. It was named for *The Black Swan,* a nineteenth-century paddlewheel steamboat that carried cargo and passengers up the Ocmulgee River that runs through downtown Hawkinsville. The inn's six guest rooms have private baths and period furnishings. A suite has a whirlpool tub. Rates of $50 to $70 include a light continental breakfast. The inn's dining room offers traditional Southern cooking with pastas; steak with mushrooms and béarnaise sauces; duck, veal, fish, and chicken dishes; and cheesecakes and European-style desserts.

Several antiques shops are on Broad Street, Hawkinsville's main street. For other information call *Hawkinsville-Pulaski County Chamber of Commerce,* P.O. 561, Hawkinsville 31036, (912) 783–1717.

That wonderful but sadly fading American landmark, the small-town cafe, is alive and well in Dublin. *Ma Hawkins Cafe* (912–275–1713), near the Laurens County Courthouse at 124 West Jackson Street, has been a citadel of Southern home cooking since 1931. Now operated by a grandson of the foundress, the cheerful cafe specializes in Southern-style breakfast—if you've been timid about sampling grits, Ma Hawkins is the place—and lunch and dinner plates highlighted by corn bread, chicken and dumplings, fried chicken, slowly simmered turnip greens and other fresh vegetables, and homemade desserts.

The cafe's front table is the traditional forum for Dublin's movers and shakers, who congregate throughout the day to jaw about the weather, crops, football, politics, and the general flow of life. The cafe is open for breakfast, lunch, and dinner Monday through Saturday. No credit cards are accepted, but it's hard to spend more than $5.00.

If you'd like to try your own hand at corn bread, using the absolutely freshest possible ingredients, head for *Chappell's Mill* (912–272–5128),

Highway 441, 13 miles north of Dublin. Built in 1811 and saved from destruction by General William T. Sherman's Union army, the old mill grinds about 15,000 bushels of corn a year into the right stuff for light, golden corn bread. Watch it ground, then buy a two-pound bag for 60 cents, five pounds for $1.10. Call before visiting.

Dublin's nineteenth-century Irish heritage is reflected in its annual *St. Patrick's Day Festival,* a lively round of parades, beauty pageants, arts and crafts, square dancing, softball, and golf tournaments. Along the emerald-green lawns of the city's *Bellevue Avenue,* many photogenic Greek Revival and Victorian showplaces parade year-round.

George L. Smith State Park, off Highway 23, 4 miles southeast of Twin City, is a quiet, lightly used retreat with twenty-one fully equipped camping sites, picnic areas, and a fishing lake with rental boats. Write P.O. Box 57, Twin City 30471, or call (912) 763-2759 or (800) 864–PARK for camping reservations. Two very nice bed and breakfasts are in the Emanuel County seat of Swainsboro: *Coleman House* (912–237–9100), 323 North Main Street ($55 to $85 a night); and *Edenfield House Inn* (912–237–3007), 358 Church Street ($45 to $65 a night). Both are in zip code 30401.

Magnolia Springs State Park, Highway 25, 5 miles north of Millen, is one of the prettiest and quietest in the whole park system. Huge old trees bend their limbs over clear springs flowing at an estimated nine million gallons a day. It's a lovely spot to spread a picnic. You can also swim, dabble your bait for fish, and walk along nature trails. You may even want to camp out overnight or stay in a furnished cottage. There is a $2.00 per visit parking fee. Contact Magnolia Springs State Park, Route 5, Box 488, Millen 30442, (912) 982–1660 or (800) 864–PARK for camping and cottage reservations.

Adjoining the park, the *Bo Ginn Aquatic Education Center* has twenty-six tanks showing off many species of Georgia fish. Call (912) 982–4160.

Tree-shaded *Statesboro* (population 21,000) is the Bulloch County seat and home of 14,000 Georgia Southern University students. The *University Museum,* (912) 681–5444, has a fascinating collection of dinosaur fossils, do-touch exhibits, and revolving scientific and technological displays. The "star" attraction is The *Plant Votgle Whale,* a 45-million-year-old leviathan that scientists believe walked on sturdy legs. It was discovered at Georgia Power Company's Plant Votgle in neighboring Burke County.

The *Center for Wildlife Education and Lamar Q. Ball Jr. Raptor*

Top Annual Events

St. Patrick's Day Festival,
March 17, Dublin, (912) 272–5546

Old South Farm Days,
mid-March, Tea Grove Plantation,
Walthourville, (912) 368–7412

Haness Racing Festival,
first weekend in April, Hawkinsville,
(912) 783–1717

Baxley Tree Festival,
early April, Tri-County Fairgrounds,
Baxley, (912) 367–7731

Sweet Onion Century Bike Ride,
early April, Vidalia, (912) 538–5892

Mossy Creek Barnyard Festival,
mid-April, I–75 near Perry,
(912) 922–8265

**Okefenokee Art Festival & Earth Day
Celebration,** mid-April, Okefenokee
National Wildlife Refuge, Folkston,
(912) 897–1184

Vidalia Onion Festival,
late April–early May, (912) 538–8687

Georgia National Fair,
early October, Georgia National
Fairgrounds & Agricenter, Perry,
(912) 988–6483

Big Pig Jig,
second weekend in October, Vienna,
(912) 268–4500

Dublin Antique Fair Show and Sale,
mid-November, National Guard Armory,
Dublin, (912) 272–5546

Buzzard Day,
first Saturday of December, Reed Bingham
State Park, Adel, (912) 896–3551

Hazlehurst Holiday Tours,
mid-December, Hazlehurst,
(912) 375–4543

Center is Georgia Southern's most popular attraction. Visitors follow a self-guided nature walk through six natural habitats that house fourteen birds of prey native to Georgia. They include bald eagles, falcons, ospreys, hawks, and several types of owls. They were rescued after being injured and can't return to the wild. Look up and you'll see a bald eagle camped in a hot tub–size aerie in the forks of a live oak tree, an osprey perched on a limb overlooking a cypress swamp, and a barred owl roosting in the rafters of an old barn strung with sheaves of drying tobacco. The center was designed by naturalist Jim Fowler, former host of Mutual of Omaha's *Wild Kingdom* TV series. Fowler also designed Albany's Chehaw Wild Animal Park. It's open Monday through Friday 9:00 A.M. to 5:00 P.M. and Saturday and Sunday 1:00 to 5:00 P.M. Free admission.

Near the campus, the ten-acre **Botanical Gardens** grow around a restored nineteenth-century farmhouse and outbuildings. After trekking around the gardens, bring your best boardinghouse reach to the **Beaver House,** 121 South Main Street, (912) 764–2821. The dining room table groans under a delicious family-style buffet that includes fried chicken, fish, baked ham, roast beef, and numerous vegetables, relishes, and desserts. It's open daily except Saturday for lunch ($6.49) and dinner ($6.99). *Vandy's Barbecue,* downtown at 22 Vine Street, (912) 764–2444, is another culinary landmark.

The Victorian/Federal-style **William Guy Raines Home,** built in the early 1900s, is a lovely bed and breakfast near downtown Statesboro and the Georgia Southern campus. It's located at 106 South Main Street, Statesboro 30458, (912) 489–8628 or (800) 846–9466, fax (912) 489–4785. Architectural features include a spacious veranda, Palladian windows and numerous brass and wood treatments. Guests stay in the main house or the adjacent Craftsman-style Brannen House. All 19 rooms have private baths, antiques, phones, and cable TV. Rates are $75 to $120. The Raines Room's upscale fare features duck, chicken, seafood, beef, and elegant desserts. Dinner Monday through Saturday.

Statesboro is a short drive off I–16, 60 miles west of Savannah. Contact Convention and Visitors Bureau, 332 South Main Street, Statesboro 30460, (800) 568–3301, or access www.visit-statesboro.com.

Sweet Vidalia Onions, Fruitcakes, Rattlesnakes

The sandy soil of Toombs, Treutlen, and neighboring southeast Georgia counties yields a favorite gourmet delicacy. The well-known *Vidalia Sweet Onion* takes its name from the Toombs County town of Vidalia. During the summer, you can buy 'em by the sackful or carload at roadside stands in and around the town of 10,000.

The **Robert Toombs Inn** in downtown Lyons (5 miles east of Vidalia) is a modern pairing of two early 1900s hotels. Fourteen single rooms and five small suites have modern baths and Early American furnishings: Rates range from $48 to $55. The dining room features Southern, American, and Tex-Mex food. The full bar is a rarity in a small Georgia town. The inn is at 101 South State Street, Lyons 30436; call (912) 526–4489.

Claxton, seat of Evans County, is famous for fruitcakes and rattlesnakes. As you drive into the small town, you're very nearly intoxicated by the sweet aroma of baking fruitcakes. More than 6 million pounds of the holiday treats are produced annually in Claxton's modern bakeries. You can get information on **Fruitcake Plant Tours** and other area attractions at the Claxton Welcome Center, 4 North Duval Street, Claxton 30417, (912) 739–2281.

If you're here in mid-March, you can take part in the festivities surrounding the annual ***Rattlesnake Roundup.*** Begun, simply, in 1968 as an effort to reduce the venomous reptile's threat to man and beast, the roundup has grown into a major happening, with a parade, hundreds of arts and crafts booths, home cooking, and such rattler-related events as awards for the most snakes brought in,

Robert Toombs Inn

the longest, the fattest, and so on. A reptile expert "milks" the snakes of their deadly venom, which is used in antivenom serums and other medicines.

In neighboring Tattnall County, ***Gordonia-Altamaha State Park,*** P.O. Box 1047, Reidsville 30453, (912) 557-6444, has twenty-five tent and trailer sites with water and electricity, hot showers, and rest rooms as well as a swimming pool, a boat dock, and plenty of good fishing places. There's also a new 9-hole golf course. Call (800) 864–PARK for camping reservations.

If you're a fishing family, you may come close to nirvana in Wayne County. One county removed from the Atlantic Coast, Wayne includes 60 miles of the ***Altamaha River,*** a waterway rich with several varieties of bass, bream, perch, and catfish. Altamaha River Campground, 249 Joe Naia Road, (912) 586-6300, has three big fishing lakes, a spring-fed swimming lake, campsites, and nature trails.

Lake Grace, on Highway 301 near the Wayne County seat of Jesup, is a local favorite. The 250 acres include plenty of secluded fishing spots, as well as opportunities for boating, swimming, waterskiing, picnics, and camping. Contact the park superintendent at (912) 579-6475.

Pine Lake Campground (912-427-3664), Highway 341 near the small community of Gardi, features a stocked twenty-acre lake tailored for bank fishing. You may also enjoy a swimming pool, shaded picnic areas, and forty campsites with electricity, water, and rest rooms.

Jaycee Landing (912–427–7987), on Highway 301 North, has a number of boat ramps in the Altamaha, as well as a general store with food and all your favorite kinds of fishing bait. Campsites have water, electricity, rest rooms, and showers.

Your camaraderie with local anglers is bound to lead you to some especially rewarding, off-the-beaten path fishing spots!

Sweet, Sweet Vidalia Onions

*V*idalia onions are so sweet that many people eat 'em like apples or dressed up like this:

HONEY BAKED ONIONS

Preheat oven to 325°.

Peel and trim 4 large, white, sweet onions. Cut in half and place in a buttered baking dish, flat sides up.

In a separate bowl mix:

1½ cups tomato juice

1½ cups water

6 teaspoons melted butter

6 teaspoons honey

Pour sauce over onions. Bake for one hour, or until soft.

VIDALIA ONION TART

This dish takes a little time, but it's worth it.

Tart dough:

2 cups plus 1 tablespoon flour

5¼ ounces butter, chilled and cut into small pieces

¼ cup ice water

Pinch of salt

Filling for tart:

3 Vidalia onions, chopped

1 tablespoon bacon, finely minced and sauteed

2 tablespoons butter

1 cup heavy cream

1 whole egg, plus one additional egg yolk

Salt, pepper, nutmeg, and cumin seeds

For the tart, place flour and salt in a mixing bowl. Add butter and work into the flour. Add water and form into dough (don't work dough too much). Chill at least two hours. Roll out dough to ⅛-inch thickness and fit into pie pan. Prick the dough all over with a fork. Set aside.

Saute onions in butter just until tender. Add heavy cream and reduce until it thickens. Remove from the heat and mix in the beaten egg and additional egg yolk. Season to taste with salt, pepper and nutmeg (freshly ground if possible). Pour filling into prepared tart shell and sprinkle finely minced bacon and cumin seeds on top. Bake on the bottom rack of a preheated 425° oven 20 to 25 minutes, or until done. Serves 6.

When you've bagged your limit, enjoy a large sample of Southeast Georgia cooking at *Jones' Kitchen,* on Main Street in Jesup, (912) 427–4100. The all-you-can-eat daily luncheon spread includes fresh local fish, chicken, meat loaf, vegetables, several kinds of salads, and a peach or apple cobbler for less than you'd pay for lunch at a fast-food outlet.

Jesup, an industrious town of 10,000, has a number of beautifully maintained Victorian homes, which you can drive past with a brochure provided by the Wayne County Chamber of Commerce, P.O. Box 70, Jesup 31545, (912) 427–2028.

The *Edwin L. Hatch Nuclear Plant Visitors Center,* on U.S. Highway 1, 14 miles north of Baxley, will tell you all you ever wanted to know about this controversial source of energy. The story is told with films, hands-on exhibits, and animated displays. Open Monday through Friday 8:30 A.M. to 5:00 P.M. Phone (912) 367–3668 or (800) 722–7774. No charge.

You can unwind at *Lake Mayers,* a locally popular resort with fishing, boating, swimming, waterskiing, and picnic areas. Lake Mayers is off U.S. Highway 341, 8 miles west of Baxley.

Nonmembers may play the Appling Country Club's 9-hole golf course. Phone (912) 367–3582.

Land of Trembling Earth

*O**kefenokee Swamp Park,*** off Highway 1, 8 miles south of Waycross, is the most popular of three entrances to the vast, mysterious "Land of Trembling Earth." Although most of the park is actually outside the boundaries of the 700-square-mile, 412,000-acre Okefenokee National Wildlife Refuge, guided boat tours and cypress boardwalks lead you well into this fascinating world.

The Swamp Park is the most casual visitor-oriented of the three entrances—the others are in neighboring Charlton County—with numerous exhibits, interpretive centers, wildlife shows, and other visual displays.

Stop first at the cedar-roofed welcome center adjacent to the paved parking areas. Mounted wildlife exhibits, and the real thing viewed through one-way windows, and a twenty-minute film are an excellent orientation. From there, climb the 90-foot observation tower, peer into the dark tannic waters from the boardwalk, and see some of the Okefenokee's three dozen varieties of reptiles at the Serpentarium.

Okefenokee Swamp Park

Gate admission—$10.00 for adults, $7.00 for ages 6 to 11, free under 6—includes a 1½-mile guided boat tour and all exhibits and shows. A two-hour boat tour ($10.00 a person) includes an even more extensive look at the hundreds of species of birds, otter, armadillo, black bear, deer, and other critters that inhabit the swamp. You'll also see some of the 15,000 gators as they cruise among the reeds and cypresses like iron-clad gunboats. (Back near the welcome center, you'll meet Oscar, the park's 15-foot, 900-pound mascot.)

If this two-hour sojourn was too brief, you may arrange with park officials for a guide who'll boat you back into really deep waters, where you may see what songwriter Stephen Foster only fantasized: the head-waters of the Suwannee River, which rise in the swamp and flow into Florida.

Okefenokee Swamp Park, Waycross 31501, (912) 283– 0583, is open daily in spring and summer 9:00 A.M. to 6:30 P.M., fall and winter 9:00 A.M. to 5:30 P.M.

Two other attractions also mirror the swamp's colorful heritage. *Obediah's Okefenok* (912–287–0090), on a small island at the swamp's southwestern edge, was the early 1800s home of the Obediah Barber family. Their restored cabin and outbuildings are filled with authentic tools and household necessities. Open daily. Adults, $4.00; ages 4 to 17, $3.00.

The *Okefenokee Heritage Center* (912–285–4260), 1460 North Augusta Avenue near downtown Waycross, is an indoor/outdoor museum with historical displays, artworks, a 1912 locomotive and depot, an 1840s farmhouse, a print shop, and antique vehicles. Open daily. Adults, $2.00; 18 and under, free. Phone (912) 285–4260.

Nearby **Laura S. Walker State Park,** Waycross 31501, (912) 287–4900, has campsites with water, electricity, showers, and rest rooms ($10.00 a night); a swimming pool; a playground; a golf course; fishing; and picnic tables. There is a $2.00 parking fee. For reservations call (800) 864–PARK.

Contact Waycross/Ware County Tourism and Conference Bureau, 200 Lee Avenue, Waycross 31501, (912) 283–3742, when you arrive for more information. Stop at the Waycross Welcome Center at the same address.

Three gateways lead you into the primeval mysteries of the 412,000-acre *Okefenokee Swamp National Wildlife Refuge.* Suwannee Canal Recreation Area and Stephen C. Foster State Park are in Charlton County, while the Okefenokee Swamp Park is near Waycross, in Ware County.

Administered by the U.S. Fish and Wildlife Service, *Suwannee Canal Recreation Area* is what remains of one man's frustrated efforts to drain the Okefenokee back in the 1880s. He left behind an 11-mile-long waterway that now provides an easy avenue for boaters, fishermen, and sightseers. Along with boat tours—one-hour trips are $7.50 for adults, $3.75 for ages 5 to 11—Suwannee Canal has several other visitor amenities.

The *Information Center Museum* has a fifteen-minute orientation film and exhibits of the swamp's plant and animal life. A boardwalk over the water leads to a 50-foot observation platform. Picnic tables and rest rooms are clustered around the information center. The concession building stocks groceries, cold drinks, insect repellents, and docks for guided boat tours.

I-Go-Pogo

"*P*ogo," the late cartoonist Walt Kelly's wise and witty opossum, is the Okefenokee's most famous citizen. In the 1940s, Kelly created the comic strip featuring Pogo, Albert Alligator, Bearegard Hound Dog, and other critter friends to focus attention on the serious environmental dangers posed to the Okefenokee and other wilderness areas. Many of Pogo's pronouncements—"We have met the enemy and it is us," for example—have become part of our language. He's run for president several times on the "I-Go-Pogo" platform. The latest threat to his realm is a controversial titanium mining operation Dupont proposes on the edge of the swamp.

A short drive from the concession building and museum, *Chesser Island Homestead* is the pine and cypress cabin once home to several generations of the Chesser family.

Suwannee Canal Recreation Area, Route 2, Box 336, Folkston 31537, (912) 496–7156, is open daily sunrise to sunset. A $3.00 gate fee is charged at the Folkston entrance by the Okefenokee Swamp National Wildlife Refuge. Drive on Highway 121/23 for 8 miles south of Folkston, then turn right (west) at the Okefenokee Refuge sign and continue 3 miles.

Overnight canoeing and two- to five-day wilderness canoeing and camping adventures are available by advance reservations from the Refuge Manager, Route 2, Box 338, Folkston 31537, (912) 496–3331.

Stephen C. Foster State Park is so far off Georgia's beaten path that to get there from Suwannee Canal you'll have to detour through northeastern Florida. From Suwannee Canal, drive 15 miles south on Highway 23 to St. George, 37 miles west on Highway 94 and Highway 2 in Florida, and back into Georgia at Fargo. From Fargo, go right on Highway 177 and for 18 miles cross a domain of sentinel pines and palmetto thickets, swampy canals, egrets, great blue heron, deer, gators, armadillos, opossum, raccoons, reptiles, and amphibians. Beyond a sign warning that the gates close between sundown and sunup, you arrive at Stephen Foster's compound.

The state park is an eighty-acre island entirely within the Okefenokee Swamp National Wildlife Refuge. Rangers conduct boat tours, replete with swamp legends and lore, practical lessons in fauna and flora, and lots of hilarious tall tales. You're bound to see plenty of gators, exotic birds and plants, turtles, and trees. You may also rent boats and canoes and venture forth on your own. There are also a ¼-mile hiking trail, picnic shelters, a playground, and a small museum.

Staying overnight, serenaded by the symphony of the swamp, is an unforgettable experience. Campsites with electricity, water, hot showers, and rest rooms are available as are two-bedroom cottages completely furnished with full kitchens and fireplaces, heat, and air-conditioning. There is a $2.00 per visit parking fee. The park's small grocery has minimal supplies, so be sure to stock up before leaving Fargo.

Stephen C. Foster State Park, Fargo 31631, (912) 637–5274, is open 7:00 A.M. to 7:00 P.M. from mid-September to the end of February and 6:30 A.M. to 8:30 P.M. from March 1 to mid-September. For cottage and camping reservations call (800) 864–PARK. When the gates are locked at night, only a dire emergency will open them before sunrise. This is done to protect you from roaming critters and the critters from roaming poachers. Also bear in mind that a swamp is full of mosquitoes, other biting pests, and uncomfortable summer heat and humidity. Bring insect repellent and dress comfortably.

In addition to the Folkston route, you may get to the park on Highway 441 to Fargo.

Valdosta and the Great Southeast

*D*epending on your perspective, *Lowndes County* is either the jumping-off place for Florida or your reentry point to Georgia. With 76,000 residents, Lowndes is Georgia's sixteenth most populous county. *Valdosta,* the county seat, with close to 50,000 residents, is the state's tenth largest city. With so much traffic flowing back and forth from Florida on I–75, much of the city is devoted to chain motels, fast-food strips, and factory outlet malls. Behind these contemporary distractions, under canopies of live oaks and palm trees and banks of azaleas and camellias, the city has many historic homes, churches, and public buildings.

Stop for free information and the *Historic Tours* self-guided map at the *Valdosta-Lowndes County Convention and Visitors Bureau's Tourism Information Center* off I–75 exit 5, 1703 Norman Drive, (912) 245–0513. Among the twenty-six landmarks, the most outstanding is *The Crescent.* Built in 1898, at a cost of $12,000 by Valdosta educator William S. West, the grand twenty-three-room neo-classical mansion is graced by thirteen Doric columns supporting a crescent-shaped portico. In 1913 President Woodrow Wilson attended a gala dinner in the ballroom. Now maintained by the Valdosta Garden Center, the mansion has been restored to its original grandeur and appointed with many original furnishings and period antiques. The gardens are always in bloom. It's at 904 North Patterson Street, (912) 244–6747.

Before heading on, relax a while at Valdosta's parks, boating and fishing lakes, and public golf courses and tennis courts.

The small Lowndes County town of *Hahira,* north of Valdosta at I–75 exit 7, is a center of Georgia's tobacco industry. From July to October you can witness the age-old ritual of tobacco auctioning at the town's warehouses. If you're here the first week of October, drop by the *Hahira Honeybee Festival.* To get the buzz on what's happening in town, and enjoy good home cooking, take a seat for breakfast or lunch at *The City*

Valdosta's "Doc" Holliday

Celebrated late-nineteenth-century Western gambler and gunfighter John Henry "Doc" Holliday began his adult life as a dentist in his hometown of Valdosta, which his father was mayor of. Plagued all his life by tuberculosis, he moved to Arizona for his health and a taste of frontier adventure. His most famous set-do came about when he sided with Wyatt Earp in the legendary "Gunfight at OK Corral." He survived that and other close calls and died peacefully in bed with his boots on.

Cafe on Main Street. The Hahira Chamber of Commerce, Hahira 31632, (912) 794–2567, offers tobacco and honey tours.

At *Reed Bingham State Park,* off Highway 37, 6 miles west of Adel, the Cook County seat, you can go boating, fishing, waterskiing, and swimming on a 375-acre lake. The park also has a nature trail, campsites, and picnic grounds—and one rather unusual event. "Buzzard Day," the first Saturday of December, hails the thousands of buzzards that roost in the park each winter. Enjoy arts and crafts and musical entertainment while you watch the skies. Phone (912) 896–3551. For campsite reservations call (800) 864–PARK.

The *Jefferson Davis Memorial Museum,* Highway 32, in the small community of Irwinville, commemorates the site where the Confederate president was captured by Union troops on May 10, 1865. The museum has Civil War artifacts and part of the tree where Davis was standing when captured. A park around the museum has nature trails and picnic areas. Open Tuesday to Saturday 9:00 A.M. to 5:00 P.M. and Sunday 2:00 to 5:30 P.M. Adults, $1.00; children, 50 cents. Phone (912) 831–2335.

After your history lesson, unwind at nearby *Crystal Lake Water Park,* which has a white sand beach, campsites, and boat rentals.

Tobacco, not java, is the economic lifeline of agrarian Coffee County. If you drop by the county seat of Douglas from midsummer through early fall, you'll see traffic jams of trucks bringing in leaf tobacco from across Southeast Georgia's "Tobacco Belt." The gold leaf is auctioned in the age-old tradition at warehouses around the town and sent off for cigarettes, pipe and chewing tobacco, and snuff. After the hullabaloo of the auction houses, unwind a while at two tranquil recreation areas.

General Coffee State Park, on Highway 32, 6 miles east of Douglas, offers a wealth of recreational opportunities. You can fish the lake and streams for catfish, gar, and bream and swim in the outdoor pool. A nature trail winding through the wooded 1,490-acre park puts you in photo range of many species of birds, reptiles, deer, and other critters. There are also playgrounds and picnic shelters. Heritage Farm has nature trails, wildlife habitats, antique farm equipment, a cane mill, and barnyard animals. You can stay overnight in full-service campsites and in a group cabin sleeping thirty-six. Phone (912) 384–7082. For camping and cabin reservations call (800) 864–PARK.

In *Douglas,* which is a pretty college town of 15,000 folks, you can either play the 18-hole *Beaver Kreek Golf Club* course (912–384–8230), or you might want to try your swing at the 9-hole *Community Golf Course* (912–384–7353). Rental clubs are available at both. After your round, drive into Douglas's revived downtown area—it's one of Georgia's Main Street Program cities—and enjoy dinner Tuesday through Saturday at *Fern Bank Bar and Grill* (912–384–4385), an historic brick-walled building with good steaks, seafood, and Southern dishes and many relics from the city's past.

The small town of *Fitzgerald* (pop. 8,600) is a living memorial to the nation's post–Civil War reunification. In the 1890s Indiana newspaper publisher P. H. Fitzgerald envisioned a place where he and other Union veterans could live in peace with their former Southern foes. When Ben Hill County farmers sent trainloads of food in response to a Midwestern drought, it became the chosen place. The town was laid out on a grid, with streets on the west side named for Confederate generals, those on the east side for Union generals. Other streets were named for Northern and Southern trees and flowers.

The *Blue and Gray Museum,* in the former train depot, displays thousands of Civil War artifacts, including uniforms, weapons, newspaper articles about Lincoln's assassination, and the history of this unique town. It's open April 1 to October 1, Monday through Friday, 2:00 to 5:00 P.M. Free admission. Phone (912) 423–5375.

Until July 4, 1986, most motorists passed through the little Telfair County seat of McRae without a second thought. Nowadays, they have a reason to stop, get out of their cars, and take a picture. Right in the middle of town, where Highways 341, 441, 280, 23, and 319 come together, there's a replica of the *Statue of Liberty,* a *Liberty Bell,* and copies of the *Declaration of Independence,* the *Constitution,* and other documents. "Miss Liberty" stands 32 feet tall—a $1/_{12}$-scale reproduction of the original in New York Harbor. And she's entirely homemade: Her head is carved from a black gum tree, her torch from cypress, and her fiberglass coating was created by a McRae boat manufacturer.

Little Ocmulgee State Park and Pete Phillips Lodge and Convention Center, off Highway 441, 2 miles north of McRae, is a resort park with lots of things to keep you happily occupied. You can challenge the park's well-maintained 18-hole, par-72 golf course and rent carts and clubs at the pro shop. You can also swim, play tennis, and hike nature trails. Pete Phillips Lodge and Conference Center has thirty modern motel-type guest rooms, an outdoor pool, a full-service restaurant, and meeting rooms. You can also pitch your tent or park your RV in full service campsites and stay in furnished cottages. For camping, cottage, and lodge reservations phone (800) 864–PARK. For general information contact the Park Superintendent, P.O. Box 149, McRae 31055, (912) 868–7474.

PLACES TO STAY IN SOUTHEAST GEORGIA

VIDALIA
Darby House,
401 Kenworth Street,
(912) 537–2618.

Six guest rooms, four with private bath, in a rejuvenated late 1920s Prairie-style house are your comfortable quarters in the Sweet Onion City. The house has numerous antiques, including a large collection of bisque dolls. Rates are $50 a double, with breakfast.

FOLKSTON
The Inn at Folkston,
509 West Main Street,
(888) 509–6246,
fax (912) 496–6256,
www folksinn@plantel.net.

After a big day exploring the Okefenokee National Wildlife Refuge or the Cumberland Island National Seashore, Roger

and Genna Wangness's restored 1920s heart-pine bungalow is only a few minutes away. Four spacious guest rooms have feather beds, private beds, and plenty of AC. You can recount your day's adventures in wicker chairs and rockers on the front veranda. A full breakfast comes with double occupancy rates of $90.

EASTMAN
Dodge Hill Inn,
105 Ninth Avenue,
(912) 374–2644.

Ann and Don Dobbs are gracious hosts at this 1912 home, filled with antiques and original art works. Five guest rooms have private baths, TV, fridges, and phones. Make yourselves at home in the parlor, read, and play the grand piano.

Favorite Web Sites

Baxley-Appling County Tourism Board,
www.applingdacoc.com

Dublin-Laurens County Welcome Center,
www.dublin-georgia.com

Folkston/Okefenokee Chamber of Commerce,
www.folkston.com

Statesboro Tourism Office,
www.visit-statesboro.com

Waycross/Ware County Tourism Bureau,
www.gacoast.com.navigator/waycross.html

Valdosta-Lowndes Convention & Visitors Bureau,
www.datasys.net/valdtourism

Breakfast, included in the $60 to $95 double rate, is one of the best reasons for staying here. The huge spread includes fresh fruit, hot baked breads, ham, biscuits, pancakes, cheese grits, and eggs.

HOMERVILLE
The Helmstead,
One Fargo Road, P.O. Box 61,
(912) 487-2222,
(888) 224-3567,
fax (912) 487-5827.

Jane Helms's four guest rooms welcome business travelers and visitors to the neighboring Okefenokee National Wildlife Refuge. Rooms have private baths, and continental breakfast is included in the $60 to $75 rates.

PLACES TO EAT IN SOUTH-EAST GEORGIA

WAYCROSS
Adolph's Family Restaurant,
410 Plant Avenue,
(912) 283-1766.

This place loads its buffet tables with fried chicken, fish, fresh vegetables, salads, and other Southern favorites.

Ocean Galley Seafood,
421 Memorial Drive,
(912) 283-8341.

Ocean Galley Seafood's "Swamp Platter" is heaped with fried 'gator tail, soft-shell crab, frog legs, turtle meat, and other Okefenokee fare.

FOLKSTON
Vickery House,
108 South First Street,
(912) 496-7942.

Cozy downtown dining room is a good choice for weekday lunch. Specialties include quiche, crepes, soups, fresh vegetables, salads, baked desserts, and daily blue-plate specials. Lunch is served Wednesday through Friday.

MCRAE
Southern Star Grill,
752 Oak Street,
(912) 868-2507.

This is where hungry folks in McRae and neighboring towns come for country fried steak, herbed roast chicken, sesame fried catfish, great desserts, and other treats. Lunch Monday through Saturday, dinner Tuesday through Saturday.

METTER
Jomax Barbecue,
Highway 121,
(912) 685-3636.

Traveling the long, lonely stretches of I-16 between Macon and Savannah, with only a few scattered fast-food outlets to sate your hunger, Jomax is a pleasant and tasty surprise. Tuck into the chopped barbecued pork or ribs, draped with a piquant house-secret sauce (available in bottles to take home), with slabs of starchy white bread and cole slaw and you'll be ready to hit the highway high on the hog. Lunch and dinner Monday through Saturday.

Northwest Georgia

Cloudland Canyon to Georgia's Rome

Cloudland Canyon State Park, in far northwest Georgia's remote and rugged Dade County, contains one of the Southeast's most awesome natural sights. The park's namesake and centerpiece is a steep canyon cut into the western flank of Lookout Mountain by *Sitton Creek Gulch.* You may stand by the rim and peer into misty reaches 1,800 feet deep. Better still, lace up your hiking boots, follow woodland trails down to three waterfalls on the canyon floor, and get really off the beaten path on 6 miles of backcountry trails.

After you hike, unwind with a swim in the park pool or a few quick sets of tennis. Also in the heavily forested 2,120-acre park are sixteen completely furnished cottages and seventy-five tent and trailer sites, with electrical and water connections, showers, and rest rooms. For camping and cottage reservations call (800) 864–PARK. Contact Park Superintendent, Route 2, Box 150, Rising Fawn 30738, (706) 657–4050.

According to tradition, Cherokee Indians named their children for symbolic signs that caught their eye after birth. So the Cloudland community of *Rising Fawn* owes its poetic name to a chief who legend says looked out of his lodge on the happy morning his son was born and saw a newborn fawn wobble to its feet by its mother's side.

After a vigorous day in the park, make tracks for *Geneva Wooten's Restaurant,* (706) 398–1749. Across Highway 136 from the Cloudland entrance, the homey cafe is the eating-meeting-greeting destination for folks from miles around. At breakfast, lunch, and dinner, country cooking just doesn't get any better.

Hidden Hollow Country Inn, 5 miles down the mountain from Cloudland Canyon, is one of those discoveries you can hardly wait to tell your best friends about. Tommy and Bonnie Jean Thomas preside over a gaggle of rustic but very comfortable family-size cabins around a small

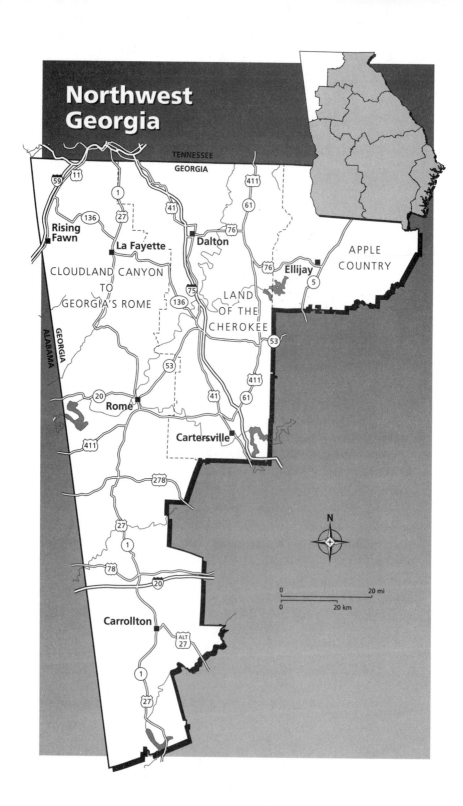

Northwest Georgia

TENNESSEE
GEORGIA

Rising
Fawn

La Fayette

Dalton

CLOUDLAND CANYON
TO
GEORGIA'S ROME

LAND
OF THE
CHEROKEE

APPLE
COUNTRY

Ellijay

ALABAMA

GEORGIA

Rome

Cartersville

Carrollton

N

0   20 mi
0   20 km

lake full of Canada geese. Cabins are filled with well-worn furniture, cards, board games, dog-eared magazines, and coffee, but there are no TVs or phones to ruffle your peaceful ruminations. For entertainment snag a fish in the lake, hike in the woods, and watch the sun come up and go down. Two persons are $55 to $75, $8 for each additional. No meals are served, but Geneva Wooten's and other restaurants are close by. The inn is at 463 Hidden Hollow Lane, Chickamauga 30707, (706) 539–2372.

Be sure to bring your fishing gear when you head for *James H. Floyd State Park.* Off Highway 27, 3 miles southeast of the Chattooga County seat of Summerville, the 270-acre park is renowned as one of the state's finest fishing places. A pair of stocked lakes—thirty and thirty-five acres—offer excellent bass-fishing opportunities from the banks. Only boats with trolling motors are allowed.

Area fishermen say you can expect to reel in impressive largemouth bass, as well as big catches of catfish and bream. Youngsters can learn some of the fine art of fishing during the park's annual fishing rodeo in mid-May. Admission is free, and prizes are awarded for the first, largest, and most fish caught.

Floyd State Park's twenty-five tent and trailer sites have water and electrical hookups and convenient showers and rest rooms. You'll also find a playground, picnic areas, and hiking trails in the neighboring Chattahoochee National Forest. Contact Park Superintendent, Route 1, Summerville 30747, (706) 857–0826. Call (800) 864–PARK for camping reservations.

Three miles north of Summerville, turn right off U.S. Highway 27 onto Rena Street (between Jim's Auto Supply and Penn Auto Parts) and prepare for an otherworldly visit to *Howard Finster's "Paradise Garden,"* (706) 857–2926. One of America's premier folk artists, Reverend Finster made his garden a jumble of gaudily painted

John Wisdom's "Midnight Ride"

Boston has its Paul Revere, and Romans remember their own courageous rider who saved the day (and their necks). Learning that Union troops were approaching the city, mail carrier John Wisdom rode off in a desperate attempt to mobilize defenders. He abandoned his mail buggy after 20 miles, begged and borrowed horses, which he changed six times, and galloped 65 miles in less than nine hours.

The approaching Union troops saw Rome's defenders armed with shotguns, squirrel guns, and muzzle-loading rifles and retreated into captivity by Confederate Gen. Nathan Bedford Forrest. Rome's grateful citizens gave him $400 and a silver service.

angels, birds, animals, 14-foot Coke bottles, heaven-bound buses, surreal images of Elvis and Marilyn Monroe—and everywhere you look, biblical passages and admonitions. Paintings and wooden figures by Finster, his son, and grandson sell from $20 to $2,500. The garden is open daily 9:00 A.M. to 5:00 P.M.

Like its Italian counterpart, Georgia's Rome spreads over seven green hills, in the foothills of the state's northwestern Appalachian Mountains. In the rivers department, the Georgia city of 30,000 has the edge. Instead of one mere Tiber, the Floyd County seat has three: the Etowah and Oostanaula, which join up downtown and form the Coosa. It may not have personages to match the Caesars, but a *dramatis personae* of Cherokee Indian chieftains, Southern aristocrats, cotton traders, Civil War soldiers, and riverboat paddle wheelers have made a rich and colorful cast, all the same. The city got its name quite by chance. In 1834 two traveling salesmen and a cotton planter put their choice of names in a hat. "Rome" was the fortuitous choice, otherwise the city might be known today as Warsaw or Hamburg. A revitalized downtown, focusing on the three rivers, ensures Rome of a future as exciting as its past.

Begin your Roman holiday at the Greater Rome Visitors Center (706–295–5576 or 800–444–1834, fax 706–236–5029, or www.romegeorgia.com), a rejuvenated Southern Railway passenger depot, circa 1900, and a retired caboose at 402 Civic Center Drive, off Highway 20 and Highway 27 near downtown. Information is available Monday through Friday 9:00 A.M. to 5:00 P.M., Saturday 10:00 A.M. to 3:00 P.M., and Sunday noon to 3:00 P.M.

"The Between the Rivers Walking Tour"—it can also be driven, of course—leads you past thirty-eight historic downtown landmarks. If you've been to the Italian Rome, you'll probably recognize the statue in front of City Hall here. The *Capitoline Wolf,* a replica of the Etruscan sculpture on ancient Rome's Capitoline Hill, depicts the city's mythical founders, Romulus and Remus, being nurtured by a she-wolf. It was a 1929 goodwill gift from Benito Mussolini.

The *Town Clock,* on Clock Tower Hill, is the city's symbol and one of its most beloved landmarks. Built in Waltham, Massachusetts, in 1871, the four 9-foot-diameter clock faces a handsome brick and cypress water tower. So many people wanted to climb the 104-foot tower that the city opened it as the *Clock Tower Museum.* You can walk up the spiral staircase and take in panoramic views of the city's hills and rivers. Also admire the handsomely restored clock works and murals depicting chapters in the city's history. It's open Saturday 10:00 A.M. to 4:00 P.M. and Sunday 1:00 to 5:00 P.M. from April to November and other times by appointment. Free admission. Phone (706) 236–4416.

Myrtle Hill Cemetery, on another of the city's seven hills, is a beautiful tree-shaded sanctuary where Mrs. Woodrow Wilson, 377 Confederate soldiers, and other notables are buried. You're welcome to stroll and admire the panoramic views of Rome's rivers and green hills.

Until recently the Etowah, Oostanaula, and Coosa had to flood before Romans would pay them any attention. Nowadays the 2½-mile *Heritage Trail* walking, biking, and hiking route, shaded by big trees, takes inhabitants and visitors along the Oostanaula from the *Rome–Floyd County Public Library* downtown to the *Chieftains Museum.* If you'd like to get out on the water, the visitors bureau can direct you to a canoe rental.

You can also unwind at *Lock and Dam Park,* a publicly owned camping/RV/fishing/boating park in a mountain setting beside a 1910 lock on the Coosa River. Facilities include twenty-five fully equipped RV camp-sites, a fishing pier, canoe rentals, boat ramp and docks, a bait shop, and a snack bar. Call (404) 234–5001 for information.

Rocky Mountain Recreation and Public Fishing Area. A joint venture of the Georgia Department of Natural Resources and Oglethorpe Power Corporation, the 5,000-acre retreat in northern Floyd County has two recreational lakes (357 and 202 acres) for swimming, fishing,

Atlanta Steeplechase, mid-April, Kingston Downs, Kingston, (404) 237–7436

Historic House & Garden Pilgrimage, late April, Rome, (706) 291–7181

Kingston Confederate Memorial Day, late April, (770) 387–1357

Cedar Valley Arts Festival, early May, Cedartown, (770) 748–0397

Prater's Mill Country Fair, Mother's Day Weekend, Dalton, (706) 275–6455

Cherokee County Indian Festival, early May, Canton, (770) 735–6275

CHVA Car Show & South-eastern National Meet, mid-June, Cartersville High School, (770) 386–2964

Georgia Apple Festival, mid-October, Ellijay, (706) 635–7400

Candles & Carols of Christmases Past, early December, Martha Berry Museum, Rome, (800) 220–5504

Coosa River Christmas Lighted Boat Parade, early December, Rome, (800) 444–1834

and boating. You can also enjoy picnic pavilions, hiking trails, and other outdoor activities and camp out at thirty-nine RV sites and nine wooded tent sites. For information call the Greater Rome Visitors Bureau at (800) 444–1834.

Rome Area History Museum, 305 Broad Street, (706) 235–8051. Walk through nearly two centuries of northwest Georgia's past at this new downtown museum. Exhibits focus on the Civil War, the Cherokees, cotton, and commerce. A *Gone With the Wind* exhibit has photos, collectibles, and costumes from the book and movie. Open Tuesday through Saturday 10:00 A.M. to 5:00 P.M. and Sunday noon to 5:00 P.M. Admission is $2.00.

If golf's your game, check out the new **Stonebridge Golf Club,** (706) 236–4400. Owned by the city of Rome, the 18-hole, par-72, 6,971-yard layout is at the base of Lavendar Mountain, on the Berry College grounds. Rolling fairways, water, and big stands of hardwoods and pines are scenic to look at and challenging to play. The course is named for an old stone bridge over a lake on the ninth fairway. Greens fees won't handicap your budget: $31.50 weekdays, $42.40 weekends, including cart fee.

The **Chieftains Museum** is Rome's oldest historical landmark. Built as a frontier log cabin in 1794, Chieftains was the home of Major Ridge, the Cherokee leader who signed a treaty with the U.S. government that partially contributed to the expulsion of the Cherokees from Georgia and the tragic "Trail of Tears." Along with Cherokee history, the museum's artifacts tell the story of Rome as a river town and its role in the antebellum South and the Civil War. An open archaeological dig and a nineteenth-century riverboat are on the grounds. It's at 80 Chatillon Road, off Highway 27, (706) 291–9494. Hours are Tuesday through Friday 11:00 A.M. to 4:00 P.M. and Sunday 2:00 to 5:00 P.M.

Rome's most inspiring personality was a determined lady named Martha Berry. Born to privilege in a white-columned Greek Revival mansion, Miss Berry in 1902 founded the Berry Schools to provide educational opportunities to impoverished Appalachian youth. Her original domain of 83 acres has grown to 28,000 acres of handsome buildings, forests, fields, mountains, lakes, and streams. Many students of today's **Berry College** earn their tuition by working on the college's farm, research facilities, and other enterprises.

"The Miracle of the Mountains" is chronicled at Oak Hill and the **Martha Berry Museum and Art Gallery,** across from the campus on Highway 27. You'll see a twenty-eight-minute film on her remarkable life and achievements and photos, furniture, and memorabilia. Nearby **Oak Hill** (706–232–5374), built in 1847, is the classic Old South mansion, filled with the Berry family's antiques and artworks. Behind the museum, an easygoing nature trail loops through woodlands, ponds, and native plants. Around Oak Hill you're free to wander five acres of tiered formal gardens. The Martha Berry Museum and Oak Hill are open Monday through Saturday 10:00 A.M. to 5:00 P.M. and Sunday 1:00 to 5:00 P.M. Admission is adults, $3.00; students, $1.50; under age 6, free.

You're welcome to drive through what's proudly called "The World's Most Beautiful Campus." Among the Berry College landmarks are the **Ford Buildings,** a cluster of hand-

Berry College

some English Gothic structures and a reflecting pool donated by Henry Ford. In the Ford Buildings' **Weaving Room,** students perpetuate a mountain craft revived by Miss Berry. During the week you can watch as afghans, rugs, placemats, and jackets are hand-loomed the age-old way. These beautiful pieces, and student-made pottery and glassware, sell for $5 to $125.

You're also invited to visit the scenic campuses of **Shorter College** and **Darlington Lower School,** neighbors on Shorter Avenue west of downtown.

If you'd like to get a little lost in the woods, make an appointment to visit **Marshall Forest,** on Horseleg Creek Road, off Highway 20, 4 miles west of downtown. The lush 170-acre preserve, administered by the Georgia Conservancy, includes ninety acres of fields and eighty acres of forests, where northern red and chestnut oaks mingle with long-leaf southern pines. About 300 species of wildflowers and other plants grow on the Flower Glen Trail. The Big Pine Braille Trail offers blind visitors the opportunity to stop at twenty stations describing fifty-three plant species, thirty-one species of trees, and nineteen species of vines and shrubs. Call the Rome Visitor Center for information, (800) 444–1834.

Cave Spring, a village of 950 residents and one traffic light 16 miles south of Rome (via Highway 411), is pure Norman Rockwell. The *Hearn House B & B,* a comfy community-owned inn in an 1840s schoolhouse, features five guest rooms with private bath and breakfast for $50 to $60 per night. When you're well rested, lace up your walking shoes and head across *Rolater Park* to the limestone cave that gave the town its name. Inside the caverns you'll see the spring whose pure water is bottled and sold in area stores.

Around the square more than a dozen antiques stores and flea markets are a collector's dream. Some of the nicest include *Asbury House* (706–777–3608); *Martha Jane's Fudge, Gifts and Collectibles* (706–777–3608); and *Christa's Etc.* (706–777–3586). More than a hundred artists and craftspeople come for the *Cave Spring Arts Festival* the second weekend of June. For information and bed-and-breakfast reservations, contact City of Cave Spring, P.O. Box 365, Cave Spring 30124, (706) 777–3382.

John Tanner State Park, off Highway 16, 6 miles west of Carrollton, is a popular getaway for west Georgians and east Alabamians. Six furnished one-bedroom cottages and thirty-six full-service campsites surround a lake with a sandy swimming beach, rental fishing boats, and tree-shaded picnic shelters. There is a $2.00 parking fee. Contact Park Superintendent, 354 Tanners Beach Road, Carrollton 30117, (770) 830–2222. For campsite and cottage reservations, call (800) 864–PARK.

Land of the Cherokee

I n the hellish heat of September 19 and 20, 1863, nearly 130,000 Americans engaged in one of the bloodiest battles of the entire Civil War. When it was over, Confederate forces under the command of General Braxton Bragg had a costly and dubious victory. They had repulsed the outnumbered Union armies under General William Rosecrans but were too weakened to pursue the Federals as they fled to safety around Chattanooga, Tennessee. Subsequent Union victories at Chattanooga's Lookout Mountain and Missionary Ridge and the capture of the city's vital railway hub opened General William T. Sherman's route to Atlanta and the sea.

The 5,500-acre Chickamauga battlefield is now part of the Chattanooga and *Chickamauga National Military Park.* The major sites are adjacent to Highway 27, near Chattanooga and Chickamauga. Stop first at the National Park Service Visitors Center for the audiovisual orientation and the many exhibits. The *Fuller Collection of Military Arms* has more than 400 weapons from the French and Indian Wars through present-day conflicts.

Park rangers in Civil War uniforms demonstrate cannon and rifles. The Chattanooga Symphony Orchestra has free outdoor concerts on summer Sunday evenings. Bring a blanket and a picnic supper and join the festivities!

From the visitors center, follow Highway 27 for 3 miles through the park. Battle sites are marked by earthworks, cannon batteries, and farm buildings. Impressive monuments have been placed by states whose sons in blue and gray died here more than 125 years ago. The park is open all the time. The visitors center is open daily from 8:00 A.M. to 5:45 P.M. Contact Park Superintendent, P.O. Box 2128, Ft. Oglethorpe 30742, (706) 866–9241.

The *Gordon-Lee Mansion,* on the edge of the battlefield park, invites you to spend the night in antebellum luxury. Built in 1847, the white-columned Greek Revival residence in seven acres of gardens and grounds served as Union headquarters and a hospital during the battle. Six guest rooms and public areas are furnished with Civil War–era antiques. Rates of $75 to $125 per night include evening wine and cheese on the veranda and a continental-plus breakfast. Contact Gordon-Lee Mansion, 217 Cove Road, Chickamauga 30707, (706) 375–4728 or (800) 487–4728, fax (706) 375–4586.

Before leaving the area, see *Lookout Mountain, Missionary Ridge,* and other major parts of the Chattanooga and Chickamauga National Military Park.

If you've been planning to recarpet your home or cover your pool deck or patio with Astroturf, put off that major purchase until you've been to **Dalton.** Seat of northwest Georgia's green and hilly Whitfield County, industrious Dalton, with a population of 25,000, is the long-reigning "Carpet Capital of the World."

About 66 percent of all the tufted carpeting manufactured in the United States rolls off the giant looms of Dalton's more than seventy-five modern plants. If you're in a buying frame of mind or would just enjoy browsing the latest styles and colors, dozens of *Dalton carpet outlets* offer a full range of floor coverings at greatly reduced prices. The Dalton Convention and Visitors Bureau, 2211 Dug Gap Battle Road, Dalton

30722, (800) 331–3258, open Monday through Saturday, can provide you with an up-to-date outlets directory. You can also find out about guided tours of area mills, Civil War and Native American sites, restaurants, and lodgings.

Dalton's $5-billion carpeting industry was born around 1900, when a Whitfield County farm girl named Catherine Evans produced a hand-tufted chenille bedspread, copied from a family heirloom, and promptly sold it for the handsome price of $2.50. Encouraged by her success, she made more of the brightly colored cotton bedspreads, and these, too, were eagerly snapped up by tourists and local homemakers. Other homebound women began following her lead, and by the early 1920s, tufted bedspreads had grown into a major "cottage industry."

The bedspreads usually featured flowers and other patterns, but the brilliantly plumed male peacock was such a runaway favorite that Highway 41, the major highway leading into Dalton, became popularly known as "Peacock Alley."

In the 1920s, a machine invented in Dalton was able to mass-produce the cotton bedspreads. Another wizard soon realized that by tufting more densely and adding a sturdy backing the same machinery could be adapted to the manufacture of carpeting. Dalton—and households the world over—were never again the same.

The original "cottage craft" of chenille bedspreads is still alive. You can find a practical souvenir with a peacock, Elvis Presley, Jesus Christ, the

Carpet Shopping Tips

*I*f you're planning to do serious carpet shopping, do your homework ahead of time. Have a good idea of what you're looking for, how much you'll need, the color and style, and what you can afford to pay. Do comparison shopping in your local stores—the more than 100 outlet stores in Dalton and neighboring towns like Calhoun and Chatsworth offer prices for up to 70 percent less than you'll pay in a retail store. You can get a list of the Carpet & Rug Out-

let Council stores from the Dalton-Whitfield Chamber of Commerce, (706) 278–7373, and the Dalton Convention & Visitors Bureau, (800) 331–3258. Most outlets deal in "seconds," that is, those with some problems that exclude them from the "A-list." It's often just a small tear or a color that doesn't match the mill's specifications. Be sure to examine it thoroughly. Having your carpet shipped will be much easier than trying to take it home yourself.

Confederate battle flag, and other designs at stores around Dalton and along Highway 41—the original "Peacock Alley"—between Dalton and the Tennessee border. Figure on paying a bit more than $2.50, however!

Some of the early chenille bedspreads are among the exhibits at **Crown Gardens and Archives,** in the original Crown Cotton Mill at 715 Chattanooga Avenue, (706) 278–0217. The museum also has historical displays, a Black Heritage room, an outdoor spring, and picnic areas. It's open Tuesday to Saturday. Admission is free.

With its influx of executives and workers from across the nation and several foreign countries, this surprisingly cosmopolitan little city is very active in the fine arts. The **Creative Arts Guild,** 520 West Waugh Street, (706) 278–0168, is a tastefully contemporary complex with two art galleries and a forum for live theater, dance, and other cultural programs. It's open daily. Admission is free.

Dalton is also a festive city. The **Red Carpet Festival,** the first weekend of May, celebrates Dalton's famous industry with parades, pageantry, square dancing, bluegrass and gospel music, and plenty of barbecue and other hearty Southern cooking.

On the second weekend of May and October, the **Prater's Mill Country Fair** centers on Benjamin Franklin Prater's circa 1859 gristmill. While the huge millstones turn out silky cornmeal, 185 artists and craftsmen sell their wares to the tune of bluegrass fiddlers, clog dancers, and gospel singers. There are pony rides and other special treats just for the youngsters.

Dalton Depot Restaurant & Trackside Cafe, 110 Depot Street, five minutes from I–75, (706) 226–3160, is the carpet city's liveliest eating and drinking address. The cleverly regeared old wooden train depot has a something-for-everyone menu: Stuffed jalapeños and quesadillas, filet mignon, baby back ribs, prime rib, ribeye and sirloin steak, chicken several different ways, fish and shrimp, sandwiches and salads, and bar drinks and 130 brands of beer. Lunch and dinner are served Monday to Saturday.

When Daltonites are in the mood for a dress-up dinner, they head for the **Cellar Restaurant and Lounge** in the Dalton Shopping Center, 1331 West Walnut Avenue, (706) 226–6029. Veal, seafood, steaks, soups, salads, cocktails, and wines are served at lunch, Monday through Friday, and dinner, Monday through Saturday, at moderate prices.

Vann House was a showplace of nineteenth-century Cherokee accomplishment. At the junction of Highways 52 and 225, 3 miles west of modern-day Chatsworth, the sturdy three-story house, with brick walls 2 feet thick, was built in modified Georgian style in 1804–1805. Owner James Vann was a half-Cherokee, half-Scot who helped create a Moravian mission for the education of young Cherokees. When Vann died in 1809, his son Joseph inherited the house and surrounding farmlands. He prospered until 1830, when the state of Georgia confiscated his lands for violating a law forbidding white men to work for Indians.

The Georgia Department of Natural Resources has restored the house and refurnished and redecorated the rooms in early-nineteenth-century style. An intricately carved "floating staircase" is one of Georgia's earliest surviving examples of cantilevered construction. Elsewhere are Bibles, dinnerware, and dining room and bedroom furnishings. Vann House, Chatsworth 30705, (706) 695–2598, is open Tuesday through Saturday 9:00 A.M. to 5:00 P.M. and Sunday 2:00 to 5:30 P.M. Adults, $2.00; ages 6 to 18, $1.00; under 6, free.

On Highway 52, 7 miles east of Chatsworth, **Fort Mountain State Park** is a superscenic park on a forested, 2,800-foot peak of the Blue Ridge Mountains' Cohutta Range. The park's namesake is a puzzling rock wall, or foundation, that winds nearly 900 feet around the mountainside. Whether it was an ancient Indian fortress, a bastion built by twelfth-century Welsh explorers, or part of some other inscrutable mission is a matter of speculation. The stone observation tower nearby is no mystery. It's a legacy of the Depression-era Civilian Conservation Corps (CCC).

History lessons aside, you may relax in Fort Mountain's lake, hike nature trails, play miniature golf, and set the kids loose on the playground. The 115 campsites have water, electricity, hot showers, and rest rooms. Fifteen two- and three-bedroom cottages come with kitchen appliances, towels, sheets, and logs for the fireplace. Contact Park Superintendent, Chatsworth 30705, (706) 695–2621. For reservations call (800) 864–PARK.

You can really get off the beaten path by plunging into the nearby **Cohutta National Wilderness,** 34,000 acres of mountains, forests, and rivers. Contact the U.S. Forest Service, 401 Old Ellijay Road, Chatsworth 30705, (706) 695–6736.

The best home cooking in these parts is at **Edna's Cafe** on Highway 441 in Chatsworth, (706) 695–4951, which puts out a superb lunch Monday through Saturday. Don't miss the coconut and peanut butter pie!

The Cherokee Indians assimilated themselves into the way of life established by the white settlers, then were ruthlessly crushed at *New Echota,* near modern-day Calhoun. In the 1820s New Echota was laid out as the capital of the Cherokee Nation that included parts of Georgia, the Carolinas, Tennessee, and Alabama. Here, the Cherokee legislature formulated laws, enforced by a series of district courts and a supreme court. The Indians wore European-style dress, used the farming methods of the white settlers, and lived in stone and frame houses with the most modern conveniences of the day. The more affluent owned Black slaves. The first North American tribe to formulate their own written alphabet, the Cherokee published a bilingual newspaper, circulated as far as Europe.

Gold discovered on Cherokee lands in the late 1820s brought it all to disaster. Supported by President Andrew Jackson, the state of Georgia confiscated all Cherokee lands and in 1838 forced the Indians into exile in what is now Oklahoma. Thousands perished along this "Trail of Tears."

New Echota has been meticulously reconstructed as a state historic site. Stop first to see the orientation slide show and exhibits in the reception center. Then take a self-guided walking tour that includes the Supreme Court Building, the printing presses of the *Cherokee Phoenix* newspaper, a tavern/general store, and the home of the Reverend Samuel Worcester, a Massachusetts minister who established a mission for the Indians. Park rangers frequently demonstrate arrowhead making and hunting techniques. Books about the Cherokee civilization are on sale at the reception center. In late October the *Cherokee Fall Festival* is a weekend of Indian crafts, cooking, and storytelling.

New Echota, Route 3, Calhoun 30701, (706) 629–8151, is open Tuesday through Saturday 9:00 A.M. to 5:00 P.M. and Sunday 2:00 to 5:30 P.M. Adults, $2.00; ages 6 to 18, 75 cents; under 6, free.

After all this history, replenish your energy at *B.J.'s Restaurant,* in a small shopping center at 102 Bryant Parkway (Highway 41), south of downtown Calhoun, (706) 629–3461. Luncheon specialties include chicken pot pie, barbecue, country fried steak, and vegetables; dinner features seafood, steaks, and pasta.

You may combine New Echota's fascinating lessons with Vann House in neighboring Murray County and the Etowah Indian Mounds, near Cartersville in Bartow County.

Bartow County, along I–75 between Atlanta and Chattanooga, is the site of a fascinating Indian temple mound complex. Here, also, you can visit

New Echota

a small gem of a mineral museum and take a minivacation at a state park on a 12,000-acre lake.

Barnsley Inn and Golf Resort, formerly the Barnsley Gardens (spring 1999 reopening), 10 miles west of I–75 Adairsville exit 128, (770) 773-7480, features a seventy-room luxury inn, championship golf course, tennis courts, swimming pools, health spa, fine dining, and other amenities, which will enhance the 1,300 acres of gardens created in the 1840s by Englishman Godfrey Barnsley and restored in the 1990s by a Bavarian entrepreneur. The gardens include a wildflower meadow, rhododendron, azaleas, dogwoods, and thousands of other trees, shrubs, and flowering plants. The boxwood parterre in front of the ghostly brick ruins of the manor house is graced by an ornamental fountain with an image of Godfrey Barnsley's wife, Julia. Some say the unfortunate Julia, who died of tuberculosis not long after moving to the estate from her native Savannah, still wanders the gardens.

Between A.D. 1000 and 1500, the Etowah Indian tribe migrated into the fertile Etowah River Valley, near today's Cartersville, and created a remarkably sophisticated culture. Beans, squash, corn, and fruit that the women cultivated complemented game trapped by the men in surrounding forests and the abundant fish in the Etowah. As part of a fast trading network, the Etowahs made tools, arrowheads, axes, and household implements from Great Lakes copper and Mississippi and Ohio Valley flint. Gulf Coast seashells were fashioned into ceremonial jewelry.

Surrounded by a deep moat and log stockade, a compact city of clay and wooden houses sheltered as many as 4,000 Indians. The heart of the city was half a dozen rectangular earthen mounds. The ***Etowah Indian Mounds*** were the forum for religious rites conducted by chiefs and priests and the final resting place of these dignitaries.

Stop first at the excellent small museum and reception center, where dioramas and artifacts from the mounds tell the story of this mysteriously vanished tribe. The exhibits are highlighted by a priest's burial chamber

Bill's Favorites

Cloudland Canyon State Park

Geneva Wooten's Restaurant

Hidden Hollow Country Inn

Howard Finster's "Paradise Garden"

Martha Berry Museum

Cave Spring Antique Shops

Chickamauga National Military Park

Fort Mountain State Park

Cohutta National Wilderness

New Echota State Historic Site

Col. Oscar Poole's Pig Hill of Fame Barbecue

and beautifully carved busts of a woman and a warrior. A film traces the history of the Etowahs. With a diagrammed map, cross the moat and explore the grass-covered mounds. Ninety-two steps take you up 63 feet to the top of Mound "A," from which the priest conducted rituals for the townspeople assembled below in the plaza. Mound "C," one of the smallest, was a principal burial site and the source of most of the artifacts in the museum. Park rangers periodically lead moonlight walks around the site.

About a fifteen-minute drive west of I–75 exit 124, via Highway 113/61, Etowah Mounds State Historic Site, Route 1, Cartersville 30120, (706) 387–3747, is open Tuesday through Saturday 9:00 A.M. to 5:00 P.M. and Sunday 2:00 to 5:30 P.M. Adults, $2.00; ages 6 to 8, 75 cents; under 6, free.

In Cartersville, a congenial town of 10,000, you may want to walk around the downtown shopping area and admire the stately **Bartow County Courthouse. Etowah Arts Gallery,** 13 Wall Street, (706) 382–8277, sells pottery, paintings, handmade quilts, and other crafts by local artists. Morrell's, a homey, family-run restaurant a quarter-mile off I–75 exit 125, (770) 382–1222, is a popular destination for fried chicken, steaks, children's plates, and Southern breakfast daily.

4-Way Lunch, Main Street, downtown Cartersville, no phone, has been a landmark of swift (not "fast") food and service with a brisk "how's-your-daddy?" smile for more than seventy years. THIS IS NOT BURGER KING, a sign over the coffeepot advises, YOU DON'T GET IT YOUR WAY, YOU GET IT OUR WAY, OR YOU DON'T GET IT. Another caution about the service: I CAN ONLY PLEASE ONE PERSON A DAY—AND TODAY AIN'T YOUR DAY. Crowds line up every weekday morning for bacon, eggs, grits, and biscuits, and many come back at lunch for first-class burgers, hot dogs, chopped steak, and stew. With only eleven seats at the red Formica counter, there's no lollygagging around—when you're done, it's time to move on and let another hungry patron have their 4-Way fix.

Red Top Mountain State Park and Lodge, on exit 123 off I–75 south of Cartersville, is one of the nicest and prettiest in the whole system. A wealth of recreational opportunities, campsites, and cottages are spread over the wooded hillsides around 12,000-acre Lake Allatoona.

During warm weather, you may sun on a sandy beach, swim, and waterski. The rest of the year, bring tennis racquets, fishing gear, picnic supplies, and hiking shoes. Boaters may bring their own or rent houseboats and pontoon boats at the park marina. A small grocery is at the reception center.

Red Top's twenty two-bedroom cottages are completely furnished and include fireplaces. The 286 camping sites have electricity, water, hot showers, and rest rooms. The park's Red Top Mountain Lodge has thirty-three modern guest rooms in a quiet cove with a full-service restaurant. The park office is open daily from 8:00 A.M. to 5:00 P.M. Contact Superintendent, Cartersville 30120, (770) 975–0055. Call (800) 864–PARK for camping, cottage, and lodge reservations.

North of Cartersville, less than a mile from I–75 exit 126, the attractive, well-planned **William Weinman Mineral Center & Museum** is an intriguing stopover for rockhounds and other nature-lovers. Gemstones, minerals, fossils, crystals, arrowheads, geodes, and other specimens are displyed in brightly lighted glass cases. Some are from right here in northwest Georgia's own mineral-mining regions; others are imports from South America, Africa, Australia, Mexico, and the Western United States.

In a simulated limestone cave, with authentic stalactites and stalagmites, you can trace the eons-long formation of caves with easy-to-follow diagrams and explanations. The cave's treasures also include a mastodon's sixty-pound molar and a fossilized box turtle. Other exhibits include a huge array of Indian arrowheads and flint weapons, fluorescent minerals, petrified wood, brilliantly polished geodes, rock crystal, and colorful birthstones. Books, jewelry, and mineral samples are for sale in the gift shop.

The museum, Cartersville 30120, (770) 386–0576, is open Tuesday through Saturday 10:00 A.M. to 4:30 P.M. and Sunday 2:00 to 4:30 P.M. Adults, $3.50; ages 6 to 12, $2.50; 5 and under, no charge.

Apple Country

ilmer County, in the Blue Ridge Mountains about ninety minutes due north of metro Atlanta, is "Georgia's Apple Capital." Dozens of orchards dotting the county's green mountainsides annually produce more than 300,000 bushels of Granny Smiths, Red and Golden Delicious, Yates, Jonathans, Stayman Winesaps, Rome Beauties, and exotic Asian newcomers such as Fujis and Mutsus. In the fall, when the trees are loaded with fruit, visitors by the thousands are invited into the orchards to pick their own basketsful. Those who'd just as soon leave the labor to somebody else can buy all they can haul home at farm stores that line the highways leading to *Ellijay,* the Gilmer County seat. They also can take away freshly squeezed apple cider, apple pies and cakes, and recipe books to prepare just about everything with apples.

To celebrate the harvest, *Ellijay's Georgia Apple Festival,* two weekends in mid-October, puts on parades, apple pie–eating and apple-cooking contests, arts and crafts, mountain music and dancing, and a host of other festivities. Ellijay is a delightful small town with 1,700 amiable inhabitants. It may remind you of Sheriff Andy Taylor's bucolic hometown of Mayberry. To find out what's going on—and enjoy some delicious home cooking—stop by the **Calico Cupboard** on the courthouse square, (706) 635–7575, and tuck into grits, biscuits, and sausage at breakfast time, and fried chicken, fried fish, biscuits, and vegetables at lunchtime, with a whopping big slice of apple cobbler, of course. Walk

Apples, Ellijay Style

*H*ere's a sweet way Gilmer County prepares its favorite fruit:

CARAMEL APPLE PHYLLO TART

l tablespoon margarine

6 Granny Smith apples cut into 16 wedges

½ cup raisins

⅓ cup firmly packed brown sugar

½ cup ground cinnamon

Butter flavored cooking spray

6 sheets frozen phyllo pastry, thawed

1 teaspoon powdered sugar

¼ cup milk

12 small soft caramel candies

In a large skillet, melt margarine over medium high heat. Add apples and sauté 15 minutes or until tender. Add raisins, brown sugar, and cinnamon; stir well. Remove from heat and let cool.

Preheat oven to 375°. Coat an 11-inch tart pan with cooking spray. Gently press 1 sheet of phyllo into pan, allowing ends to extend over edges; lightly coat phyllo with cooking spray. Place another sheet of phyllo in crisscross design; coat phyllo with cooking spray. Repeat process with remaining 4 phyllo sheets. Fold in phyllo to fit pan and form a rim. Bake for 15 minutes or until golden. Cool on wire rack.

Sprinkle phyllo shell with powdered sugar. In small saucepan, combine milk and caramels and cook over medium heat until caramels melt, stirring constantly. Remove from heat. Spoon apple mixture into phyllo shell and drizzle caramel mixture over apples. Makes 8 servings.

it off with a stroll around the corner to **Penland Brothers Store,** a bona fide general merchandise emporium, which has been supplying Gilmer Countians with all their necessities since 1913. Several antiques and craft shops are also around the square.

When your appetite's worked up again, get ready for some serious barbecue. As you drive into town on the four-lane Zell Miller Mountain Parkway (Highway 515), you can't help but notice **Col. Oscar Poole's Pig Hill of Fame.** For $5.00 you, too, can have your name painted on one of thousands of little plywood piggies that graze on the hillside beside Col. Poole's yolk-yellow **Real Pit Bar-B-Q** establishment, (706) 635–4100. (Col. Poole is also a Methodist minister, and your $5.00 goes to church missions.) Inside, the barbecue is seriously delicious.

Col. Oscar Poole's Pig Hill of Fame

In contrast to Col. Poole's flamboyant stand, you'll have to look closely to find **Holloway's Pink Pig,** (706) 276–1700, on Highway 515 in the community of Cherry Log, 8 miles north of Ellijay. The giveaway is the tantalizing aroma of the 'cue that saturates the mountain air. The Pink Pig is locally renowned for its tangy barbecue sauce and Brunswick stew— loaded with meat and vegetables in a tangy tomato-based sauce—but its trademark dish is fresh garlic salad. As owner Bud Holloway is fond of saying, "When you get back to Ellijay, people won't need to ask where you had lunch." Jimmy and Rosalynn Carter 'cue up at Holloway's while staying at their mountain home outside Ellijay.

Whitewater rafters, canoeists, and kayakers flock to the Ellijay and Cartecay Rivers that flow out of the mountains, right into Ellijay. Contact Mountaintown Outdoor Expeditions, (706) 635–2524; Beacon Sports Center, (706) 276–3660; and the Gilmer County Chamber of Commerce, 5 Westside Square, Ellijay 30540, (706) 635–7400.

ROME
*Chandler Arms
Bed & Breakfast,*
2 Coral Avenue
(706–235–5702 or
800–438–9492).

This B & B is infused with
the English hospitality and
effervescent personality of
innkeeper Rosemary
Chandler, a transplanted
Brit. Each guest room in
her 1902 Victorian home
has a different turn-of-the-
century motif and private
bath. The Honeymoon
Suite has a brass canopy
bed and whirlpool. Full
English breakfast,
afternoon high tea, and
wind-down wine enhance
the gracious ambience.
Doubles are $60 to $75.

*Claremont House
Bed & Breakfast,*
906 East Second Avenue
(706–291–0900 or
800–254–4797).

This is a showplace
Victorian Gothic mansion
built in 1882. Innkeeper
Patsy Priest has lavished
her public spaces and guest
rooms with antiques,
wood-burning fireplaces,
and elaborately carved
woodwork. Champagne in
the parlor, rocking chairs
on the verandas, and full
gourmet breakfast served
in the dining room are part
of the experience of this
historic downtown home.
Doubles are $60 to $80.

ROME
*La Scala Restaurant
& Bar,* 400 block Broad
Street, downtown
(706–238–9000).

This attractively done
Italian dining room does a
bella job with pasta,
seafood, chicken, and veal
dishes and offers many
innovative surprises.
Signature dishes include
chicken Margherita,
"dedicated to a beloved
young woman," grilled
sliced chicken with
spinach, red roasted bell
peppers, black olives, and
ziti pasta; salmon
Florentine on a bed of fresh
spinach; and *cioppino posil-
lipo,* a hearty stew of calamari, mussels, shrimp and
bay scallops in a tomato-
based sauce, served over
angel hair pasta. Lunch,
including buffet, Monday
though Friday, dinner Monday through Saturday.

Longhorn Steaks,
Midtown Crossing
Shopping Center,
Shorter Avenue
(706–235–4232).

Grilled steaks and salmon,
with bodacious baked
potatoes and other
trimmings, in a kicked
back faux-Western saloon
setting. Lunch and dinner
daily.

Partridge Cafe,
300 block of Broad Street
(706–291–4048).

Good ol' Southern home-
cooking has made this
downtown eatery a land-
mark for more than sixty
years. Lunch and dinner
daily.

DALTON
The Oakwood Cafe,
downtown at 201 West
Cuyler Street,
(706) 278–4421.

Legions of Daltonians
wouldn't think about
starting their day without
Oakwood omelets, hot
cakes, and ham and
sausage biscuits. They're
back at lunch and dinner
for steaks, chicken, chops,
and seafood. Breakfast,
lunch, and dinner are
served Monday to Saturday.

Helpful Web Sites

Dalton Convention & Visitors Bureau, *www.northga.net/whitfield/*

Northwest Georgia Travel Association, *www.ngeorgia.com*

Rome Convention & Visitors Bureau,
www.romegeorgia.com

Cartersville-Bartow County
Convention & Visitors Bureau,
www.notatlanta.org

Middle Georgia

Cherry Blossoms and Fried Green Tomatoes

*F*or travelers caught in the relentless grind of interstate traffic, Macon can be a quick and refreshing retreat to a slower, easier era. Only a few minutes from the major highways, ***Downtown Macon Historic District*** offers a glimpse at beautifully restored Greek Revival and Victorian homes, churches, and public buildings on quiet, tree-shaded streets. Three landmark houses are open year-round. Others invite guests during the late March Cherry Blossom Festival and September Jubilee.

Your first stop should be the ***Macon-Bibb County Convention and Visitors Bureau***, in Terminal Station, downtown at 200 Cherry Street, Macon 31201, (800) 768–3401 and (912) 743–3401. You can pick up free maps, brochures, information, and self-guided tours. You can also sign on for ***Sidney's Historic Tours***. Named in honor of Macon's beloved poet, Sidney Lanier, the tour blends historical narrative, humor, anecdotes, and passages of Lanier's romantic poetry. It includes stops at four attractions: Hay House, Cannonball House, Lanier Cottage, and Tubman Museum. ***Colonel Bond's Horsedrawn Carriage Tours*** depart from the Green Jacket Restaurant across from the Terminal, (912) 749–7267.

Whether with a guide or on your own, the ***Hay House*** (912–742–8155) will be a highlight. Five years abuilding, the opulent Italian Renaissance palazzo was finished in April 1861 just as Macon and Georgia were marching off to the War Between the States. Behind the stately redbrick facade, the twenty-four rooms are a treasure trove of stained glass, statuary, European and American furnishings, silver and crystal, paintings, and silk and damask draperies and wall coverings. Long before air-conditioning, a cleverly concealed ventilation system kept the high-ceilinged rooms surprisingly cool even on the most torrid summer days. Located at 924 Georgia Avenue, Hay House is open Monday through Saturday 10:00 A.M. to 4:30 P.M. and Sunday

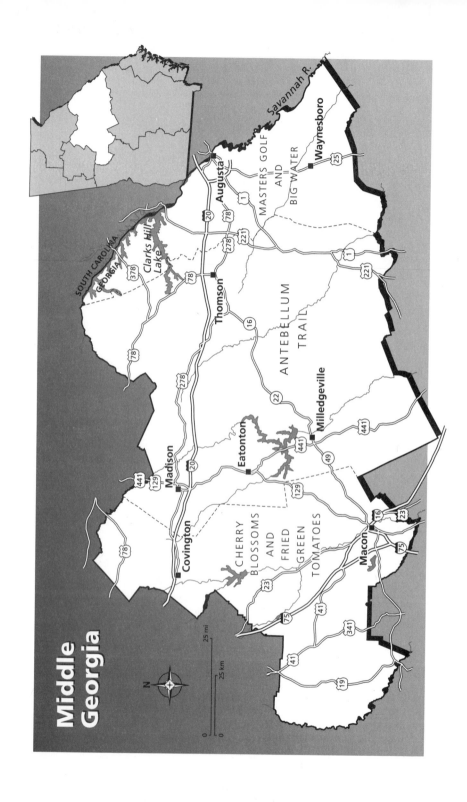

1:00 to 4:30 P.M. Admission for adults is $6.00; students, $2.00; and ages 6 and under, free.

Just around the corner at 856 Mulberry Street, a white-columned Greek Revival achieved lasting notoriety when a Union shell crashed through the facade and landed in the front hallway. Walk through the **Old Cannonball House** and adjoining **Macon Confederate Museum** (912–745–5982) for a look at the stray missile, Civil War photos, artifacts, china, crystal, weapons, uniforms, and such rare treasures as Mrs. Robert E. Lee's rolling pin. It's open Monday through Saturday 10:00 A.M. to 4:00 P.M. Adults are $3.00; senior citizens, $2.50; students, $1.00; children 12 and under, 50 cents.

Every Georgia schoolchild learns, at least for the moment, Sidney Lanier's romantic poems "The Marshes of Glynn" and "The Song of the Chattahoochee." Poet, lawyer, linguist, and musician, Lanier was born in 1842 in the tidy Victorian cottage at 935 High Street. His desk, furnishings, and personal effects are displayed at **Lanier Cottage** (912– 743–3851)

Monday through Friday 9:00 A.M. to 4:00 P.M. and Saturday 9:30 A.M. to 12.30 P.M. Adults are $2.50; students, $1.00; and children 12 and under, 50 cents.

Macon's modern musical heritage includes Rock 'n' Roll Hall of Famer "Little Richard" Penniman, soul singer Otis Redding (a bridge over the Ocmulgee River is named for him), and the Allman Brothers Band. Duane Allman and fellow band member Berry Oakley—both killed in 1970s motorcycle accidents—are buried in much-visited graves at *Rose Hill Cemetery.* Maconites from all the way back to the 1830s and 600 Confederate and Union soldiers are also in the historic cemetery at 1091 Riverside Drive. Call (912) 751–9119 for information.

The Tubman African American Museum, downtown at 340 Walnut Street, (912) 743–8544, displays paintings, sculpture, and other creative endeavors by Black American, African, and Caribbean artists and craftspeople. The *Resources Room* has available reference materials and books on Black Americans. The museum's shop sells handcrafted jewelry, paintings, posters, recordings, and books. A mural depicting contemporary Black characters features Colin Powell as a military hero. Open Monday through Saturday 10:00 A.M. to 5:00 P.M. and Sunday 2:00 to 5:00 P.M. Admission is $3.00 for adults, $2.00 for ages 6 to 12, and under 6, no charge.

Ocmulgee National Monument, a short drive from downtown, is a must-see for anyone fascinated by ancient American Indian civilization. A dozen ceremonial and burial mounds, the highest nearly 45 feet, were built by Mississippian Indians between about A.D. 900 and 1100. They were succeeded at the site by Creeks, who remained here until their expulsion to Oklahoma in the 1830s.

Stop first at the National Park Service Visitors Center and see a short film, artifacts unearthed from the mounds, and dioramas on the cultures that flourished here. You may climb steep wooden stairs to the flat top of the 45-foot-high *Great Temple Mound* and to the crest of the surrounding smaller mounds. You may also see them from the comfort of your car. A sound-and-light presentation brings the circular *Earthlodge* back to life, as tribal elders discuss plans for a war, the effects of a drought, and other important issues. The monument is at 1207 Emery Highway, (912) 752–8257. Hours are (daily) 9:00 A.M. to 5:00 P.M. Free admission.

The *Georgia Music Hall of Fame,* 200 Martin Luther King, Jr., Boulevard, (912) 750–0350, takes you on a delightful tune-filled stroll through the Peach State's incredibly rich musical heritage.

Opened in 1996, the $6-million, 43,000-square-foot downtown Macon "musical village" showcases such varied homegrown talents as Ray Charles, Lena Horne, Travis Tritt, Trisha Yearwood, Savannah songwriter Johnny Mercer, Augusta-born opera diva Jessye Norman, the Allman Brothers Band, Capricorn Records, bandleader Harry James, and Macon's own Otis Redding and "Little Richard" Penniman. You can sit in theaters and watch music videos of gospel, pop, and rock performers and listen to dozens of your favorites on headphones placed around the museum. The indoor "musical village" also has a 1950s soda fountain and a gift shop with recordings by 115 Georgia artists. Open Monday through Saturday 9:00 A.M. to 5:00 P.M. and Sunday 1:00 to 5:00 P.M. Adults, $7.50; senior citizens, $6.50; ages 6 to 16, $3.50.

The **Georgia Sports Hall of Fame,** a 43,000-square-foot museum opening in mid-1999 across from the Music Hall of Fame, 301 Cherry Street, (912) 752–1585, showcases heroes of golf, football, baseball, basketball, and other endeavors. You'll be able to test your skills on interactive and virtual reality games.

To get in the proper antebellum spirit, make reservations at the **1842 Inn,** 353 College Street, Macon 31201, (912) 741–1842 or (800) 336–1842. The twenty-two guest rooms in the circa-1842 Greek Revival showplace and an adjacent cottage are decorated with antiques, fresh flowers, fireplaces, and all the contemporary comforts. Double rates of $125 to $185 include continental breakfast.

During the last ten days of March, more than 200,000 Japanese cherry trees set the stage for the city's annual **Cherry Blossom Festival** highlighted by concerts, home and garden tours, parades, and other activities. You won't be in town very long before proud Maconites tell you that in sheer numbers of blossoming trees, if nothing else, their festival is bigger than Washington, D.C.'s.

Top Annual Events

Macon Cherry Blossom Festival, mid-late March, *(800) 768–3401*

Madison's Spring Tour of Homes, mid-April, *(706) 342–4743*

Washington-Wilkes Tour of Homes, early April, Washington, *(706) 678–2013*

Masters Golf Tournament, early April, Augusta, *(800) 726–4067*

Riverwalk Bluegrass Festival, early May, Augusta, *(706) 592–0054*

Oliver Hardy Festival, early October, Harlem, *(706) 556–3448*

Blind Willie McTell Blues Festival, early October, Thomson, (706) 595–5584

Ocmulgee Indian Celebration, late September, Ocmulgee National Monument, Macon, *(800) 768–3401*

Twelve Days of Christmas, mid-November to end of December, Milledgeville, *(800) 653–1804*

Christmas at Callaway Plantation, early December, Washington, *(706) 678–7060*

Cherry Blossom season or not, you'll still enjoy a drive by the stately homes on north Macon's *"Cherry Blossom Trail,"* several miles of streets marked by pink and white signs.

Sweet Sue's Tea Room & Soda Fountain, Highway 41, just off the I-75/Bolingbroke exit 58, (912) 994-0031, is a sweet old-fashioned retreat from the crass commercialism and junk food of I-75. Beverly and Jim Mickle's soda fountain and lunchroom is a delightful place to sip sodas; sundaes; phosphates; cherry, vanilla, and lemon Cokes; a big choice of teas (served English style with finger sandwiches, scones, and shortbread tea cakes); and lunch on salads, house-made soups, and a variety of nutritious sandwiches. It's open mornings and afternoons Monday through Saturday. Afterward stroll around the small community of Bolingbroke, and visit a pair of antiques shops and an arts and crafts store.

Jarrell Plantation is a homespun juxtaposition to the romanticized Old South of Tara and Twelve Oaks, dashing beaux and ladies fair. At the end of a tree-shaded graveled road off Highway 18 between Forsyth and Gray, you enter a world where unrelenting hard work—not flirtation and idle mint juleps—was the rule of society. From the early 1840s, when John Fitz Jarrell built the first dwelling, until 1958 when the last direct heir died, the plantation was worked by three generations of Jarrells. They planted cotton, ran gins and gristmills, and battled boll weevils, depressions, and General William Tecumseh Sherman himself. Nowadays, the dwellings, work buildings, barnyards, and fields are

Harlem's Oliver Hardy

*O*ne of the silver screen's most popular and recognizable comedians was born in 1892 in the small east Georgia town of Harlem. Rotund fussbudget Oliver Hardy left home when he was eight years old and joined a traveling show as a boy soprano. Weary of the road, he attended Georgia Military Academy and studied law at the University of Georgia.

But greasepaint was apparently in his blood. He opened Milledgeville's first movie house and was so intrigued by the films, he became a comic villain in a theater company. In the mid-1920s, he went to Hollywood and teamed up with his sidekick and foil, Stan Laurel. It was a match made in the stars. They appeared together in more than 100 pictures and performed on radio, stage, and TV. Hardy died in 1957, and his memory lives on at Harlem's Oliver Hardy Festival in early October. Visitors enjoy a Laurel and Hardy film fest and a look-alike contest.

maintained by the Georgia Department of Natural Resources as a living memorial to the state's agricultural heritage.

You'll enter the plantation through the scuppernong arbor, whose juicy fruit Jarrell women turned into pies and jellies. A flock of guinea fowl, squawking like so many feathered burglar alarms, alerted the family that visitors were approaching. These days, the guinea fowl still sound off, and an assortment of barnyard animals—a goat, a horse, a brown milk cow, a burro, a couple of sheep—press against the fence for the hay held out by children.

At the modern new visitors center, you can watch a film on the plantation's history and pick up a self-guided walking-tour map.

At the 1847 plantation's plain first dwelling, you can visualize the womenfolk sitting in a circle, their hands busily making quilts and clothes while hearty stews bubbled on the wood-burning stove. At the mill complex down the hill from the house, workmen get the steam engine ready to grind the sugar cane into syrup.

Jarrell Plantation—Route 1, Box 40, Juliette 31046, (912) 986–5172—is open Tuesday through Saturday 9:00 A.M. to 5:00 P.M. and Sunday 2:00 to 5:00 P.M. Adults are $2.00; children 6 to 18, $1.00; 5 and under, free.

The *Piedmont National Wildlife Refuge,* 10 miles down the graveled road from the plantation, has a visitors center and hiking trails. You can bring your fishing gear and try your luck in the Ocmulgee River.

If you saw the movie *Fried Green Tomatoes* or read the Fannie Flagg novel it was based on, you'll be glad to know it wasn't pure fiction. After the movie's highly successful 1991 run, enterprising folks in the almost-ghost town of *Juliette* bought up the store that served as the movie's cafe and reopened the "new" *Whistle Stop Café,* (912) 994–3670. Fried green tomatoes are served, along with barbecue, fried chicken, meat loaf, pork chops, and other home-cooked favorites. Southern-style breakfast is also served. The block of stores and the white frame depot around the cafe have also been revived as antiques and gift shops. And, adding to the atmosphere, local kids dive off the dam near the textile mill, just as they did in the film. The Whistle Stop Café is open daily. It's in downtown Juliette, 10 miles off I–75 North and South exit 61.

A quiet and peaceful recreation place now, *Indian Springs State Park,* near Jackson, has a long, colorful, and tragic history. For many centuries Creeks and other Indians gathered at a sulfur spring whose waters were believed to have magical powers to cure ailments and restore vitality. In the spring in 1825, Creek Indian Chief William

McIntosh signed an illegal treaty ceding all tribal lands to the state of Georgia. The fraudulent treaty so enraged the dispossessed Indians that they murdered McIntosh and several of his followers. A valid treaty in 1828 finally ended Creek dominion. The town of Indian Springs was founded, along with what's believed to be the oldest state park anywhere in the United States.

Nowadays people still flock to the sulfur springs and take home jugs of the strong-smelling water. They swear by its ability to restore health and vitality and offer this advice to those who quail at the rotten-egg smell: Just let it sit for two to three days, and the aroma will vanish, but not the curative strength of the minerals.

The handsome fieldstone buildings in the park were built during the Great Depression by the Civilian Conservation Corps. Along with the mineral waters, artifacts and historical displays are on view at the **Indian Museum.** Around a 105-acre lake are a swimming beach, fishing, rental boats, nature trails, and picnic areas. Campsites with electrical and water hookups are $10 a night. Completely furnished two-bedroom cottages, with log-burning fireplaces, are available. There is a $2.00 per visit parking fee. Contact Park Superintendent, Indian Springs 30231, (770) 504–2277. For reservations call (800) 864–PARK.

Fresh Air Bar-B-Que (770–775–3182), on Highway 42 between Jackson and the park, is one of the holy grails of this savory Georgia art form. Except for wooden planking that covered the old sawdust floor a few years ago, and one change of ownership more than fifty years ago, this rambling, wooden barbecue shack has changed only marginally since it served its first platter in 1929.

The pine board tables have been in place for more than forty years. Pork is slowly cooked over hickory and oak coals right behind the ordering counter. It's sweet and succulent, with a tangy pièce de résistance provided by a secret sauce prepared every day by G. W. "Toots" Caston, the patriarch of the family that has operated the place since the early 1940s. Along with barbecued pork, the simple menu includes only Brunswick stew, cole slaw, slabs of starchy white bread, soft drinks, and iced tea. It's open Monday through Thursday 7:00 A.M. to 7:30 P.M., Friday and Saturday until 9:30 P.M., and Sunday until 8:30 P.M. During the summer, it usually remains open a half hour to an hour later.

High Falls State Park, off Highway 36, about 12 miles south of Indian Springs, is another rustic off-the-beaten-path retreat. The centerpiece is a series of scenic whitewater cataracts of the **Towaliga River** rushing over mossy rocks. According to legend, Creek Indians "cured" their victims' scalps around the Towaliga—hence the name, which means "roasted scalp."

Two hiking trails offer views of the falls, the river, and adjacent woodlands. You can wade into the river, but be extremely careful of the slick, mossy rocks. Also in the 995-acre park, you'll find a 650-acre lake for fishing and boating, a swimming pool, and 142 tent and trailer sites, with water and electrical hookups. There is a $2.00 per visit parking fee. Contact Park Superintendent, Route 5, Box 108, Jackson 30233, (912) 993–3053. For reservations call (800) 864–PARK.

The little Walton County town of *Social Circle,* about 8 miles west of Hard Labor Creek on Highway 11, is a delightful place to stroll and browse. The nineteenth-century storefronts have been brightly repainted, and three are antiques shops. The wooden shelves in Claude Wiley's Store are stacked to the ceiling with canned goods, overalls, farm products, and household necessities. The town allegedly got its name when a stranger happened onto a cluster of idling locals and found them so friendly he proclaimed, "Why, this is sure some social circle."

The *Blue Willow Inn Restaurant* (770–464–2131) is like an old-fashioned Sunday dinner at grandma's. The dining room of the 1890s Victorian house is filled with a bountiful buffet that includes fried chicken, pork chops, chicken and dumplings, baked ham, an array of vegetables (including state-of-the-art fried green tomatoes), congealed salads, cake, and fruit cobbler—all at astonishingly modest prices. After your feast, sit on front porch rockers, walk in Billie and Lewis Van Dykes's gardens, and stroll down Social Circle's Main Street. Open daily.

Lake Oconee, a mammoth Georgia Power Company impoundment of the Oconee River, is a major destination for outdoor recreation. The 19,000-acre lake, with a 375-mile shoreline, has numerous marinas, campsites, picnicking areas, and swimming beaches. The Georgia Power Company office at the lake (800–886–LAKE) can supply further information about recreational facilities. The lake is easily accessible from I–20.

Three country club and golf communities on Lake Oconee welcome overnight guests in cottages and villas. Guests enjoy championship-style golf courses, lighted tennis courts, fitness centers, swimming pools, croquet, horseback riding, marinas, dining, and other first-class

Bill's Favorites
Cherry Blossom Festival
Hay House
Indian Springs State Park
The buffet tables at the Blue Willow Inn
Old Governor's Mansion
Antebellum Milledgeville
Antebellum Madison
Antebellum Washington
Riverwalk Augusta
Fort Discovery Science Center
Morris Museum
Lunch at Len Berg's

facilities. Contact **Harbor Club,** One Club Drive, Greensboro 30642, (770) 453–4414; **Port Armor,** One Port Armor Parkway, Greensboro 30642, (770) 453–4561; and **Reynolds Plantation,** 100 Linger Longer Road, Greensboro 30642, (770) 467–3151.

Antebellum Trail

Milledgeville was Georgia's capital city from early after the Revolution until after the War Between the States. Laid out in 1803–1804 on a precise grid of broad streets and public squares, it was the only American city, other than Washington, D.C., specifically planned as a capital. In its own way, it was to post-Revolutionary Georgia what Brasilia was to mid-twentieth-century Brazil: a magnet intended to lure settlers away from the comforts of the Atlantic coast.

Statesmen and public officials eased the burdens of the wilderness by building palatial Greek Revival mansions filled with the finest American and European furnishings, books, and art. Halcyon days ended in the fall of 1864 when General William T. Sherman's Union army, marching from Atlanta to Savannah, captured the city.

According to which legend you choose to believe, Milledgeville was spared Sherman's torch because (a) he was met at the outskirts by fellow brothers of the local Masonic lodge, who pleaded for leniency; (b) he didn't want to burn a town he'd chosen as temporary headquarters; (c) he had a local lady friend and did not wish to break her heart.

Whatever the reasons, Milledgeville's peaceable surrender was accomplished when Governor Joseph E. Brown stood in the rotunda of the Governors Mansion and handed his sword to General Sherman. When the "March to the Sea" resumed, the Governors Mansion and everything of nonmilitary importance was left unharmed. The Reconstruction government moved the capital to Atlanta, an action ratified by the state's voters in 1868.

Built in 1835 to 1838 in Palladian design Greek Revival style, the **Old Governors Mansion** (912–453–4545) has been beautifully restored and refurnished. Guided tours of public rooms rich with original furnishings and fascinating architectural features are conducted Tuesday through Saturday 10:00 A.M. to 4:00 P.M. and Sunday 2:00 to 5:00 P.M. Adults are $3.00; students, $1.00. It's in the center of the town at 120 South Clark Street.

American literature fans should also visit the **Flannery O'Connor Room** (912–455–4047) in the library of neighboring Georgia College.

The late author wrote her two novels (*The Violent Bear It Away* and *Wise Blood*) and short story collections while living here. She died in 1964 and is buried in Memory Hill Cemetery. The Flannery O'Connor Room at her alma mater displays first editions, manuscripts, gifts from admirers, memorabilia, and drawings she did as a hobby. It's open by appointment.

The best way to enjoy the town's heritage is on a two-hour motorized **Milledgeville Trolley Tour,** which covers the major landmarks and includes a visit to the Governors Mansion. Guides weave a wealth of humor and anecdotes into their historical narrative. Tours leave the Milledgeville Convention and Visitors Bureau, 200 West Hancock Street, Milledgeville 31061, Tuesdays and Fridays at 10:00 A.M. Adults are $7.50; ages 6 to 12, $3.50. The tourism office (912–452–4687 and 800–653–1804) also has free maps and information for self-guided walking tours. It's directly across the street from the handsome **Baldwin County Courthouse.**

Milledgeville is a "high-spirited" town. If you'd like to hear about some of its specters, join the **Milledgeville Ghost Walk.** The hour-and-a-half stroll through the historic district begins at dusk Wednesday through Saturday, and you never know who (or what) you'll encounter along the way. Adults are $6.50; ages 6 to 12, $4.50. Phone (706) 485–0741 for reservations.

For dinner Tuesday through Sunday, try the crisply fried catfish and hushpuppies, shrimp, and other fresh seafood at **Chobys Landing** (912–453–9744), 3090 Highway 441 North, and **Totten's Fisherman's Wharf** (912–452–0161), 170 Sinclair Marina Road. Both are on **Lake Sinclair,** north of town, with docking facilities near the door.

Two historic Milledgeville homes invite bed-and-breakfast guests: **Mara's Tara,** 330 West Greene Street, Milledgeville 31061, (912) 453–2732; and **Hinson House,** 200 North Columbia Street, Milledgeville 31061, (912) 452–4687. Both have beautiful antique furnishings, private baths, and breakfast for about $60 a double.

After Milledgeville's history lesson, you'll probably be ready for some quiet relaxation. Lake Sinclair, a 15,330-acre, 420-mile shoreline impoundment of the Oconee River, has plenty of stretching room. Marinas, fishing docks, and campgrounds are off U.S. Highway 441 north of Milledgeville.

Milledgeville's literary lioness was Flannery O'Connor. Eatonton, about 15 miles north on U.S. 441, was the birthplace in 1848 of Joel Chandler

Harris, who turned the slave legends he heard as a youngster on a Putnam County plantation into the *Uncle Remus: Tales.*

The Uncle Remus Museum (706–485–6856), on Highway 441 south of the town of 4,800 has Harris's personal mementos and illustrations of the tales of the devilish Br'er Rabbit, sly-but-perpetually-outwitted Br'er Fox, dumb ole Br'er Bear, and, of course, the Tar Baby. Also in the log cabin, which was created from two original slave cabins, you'll see first editions, a diorama of an antebellum plantation, and other historical artifacts. The museum is open daily during the summer 9:00 A.M. to 5:00 P.M. and closed on Tuesday the rest of the year. Adults are $1.00; children, 50 cents. Eatonton also is the home of Alice Walker, Pulitzer prize–winning author of *The Color Purple.*

As you drive past the Putnam County Courthouse in the center of Eatonton, look for the little likeness of Br'er Rabbit on the lawn facing

The Ghost and Miss Katherine

*M*y only encounter with a ghost was one dark and stormy night in Milledgeville. A photographer and I were guests of Miss Katherine Scott, who'd lived in her antebellum home on North Jefferson Street since early in the century. Wise and witty, she'd been an English professor at Georgia College for Women for many years and wasn't pleased with the way her teachings had influenced her most famous student, Flannery O'Connor. "I read one of her books," she bristled, "and Flannery could have done the world a big favor by killing off that odious main character on the first page instead of the last."

Her home's original owner was an unsavory character named Sam Walker, who'd reputedly buried several slaves and a few wives in his backyard. When his son came home from boarding school with typhus, skinflint Sam refused him a doctor. The boy eventually died in the four-poster bed at the top of the stairs.

Sam saw a vision of his deceased son, condemning him to walk the staircase to the bedroom (where I was to spend a sleepless night) as long as the house stood.

In the wee hours of that night, with rain, thunder, and lightning crashing, and a grandfather clock bonging every quarter hour, I heard a heavy tread on the staircase, then another, and another. Something crashed onto the floor downstairs. I didn't come out from under the covers until first light. "Well, I guess you heard Sam doing his mischief last night," Miss Katherine smiled. "See, he even threw that picture on the floor. The hook's still in the wall."

The photographer was staying in the room next to Miss Katherine's and swore she didn't get up and do the ghostly walk herself. When he processed his pictures, a vaporous image was clearly visible, lurking over the top of the stairs.

Highway 441. Many well-kept antebellum homes are on the shady streets leading off the courthouse square. Putnam County is also the center of Georgia's dairy industry, so you'll also spot several contented herds as you drive out of town.

Rock Eagle, 4 miles north of Eatonton, is a relic of Indian civilizations that flourished here more than 6,000 years ago. A creamy white quartz effigy—about 10 feet high, 103 feet from its head to its tail, 32 feet from wingtip to wingtip—the great bird seems poised for flight. Archaeologists believe Rock Eagle was a focus for Indian tribal rituals. The best views are from an observation tower. It's located in a 4-H Club Center, on Highway 74, off Highway 441.

Morgan County, between Augusta and Atlanta, claims Madison, one of Georgia's prettiest antebellum towns.Before leaving, you can relax at a state park with an 18-hole golf course, fish and swim at a 19,000-acre lake, and hunt quail on a private preserve.

Strolling along the tree-shaded streets and picturesque town square, admiring Madison's treasury of glorious antebellum architecture, we should say "thank you" to a United States senator who put himself between the town and General William T. Sherman's torch. In late 1864, Atlanta in ruins 60 miles away and the cruel "March to the Sea" in full stride, Sherman's Union army approached Madison's outskirts. They were met by former Senator Joshua Hill, a foe of secession who'd been acquainted with Sherman in Washington. He peacefully surrendered the town, which was miraculously spared war's ravages.

Your first stop should be the ***Madison–Morgan County Chamber of Commerce Welcome Center,*** 115 East Jefferson Street, Madison 30650, (706) 342-4454. In this former 1880s fire station on the courthouse square, you can load up on walking-tour maps and brochures and get any information you may need on festivals, bed and breakfasts, and restaurants. Stop next at the ***Madison–Morgan County Cultural Center,*** 434 South Main Street, Madison 30650, (706) 342-4743. The Romanesque-style redbrick schoolhouse, circa 1895, is now the hub for regional arts, theater performances, and the source of walking-tour maps of the fetching little town of 3,000. The former schoolrooms now show pottery, weaving, paintings by Georgia artists and traveling exhibitions, nineteenth-century furniture, farm implements, clothing, and Civil War artifacts. You may also see a log cabin from the early 1800s and an 1890s schoolroom, complete with pot-bellied stove and hickory switch. The center's August theater festival features everything from Shakespeare to Tennessee Williams. The center is open Tuesday through Saturday 10:00 A.M. to 4:30 P.M. and Sunday 2:00 to 5:00 P.M. Admission is $2.50 for adults; students, $1.50; no charge on Wednesday.

With a self-guided tour map, walk through the *Madison National Historic District* and admire more than three dozen gorgeous Greek Revival, Neoclassical, Victorian, Federal, and Romanesque homes, many of them graced by gardens and stately trees. A number of these old beauties are open to the public during Madison's May and December festivals.

The *Morgan County African-American Museum,* 156 Academy Street, (706) 342–9191, documents the contributions Blacks have made to the area's cultural and social life. Located in the 1895 Horace Moore House, the museum has rooms with period furnishings, a reference library, paintings, books, and exhibits. Open Tuesday to Saturday. Adults are $2.00; children, $1.00.

You may take a guided tour of *Heritage Hall,* 277 South Main Street, (706) 342–9627, a white-columned 1830s Greek Revival showplace near the courthouse square. Look for romantic messages etched on the windows, and be mindful of a mysterious presence that sometimes evidences itself in an upstairs bedroom. Open daily. Adults are $2.50; seniors, $2.00; students, $1.00.

Madison's town square is one of Georgia's most delightful, and the *Morgan County Courthouse* one of the grandest of the 159 counties. Several antiques and handicraft stores will draw your attention as you stroll around the square. When hunger strikes, head for the cafeteria line at *Ye Old Colonial* (706–342–2211), a unique dining landmark on the square. Once upon a time the building was a bank, which accounts for the high ceilings, tiled floors, and a small dining room in the one-time vault. These days you can cash in on excellent fried chicken, barbecue, fish, Southern-style vegetables, and hearty breakfasts with biscuits and buttery grits. Service is continuous from breakfast through lunch and dinner Monday through Saturday.

Three of Madison's loveliest homes welcome bed-and-breakfast guests: *Brady Inn,* 250 North Second Street, (706) 342–4400; *Burnett Place,* 317 Old Post Road, (706) 342–4034; and *The Farmhouse Inn,* 1051 Meadow Lane, (706) 342–7933. All are in zip code 30650.

Hard Labor Creek State Park, 12 miles west of Madison, near the small community of Rutledge, is a nice place to relax for a day, or several days. The recreational possibilities include a very good 18-hole golf course and a lake for swimming, boating, and fishing. Plenty of picnic tables are spread among the pines, and there's a playground for the youngsters. If you're planning to play the 6,682-yard, par-72 course, bring your own clubs. You may rent an electric cart in the clubhouse, which has showers and a snack bar. The park's fifty campsites have water, electricity, rest rooms, and showers; twenty two-bedroom cottages are completely furnished, including towels, sheets, and kitchen utensils. There is a $2.00 per visit parking fee. The park office is open daily 8:00 A.M. to 5:00 P.M. Contact Superintendent, Rutledge 30663, (706) 557–3001. For reservations call (800) 864–PARK.

Until recently Rutledge was a couple of blinks you passed through on the way to Hard Labor Creek. During the past few years, a group of citizens has bought up much of the town of 650 and attracted a cadre of artists and craftspeople from as far away as New England. *Rutledge antiques and craft stores* on the main street sell handmade quilts, handcrafted furniture, original art work, pottery, and antiques. Have lunch or dinner at *The Yesterday Cafe,* (706) 557–9337, a handsomely redone turn-of-the-century drug store with bare brick walls and a tiled floor, which blends Southern cooking with trendy pasta, veal, beef, and chicken dishes, and sandwiches and salads. Lunch daily; dinner Thursday through Saturday. Take the Rutledge/Hard Labor Creek exit from I–20.

Burnt Pine Plantation, a 10,000-acre spread of fields, woodlands, and hedgerows near Madison, is a private preserve dedicated to the sport of quail and dove hunting. Guests are furnished with guides and dogs. Accommodations and meals are at a comfortable lodge and at adjacent, fully furnished cottages. Contact Burnt Pine Plantation, 2941 Little River Road, Madison 30650, (706) 342–7202.

A. H. Stephens State Historic Park, outside the small town of Crawfordville, includes the home and gravesite of Alexander Hamilton Stephens, governor of Georgia and vice-president of the Confederacy. *Liberty Hall,* the two-story frame house Stephens built around 1830, is filled with his furnishings, personal effects, and the wheelchairs to which he was bound much of his life.

The adjoining *Confederate Museum* (706–456–2602) is highlighted by a bronze statue of Stephens by Gutzon Borglum, sculptor of the U.S. presidents on Mount Rushmore, South Dakota. This fine collection of memorabilia also includes dioramas of soldiers in the heat of battle and the quiet of the campfire; rifles and shot; field gear; battle flags; and touching personal belongings—Bibles, prayer books, and bloodstained photos of wives and sweethearts.

As in all wars, Civil War soldiers used sharp-edged humor to help blunt the insidious enemies of fear and homesickness. "In this army," a Con-

A. H. Stephens State Historic Park

federate foot soldier wrote, "one hole in the seat of the breeches indicates a captain, two holes is for a lieutenant, and the seat of the pants all out is for us privates." Liberty Hall and the Confederate Museum are open Monday and Wednesday through Saturday 9:00 A.M. to 5:00 P.M. and Sunday 2:00 to 5:30 P.M. Closed Tuesday. Adults are $2.00; ages 5 to 18, $1.00; under age 5, no charge.

After your history lesson, relax at the park's recreation area. A quarter-mile from Liberty Hall, you'll find a swimming pool, two fishing lakes, picnic shelters, and thirty-six tent and trailer sites, with water and electrical hookups, showers, and rest rooms. The museum and park are 2 miles from I–20 exit 55. For reservations call (800) 864–PARK. There is a $2.00 per visit parking fee.

Incorporated in 1780, the picture book little town of Washington was the first American community named in honor of the father of our country. Skirted by General William T. Sherman's rampaging "March to the Sea" and treated kindly by progress and time, the town of about 5,000 is today like a living Williamsburg. More than thirty Greek Revival homes, churches, and public buildings predate 1850. Most of them are still well-maintained residences. Three antebellum landmarks are open to visitors year-round.

The **Robert Toombs House State Historic Site,** 216 East Robert Toombs Avenue, (706) 678–2226, was the home of Georgia's "Unreconstructed Rebel," U.S. senator, and Confederate secretary of state. At odds with the Confederacy—he was resentful of Jefferson Davis's presidency—as well as the Union, he fled to the Caribbean and Europe after the war. Returning in 1880, he scorned political pardon. "I am not loyal to the government of the United States," he declared, "and do not wish to be suspected of loyalty." The guided tours of his Greek Revival house include a documentary film, anecdotes, historical exhibits, and several rooms with period furnishings. Open Wednesday through Saturday 9:00 A.M. to 5:00 P.M. and Sunday 2:00 to 5:30 P.M. Adults, $2.00; ages 6 to 18, $1.00; under age 5, no charge.

The *Washington Historical Museum,* 308 East Robert Toombs Avenue, (706) 678-2105, houses an outstanding collection of Civil War artifacts including Jefferson Davis's camp chest (given to him by English sympathizers), weapons, uniforms, signed documents, photographs, and furnishings. The main floor of the circa 1835–1836 two-story frame house is furnished as a typical nineteenth-century double parlor, dining room, and bedroom. The ground floor has been restored as a period kitchen. The grounds are noted for beautiful landscaping and one of Georgia's largest camellia gardens. Hours are Tuesday through Saturday 10:00 A.M. to 5:00 P.M. and Sunday 2:00 to 5:00 P.M. Adult admission is $1.50; ages 12 to 18, $1.00; children 6 to 11, 75 cents.

Callaway Plantation, 5 miles west of Washington on Highway 78, (706) 678-7060, is a living heritage museum rich in lessons about Southern antebellum life. Three restored homes and the adjoining farm are like a walk back in time. The redbrick, white-columned manor house was the heart of a 3,000-acre cotton plantation. Rooms are furnished with period antiques and many unique architectural features. The outbuildings include a hewn log cabin, circa 1785, with early domestic and agricultural tools and primitive furniture and a smokehouse, barn, pigeon house, and cemetery. Surrounding fields are planted with cotton, corn, cane, and vegetables, just as they were in the mid-nineteenth century. The plantation has been owned by the same family since the late eighteenth century, and it's open Tuesday through Saturday 10:00 A.M. to 5:00 P.M. and Sunday 2:00 to 5:00 P.M. Adults are $4.00; ages 12 to 18, $1.50; children ages 6 to 11, $1.00.

Washington also figured in the Revolutionary War. A marker at *Kettle Creek Battleground,* 8 miles south of town on Highway 44, commemorates the patriots' 1779 rout of the British and the Redcoats' subsequent withdrawal from this area of Georgia. Picnic tables are at the site. Call (706) 678-2013.

When hunger overwhelms your hunt through history, head for *Another Thyme* (706-678-1672), an attractive cafe in the lobby of the Victorian Fitzpatrick Hotel on the courthouse square. Midday fare includes sandwiches, soups, salads, plate lunches, and homemade desserts Monday through Saturday, and dinner is served Tuesday through Saturday.

Many of Washington's most magnificent homes are open during the early April *Washington-Wilkes Tour of Homes.* Contact Washington-Wilkes Chamber of Commerce, P.O. Box 661, Washington 30673, (706) 678–2013.

If your group numbers at least ten, you can take a trip through history on the *McDuffie County Upcountry Plantation Tour.* You'll set out from the Thomson–McDuffie County Tourism Bureau in the restored train depot and stop at the *Rock House,* a 1785 fieldstone farmhouse; *Alexandria,* a stately Virginia-influenced brick plantation house and boxwood gardens from 1805; and the site of November's *Belle Meade Fox Hunt.* A number of gracious antebellum homes line Thomson's tree-shaded streets. Contact Thomson–McDuffie County Tourism Bureau, 111 Railroad Street, Thomson 30824, (706) 595–5584. You can stay overnight at the *1810 West Inn,* built sometime around that year. Ten guest rooms have antiques and private baths. The house has original heart pine walls, antiques, eight fireplaces, and a restored smokehouse. Rates of $45 to $55 include an elaborate continental breakfast. Contact 1810 West Inn, 254 North Seymour Drive, Thomson 30824, (706) 595–3156.

The *Old Market House* is a souvenir of the period from 1796 to 1805 when little Louisville ("Lewis-ville") was Georgia's capital. Built in the 1790s, the Market's weathered timbers are held together by 1-inch-diameter wooden pegs. The Market's bell was cast in France in 1722 and was on its way to a New Orleans convent when it was hijacked by pirates and somehow ended up in Louisville. Louisville's tenure as state capital was immortalized by the Great Yazoo Land Fraud of 1795, which cost Georgia the territory that later became the states of Alabama and Mississippi.

Blind Willie McTell

*L*egendary blues singer and guitarist Blind Willie McTell was born in Thomson in 1901. From that small east Georgia town, he went on to fame as a composer and singer of blues, ragtime, pop, ballads, and folk songs. Unfortunately, financial success eluded him and he bolstered his small income by playing carnivals, sideshows, fairs, medicine shows, and private parties. He died in 1959 and was buried in Thomson. In the 1970s, Macon's Allman Brothers Band recorded his "Stateboro Blues" and gave him posthumous fame with modern audiences. The Blind Willie McTell Blues Festival, early October in Thomson, honors the man and his music.

Wind up your sightseeing with some historic Southern cooking at *Pansy's Restaurant* on Louisville's main street, (912) 625–3216.

Masters Golf and Big Water

Augusta, a city of 45,000 with 300,000 in the metropolitan area, traces its heritage back to 1736, when General James Edward Oglethorpe, father of the Georgia Crown Colony, laid it out as the state's second city, after Savannah. Fought for during the Revolutionary War and skirted by General William T. Sherman's "March to the Sea," Augusta has mild winters and a genteel Old Southern lifestyle that caught the attention of post–Civil War Northern aristocrats, who found the right formula for golf—a pastime that symbolizes this city to sportsmen around the world.

For many years Augusta almost forgot that the Savannah River ran by its doorstep. All that is changing rapidly as *Riverwalk Augusta* becomes a new center of downtown activity. The main entrance to Riverwalk is at Eighth and Reynolds Streets, a block off Broad Street. The top of the old river levee has been turned into an inviting brick esplanade with seating clusters overlooking the river, historical displays, and playground and picnic areas. Major hotels, shops, and dining are along the Riverwalk. Stop first at the Cotton Exchange Welcome Center, Eighth and Reynolds Streets, for information and historic exhibits on Augusta's once-lucrative trade in "white gold." It's open Monday through Saturday 9:00 A.M. to 5:00 P.M. and Sunday 1:00 to 5:00 P.M. Phone (706) 724–4067 or (800) 726–0243. Self-guided walking and driving tours as well as group tours are available at the welcome center.

The *Augusta-Richmond County Museum* is now part of Riverwalk's excitement. Early in 1996 the sixty-year-old "municipal attic" moved into a new 48,000-square-foot home at Sixth and Reynolds Streets. The twenty-three permanent galleries are filled with Revolutionary and Civil War weapons and uniforms, Native American culture, natural history (including a major dinosaur exhibit), space exploration, communications, vintage photographs, and a tribute to the city's and Georgia's founding father, Gen. James Edward Oglethorpe. Savannah River marine life inhabits a small aquarium. Train buffs shouldn't miss "Old No. 302," the Georgia Railroad's last steam engine. Open Tuesday to Saturday 10:00 A.M. to 6:00 P.M., Sunday 2:00 to 5:00 P.M. Adults are $4.00; children and seniors, $2.00. Phone (706) 722–8454.

National Science Center's Fort Discovery, Seventh Street at River-walk, (800) 325–5445, www.nscdiscovery.org, one of Riverwalk's newest attractions, is a world of fun and educational experiences for people of all ages. The 200 hands-on, interactive exhibits range from simple games for young children to more complicated lessons to tax the brain power of serious science students. You're invited to ride a bike on a high wire, walk on the moon, maneouver robots, and play the newest multimedia games. Special shows are held in the 250-seat Paul Simon Theater, and there's a snack bar when all this fun works up your appetite. The two-story, 128,000-square-foot museum is open Monday through Saturday 10:00 A.M. to 6:00 P.M. and Sunday noon to 6:00 P.M. Adults, $8.00; children, $6.00.

Morris Museum of Art is at Riverfront Center, 1 Tenth Street at River-walk, (706) 724–7501. Two centuries of Southern art are represented in this new museum designed like a private home. The permanent collection includes works by Augusta native Jasper Johns and mixed media artist Robert Rauschenberg. Special exhibits are held throughout the year. Open Tuesday through Saturday 10:00 A.M. to 5:30 P.M. and Sunday 12:30 to 5:30 P.M. Admission is $2.00.

The *Georgia Golf Hall of Fame,* Reynolds Street between Eleventh and Thirteenth Streets, (706) 724–4443, open in 1999, includes a museum highlighting the Masters and Georgia's many golfing greats, and interactive exhibits that will challenge the skills of "pros" and weekend hackers.

You can stay in the heart of the Riverwalk at the *Radisson Riverfront Hotel,* 2 Tenth Street, Augusta 30901, (706) 722–8900. The modern 234-room hotel has full-service dining, entertainment, health club, and many other amenities. Rates run about $100 for a double.

Sacred Heart Cultural Center, 1301 Greene Street, (706) 826–4700, is a heartening and very spectacular example of a cherished piece of architectural heritage, down on its luck, given a new lease on life. Consecrated in 1901, the redbrick, twin-spired Romanesque Catholic church summed up the highest skills of European artists. Jewel-like tones of German stained-glass windows played against the creamy white Italian marble columns, stations of the cross, and the ornate high altar. In the early 1970s, with much of its congregation now in the suburbs, Sacred Heart's doors were closed and the church deconsecrated and left to the mercy of the elements and vandals.

The church would probably have kept a date with the wrecking ball if an "angel" in the form of an affluent and civic-minded corporate executive hadn't come to the rescue. Following an extensive renovation,

Sacred Heart Cultural Center is now the scene of banquets, wedding receptions, fashion shows, chamber concerts, and numerous other functions. A gift shop on the lower floor sells works by local artists and authors. You may take a self-guided tour of the sanctuary Monday through Friday between 8:30 A.M. and 5:30 P.M.; donations are accepted. Guided tours are by appointment 1:00 to 4:00 P.M. Adults are $2.00; senior citizens and students, $1.00.

Ezekiel Harris House, 1840 Broad Street, (706) 724–0436, is Augusta's second-oldest structure. In 1797 Harris came to the area from South Carolina with plans to build a town to rival Augusta as a tobacco market. On a hill overlooking Augusta, the house is an outstanding example of post-Revolutionary architecture. The gambrel roof and vaulted hallway are reminiscent of New England. Tiered piazzas are supported by artistically beveled wooden posts. Rooms are furnished with period antiques. It's open Monday through Friday 1:00 to 4:00 P.M. and Saturday 10:00 A.M. to 4:00 P.M. Adults are $2.00; students, 50 cents.

Meadow Garden, Independence Drive near the intersection of Walton Way and Thirteenth Street, (706) 724–4174, was the home of George Walton, one of Georgia's signers of the Declaration of Independence.

Pecan-Crusted Peach Crisp

This dessert marries two of middle Georgia's favorite things and serves 4.

Pecan crisp topping:

1 cup pecan pieces

½ pound butter

6 ounces all-purpose flour

6 ounces brown sugar

Peaches:

Four whole peaches (preferably, fresh, ripe Georgia peaches), cut into halves and pitted

½ pound butter

6 ounces brown sugar

1 teaspoon cinnamon

½ cup brandy

Combine pecans, ½ pound butter, flour, and 6 ounces brown sugar until crumbly. Place on a sheet pan and bake in a 350° oven until crisp. Set aside.

In a saucepan place ½ pound butter, 6 ounces brown sugar, and cinnamon over low heat until butter is melted. Add peaches and cook until tender and syrup forms. Add brandy and flambé. Set two peach halves and syrup into a serving dish and spoon on pecan crisp topping.

Built around 1791, it's the city's oldest documented structure and has been restored and refurnished by the Georgia Society, Daughters of the American Revolution. Hours are Monday through Friday 9:00 A.M. to 4:00 P.M., Saturday 10:00 A.M. to 4:00 P.M., Sunday 1:00 to 4:00 P.M. Admission is $2.00 for adults and 50 cents for children.

Gertrude Herbert Institute of Art, 506 Telfair Street, (706) 722–5495, is an architecturally outstanding early nineteenth-century residence that showcases regional and Southeastern contemporary art. Built in 1818 by Augusta Mayor Nicholas Ware, the elliptical three-story staircase, Adam-style mantels, and other rich ornamentation earned it the name "Ware's Folly." Hours are Tuesday through Friday 10:00 A.M. to 5:00 P.M. and Saturday 10:00 A.M. to 2:00 P.M. Admission for adults is $2.00; children and seniors, $1.00.

If you're into antiquing, head for the 1200 block of Broad Street, where you'll find an extensive cluster of shops and flea markets.

Kids and kids at heart shouldn't miss *Fat Man's Forest* (706–722–0796). A rambling array of added-on buildings at 1545 Laney-Walker Boulevard, Fat Man's is locally renowned for its holiday paraphernalia. At Halloween people come from miles around to rent costumes, purchase pumpkins and made-to-order jack-o'-lanterns, and send their youngsters through the haunted house. At Christmas the kids ride a festive train while grownups browse for trees, gifts, and decorations. Whatever the season it's a fun place to wander and marvel at the Fat Man's ingenuity.

For golfers around the globe, Augusta is Christmas, the World Series, the rainbow's end. In late March and early April, fortunate faithful congregate along the dogwood- and azalea-rimmed fairways of storied *Augusta National Golf Club* to hail the game's elite as they pursue the Green Jacket, symbolic of the *Masters Golf Tournament* championship. Unless you know a player or a club member, tickets to the championship rounds will be impossible to find. But don't despair. You can see all the greats up close—even take their pictures—during the practice rounds preceding the tournament. The bad news is the *Masters Practice Rounds* have become so popular that tickets must now be purchased in advance, $16 to $21 per day. To receive an application form write to Masters Tournament Practice Rounds, P.O. Box 2047, Augusta 30903-2047.

If you'd like to play, the *Jones Creek Course,* an 18-hole public layout at 4101 Hammonds Ferry Road, (706) 860–4228, is considered the "poor man's" Augusta National. Designed by renowned golf architect Rees Jones, it has an excellent practice facility and professional instructors. Rental clubs and carts are available.

Ever wondered how a daily newspaper is put together? *The Augusta Chronicle-Herald*'s free tour has all the answers. The one-hour guided tour—by appointment from 10:00 to 11:00 A.M. Fridays— takes you through the busy newsrooms and feature departments and into the printing plant, where type is set and pages assembled and published on high-speed presses. *The Herald* is located at Broad Street, downtown, (706) 724–0851.

Bass fishermen and those seeking more off-the-beaten-path relaxation should look into a minivacation at *Mistletoe State Park.* About 35 miles north of Augusta, on 76,000-acre Clarks Hill Reservoir, this very tranquil park reputedly commands some of America's finest bass fishing waters. You may also swim and boat in the lake, hike 5 miles of woodland trails, and ride rental bikes around the 1,920 acres. Two-bedroom furnished cottages and camping sites with water, electricity, showers, and rest rooms are available. There is a $2.00 per visit parking fee. Contact Park Superintendent, Appling 30502, (706) 541–0321. For camping and cottage reservations call (800) 864–PARK.

Elijah Clark State Park, north of Mistletoe, is another wooded retreat on the western shores of Clarks Hill Lake. Twenty furnished cottages and 165 tent and trailor sites are a few steps from the water. You'll also find marinas, docks, boat ramps, a swimming beach, nature trails, and plenty of picnic areas. The park was named for Revolutionary War hero Elijah Clark. A Colonial museum displays relics from the period. The park is on Highway 378, 7 miles east of Lincolnton. Phone (706) 359–3458 for information. For reservations call (800) 864–PARK.

Burke County, between Augusta and Savannah, hails itself as "The Bird Dog Capital of the World." You can test its veracity with an organized bird and game hunt at *Boll Weevil Plantation,* Route 2, Box 356A, Waynesboro 30830, (706) 554–6227. You can stay overnight at *Georgia's Guest Bed & Breakfast,* 640 East Seventh Street, Waynesboro 30830, (706) 554–4863.

WHERE TO STAY IN MIDDLE GEORGIA

MACON
The Crowne Plaza Macon,
108 First Street,
(912) 746–1461,
fax (912) 746–7420.

This is downtown Macon's only full-service first-class hotel. The 177 guest rooms and public areas were a $10-million redo in 1997–98. The Bourbon Street Cafe serves New Orleans and Cajun cuisine in a faux-Bourbon Street setting. Bogart's Martini and Cigar Extravaganza and the Big Easy Lounge are popular gathering places for downtown workers, residents, and visitors. The hotel also has an outdoor pool and a fitness center. Doubles are $79 to $89.

EATONTON
Crockett House,
671 Madison Road,
(706) 485–2248.

Rosewood Bed and Breakfast,
301 North Madison Avenue,
(706) 485–9009,
fax (706) 485–3277.

Both these inns offer you Victorian splendor. Double, with breakfast, go for $65 to $90.

WASHINGTON
Blackmon-Wingfield House, 512 North Alexander Avenue, (706) 678–2278; $60 double.

The Cottage at Poplar Corner, 210 West Liberty Street, (706) 678–2453; $85 double.

Hill and Hollow Farm, 2090 Thomson Road, (706) 678–4439; $65 double.

Holly Ridge Country Inn, 2221 Sandtown Road, (706) 285–2594; $75 double.

Maynard's Manor, 402 North Alexander Avenue, (706) 678–4603; $75 double.

You'll sleep in the bower of history at any of these Washington inns.

AUGUSTA
Azalea Inn, 312–316 Greene Street, (706) 724–3454.

Twelve large suites in a redone Victorian home have queen or king beds, private baths with whirpool tubs; some have kitchenettes. Rates of $80 to $100 include continental breakfast.

Partridge Inn, 2110 Walton Way, (706) 737–8888 and (800) 476–6888, fax (706) 731–0826.

This full-service inn has 155 executive, studio, and deluxe suites. Many have kitchens and balconies. Dining room serves upscale American and continental lunch and dinner; there's also a full bar. Southern buffet breakfast is included in rates of $100 to $145.

Perrin Guest House, 209 LaFayette Drive, (800) 668–8930.

Ten large guest rooms with private baths and fireplaces in an antebellum-style house close to Washington Road and I–20. Rates of $75 to $130 include continental breakfast and afternoon wine and tea.

The Telfair Inn, 326 Greene Street, (404) 724–3315.

Here is a beautiful example of practical restoration. Seventeen Victorian residences were rejuvenated, redecorated, and refurnished in nineteenth-century fashion, with wood-burning fireplaces and all the modern comforts, and turned into a lovely downtown inn. Rates are $57 to $97 single, $67 to $107 double.

WHERE TO EAT IN MIDDLE GEORGIA

MACON

The Boulevard Serenade,
401 Cherry Street,
(912) 742-2583.

Cozy, brick-walled cellar restaurant and piano bar symbolizes downtown Macon's resurgence. Chef Jennifer Caroway's American/continental menu features her much-asked-for seafood lasagna; trout stuffed with crabmeat, spinach, and mushrooms in garlic lemon butter sauce; burgundy rib eye; lamb chops and chicken teriyaki. It's a popular luncheon destination for downtown residents and workers, who also enjoy the lighter fare and outdoor tables at owner Nancy Pierron's neighboring Boulevard Bistro & Bakery. The Serenade and Bistro are open for lunch Monday through Saturday and dinner Tuesday through Saturday.

Len Berg's,
240 Post Office Alley,
(912) 742-9255.

A downtown Macon landmark for eons, this comfy ensemble of small rooms and booths serves homecooking the way "your-mama-made-it," or at least wished she had.

Time-honored favorites include salmon croquettes, turkey and dressing, mac-and-cheese, fried catfish, and an array of Southern-style veggies, biscuits, and cornbread. If you're here in June and July, top off your lunch with "HMFPIC," homemade fresh peach ice cream, made from Middle Georgia's abundant fruit. Lunch Monday through Saturday. Len Berg's Takeout, in Ingleside Village, Ingleside and Corbin Avenues in North Macon, (912) 743-7011, serves the original's delicious food to take home or enjoy in dine-in booths. Lunch and dinner Monday though Saturday. Upscale Ingleside Village also has many gift, antique, art, and apparel shops under brightly colored awnings.

Music City Brewery & Grill,
2440 Riverside Drive,
(912) 744-1144.

This is the perfect prelude or encore to your visit to the Georgia Music Hall of Fame. While you enjoy steaks, seafood, pastas, and sandwiches, with a selection of house-brewed beers and ales, feast your eyes on walls covered with musical instruments, posters, and other memorabilia of Maconxx and Georgia's celerbated performers. Lunch and dinner are served daily.

Nathalia's,
2720 Riverside Drive,
(912) 741-1380.

Nathalia's has satisfied Macon's hunger for classical Italian cooking since 1984. Grilled veal chops, risotto, osso buco,

---

Helpful Web Sites

Macon Convention & Visitors Bureau,
www.maconga.org

Augusta Convention & Visitors Bureau,
www.augustaga.org

National Science Center,
www.nscdiscovery.org

Washington-Wilkes Chamber of Commerce,
www.washingtonga.org

Blue Willow Inn.
www.bluewillowinn.com ##

seafood, pasta, and chicken dishes are complemented by light, delicate sauces. (No heavy red sauces). French, Italian, and American wines, many available by the glass. Dinner is served Monday through Saturday.

AUGUSTA

French Market Grille,
Surrey Center,
425 Highland Avenue,
(706) 737–4865.

Chuck and Gail Baldwin's spicy Louisiana Cajun cooking has kept Augustans coming back for more than 15 years. They can't seem to get enough of the Baldwins' delectable gumbo, Cajun crawfish etouffe, jambalaya, and pecan praline pie. Lunch and dinner are served daily.

King George Restaurant & Riverwalk Brewery,
Eighth Street at Riverwalk.

After a busy day on the Riverwalk, slake your thirst with the home-brewed beers and ales at Augusta's first brewpub. The veddy British pub's traditional fare includes fish and chips, Scotch eggs, salads, soups, and sandwiches. Sample the house-brewed beers and ales or 25 brews from around the drinking world. Folk music is frequently featured. Lunch and dinner are served daily and Sunday breakfast.

La Maison,
in a restored mansion in the Old Town Historic District at 404 Telfair Street, (706) 722–4805.

Prepares the city's most sophisticated cuisine. Former Atlanta chef Heinz Sowinski's repertoire includes a wide range of French, German, Swiss, and other specialties. For adventurous tastes, the "Game Sampler" is a platter of three or four exotic, richly sauced meat dishes such as pheasant, smoked venison, quail, or wild boar. Magnificent desserts reflect Sowinski's European culinary heritage. Cocktails and a large selection of American, Australian, and European wines round out the menu. Dinner is served Monday through Saturday.

Le Cafe de Teau,
1855 Central Avenue,
(706) 733–3505.

First-rate lamb, steaks, grilled duck, and seafood are accompanied by dinnertime jazz at this upbeat cafe. Dinner is served daily except Monday.

The Town Tavern,
15 Seventh Street at the Riverwalk, (706) 724–1030.

The tavern recently celebrated its fifty-fifth anniversary. The American menu includes seafood, steaks, salads, and full Southern breakfast in an attractive Early American motif. It's open for lunch and dinner Monday through Saturday. Credit cards are accepted, and prices are moderate.

Coastal Georgia

Historic Savannah

Founded in 1733, Savannah is one of America's truly special cities. Not long after founding father, General James Edward Oglethorpe, came ashore on Yamacraw Bluff and dispersed his 144 settlers, he set about planning Savannah in a style befitting the capital of a crown colony named for His majesty, King George II. He hunkered down in his damask tent on the bluffs and with military precision laid out a grid of straight, broad streets, braided at 2-block intervals by spacious public squares. Initially, the twenty-four squares were mustering places for troops and convenient locales for citizens to draw water and exchange news.

In 1793, Eli Whitney, a visiting New Englander given to tinkering with gadgets, devised a mechanized way to separate cotton seeds from the fluffy white bolls. His cotton gin revolutionized Southern planting. On the tragic downside, it also perpetuated the waning practice of slavery and indirectly led to the Civil War. Soon, real gold earned from "white gold" enabled planters, merchants, and shipbuilders to embellish Oglethorpe's squares with English Regency, Georgian, Federal, and Gothic Revival showplaces, filled with fine furniture and art objects shipped from Europe. As "front yards" for the affluent, the squares were dressed up with trees, flowering plants, benches, fountains, and memorials to Revolutionary heroes and other notables.

In the 1950s, much of the city's heritage teetered on the brink of extinction. Scores of venerable landmarks, even a couple of Oglethorpe's squares, were crunched in the jaws of progress before the Historic Savannah Foundation rode in like the cavalry and saved the day. To date, more than 1,500 historic structures have been restored in the 2.2-square-mile *Savannah National Historic District,* the nation's largest.

Before you leave home, phone the Savannah Convention & Visitors Bureau, (800) 444–2427, for advance information. When you arrive, stop first at the Savannah Visitors Center, 303 Martin Luther King Jr. Boulevard, (912) 238–1779. Inside the former 1860s Central of Georgia Railway depot you'll find everything you need: free brochures, tour and

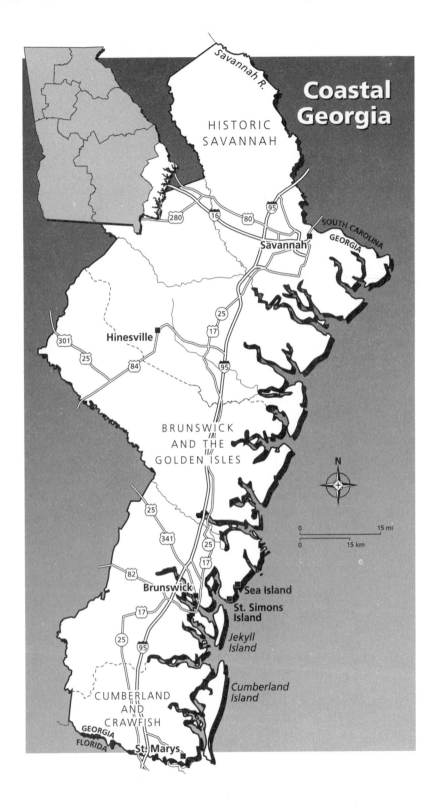

Coastal Georgia

Savannah R.

HISTORIC
SAVANNAH

SOUTH CAROLINA
GEORGIA

280 16 80 95

Savannah

301 25 17 95

Hinesville

84 25

BRUNSWICK
AND THE
GOLDEN ISLES

N

0   15 mi
0   15 km

25

341 25 17

82

Brunswick Sea Island
St. Simons
Island

17

Jekyll
Island

25 95

Cumberland
Island

CUMBERLAND
AND
CRAWFISH

GEORGIA
FLORIDA St. Marys

restaurant information, lodging reservations, and an orientation film. The center adjoins the *Savannah History Museum,* with displays, multimedia presentations, a steam locomotive, and homage to famous citizens like songwriter Johnny Mercer ("Moon River," "Moonlight in Vermont," and countless other standards). You can also see the movie prop bus stop bench where Tom Hanks told his tale in the Oscar winning film, *Forrest Gump.* Outside the Visitors Center, take one of the many guided orientation tours in an open-air tram or air-conditioned van or minibus.

When you're ready to head off on your own, *River Street,* a wide brick, pedestrian esplanade also known as Riverfront Plaza, is the best place to start. As a major plank in the restoration movement, the antebellum brick cotton warehouses were refashioned as seafood restaurants, taverns, touristy shops, and art galleries. Recessed benches are great places to sit and watch the humongous cargo ships cruising to the Georgia Ports Authority docks and heavy industries upriver and the open Atlantic 20 miles downriver.

Climb up the cobblestone ramps to Bay Street and you're ready for your walk on Savannah's most beautiful street. Few cities are fortunate to be blessed by a thoroughfare as charming as the 20 blocks of *Bull Street* from Savannah's gold-domed City Hall to the green bower of Forsyth Park. Five of Oglethorpe's most picturesque squares are set like gems on this glorious avenue named for a British colonial officer. It divides the historic district into east and west halves. Before you leave, you'll be drawn back time and again to this wonderful, old-worldly street. Revolutionary hero Gen. Nathanael Greene is buried under the granite shaft in Johnson Square. Wright Square honors the founder of the Central of Georgia Railroad.

At Bull Street and Oglethorpe Avenue, Girl Scouts and students of American history should pause at the Juliette Gordon Low Girl Scout National Center, (912) 233–4501. Designed by noted early nineteenth-century

English architect William Jay, the dignified English Regency mansion was the 1860 birthplace of "Daisy" Low, founder of the Girl Scouts of America. Her paintings and sculpture, personal effects, and GSA mementos are in the high-ceiling rooms. It's open Monday through Saturday 10:00 A.M. to 4:00 P.M. and Sunday 12:30 to 4:30 P.M.; closed Wednesday. Adults $5.00, senior citizens and students $4.50, children $4.00.

A bronze statue of General Oglethorpe, by Daniel Chester French (who sculpted the seated statue at Washington's Lincoln Memorial) looks south from its pedestal in Chippewa Square, daring the Spanish in Florida to move against his city. Sgt. William Jasper, killed in the 1779 British siege of the city, brandishes the flag atop the monument in the center of Madison Square. The tree-shaded benches are usually filled with earnest-looking young people who've drifted over from the Savannah College of Art and Design. Chartered in 1979, with seventy-one students and four faculty, SCAD has grown from the redbrick, late-1800s Guards Armory on the square's east side into an internationally known institution with 3,500 students and 500 faculty and staff. SCAD has restored more than three dozen buildings in the historic district, and all those students infuse the area with electrifying energy.

A Taste of Savannah

*R*estaurants have notoriously short lives, but River House Seafood, 125 West River Street (912–234–1900), has thrived for seventeen years with a loyal mix of Savannahians and out-of-towners. This tangy concoction is one of the dishes that keeps 'em coming back:

SHRIMP AND SAUSAGE STEW

2 pounds large shrimp, peeled and deveined

1 pound andouille sausage, sliced

1 small red onion, chopped

4 cloves garlic, minced

8 ounces beer

16 ounces shrimp stock

2 tablespoons fresh basil, chopped

Tabasco sauce, to taste

1 teaspoon Worcestershire sauce

4 tablespoons whole butter, cut in pieces

Saute shrimp for 2 minutes in a little olive oil. Add the sausage and cook together for 1 minute. Add the onion and garlic. Cook 1 minute more then deglaze pan with beer. Bring to a boil, then add vegetables and basil. Pour in the shrimp stock. Cover and cook for 3 minutes. Season with Tabasco and Worcestershire. Swirl in whole butter. Taste and adjust seasonings if necessary. Serve in large bowls with fried grits cakes or rice pilaf.

COASTAL GEORGIA

Top Annual Events

When Savannah peacefully surrendered to the Union Army in December 1864, General William T. Sherman lodged in the Gothic Revival *Green Meldrim House* (now St. John's parish house) on Madison Square's west side, (912) 233-3845. From the house, he sent a telegram to his commander-in-chief. "Dear Sir, President Lincoln: I beg to present you as a Christmas gift, the city of Savannah with 150 heavy guns and also about 25,000 bales of cotton." You're welcome to walk in and admire magnificent Gothic wood carvings, plaster work, and spacious rooms. Open Tuesday through Saturday 10:00 A.M. to 4:00 P.M. Adults, $4.00; students, $2.00.

If you starting to flag a bit, pep up with a cappuccino or latte at Expresso Gallery's indoor or sidewalk tables on Liberty Street, across from the DeSoto Hilton Hotel. Or have a salad, soup, sandwich or coastal seafood at Chutzpah, a quirky cafe at Bull and Liberty, and afterwards browse the kicky clothes at companion Panache. You can also tuck into shepherd's pie and a pint of something from the bar at Six Pence Pub, a bit of Olde England at 245 Bull Street, (912) 233-3156.

Patriotic Savannahians named *Monterey Square* for an American victory in the 1840s Mexican War. The monument that's usually in the center of the square salutes Count Casimir Pulaski, a Polish nobleman who gave his all for the American cause during the 1779 British siege. The crumbling, century-old marble shaft was taken down for restoration in 1996 and may or may not be back in place when you visit. *Temple Mickve Israel,* on the east side, is Georgia's oldest Jewish congregation. Spanish and German Jews who landed five months after Oglethorpe brought Torahs and other sacred objects and documents that are now part of a collection you're welcome to see. Just knock on the side door Monday through Friday 10:00 A.M. to noon. No charge.

Savannah's most famous house is directly across the square. Some tour guides used to tell visitors that the *Hugh Mercer House* was songwriter Johnny Mercer's boyhood home. Mercer's grandfather build it after the Civil War, but the family never lived in the stately red-

St. Patrick's Celebration, *downtown Savannah,* *for several days leading up to* *March 17, (800) 444-2427*

Jekyll Island Arts Festival, *Goodyear Cottage,* *mid-March, (912) 635-3920*

Savannah Tour of *Homes & Gardens,* *late March, (912) 234-8054*

Night in Old Savannah, *mid-April, (912) 650-7846*

N.O.G.S. Tour of Hidden *Gardens, walled gardens* *north of Gaston Street, downtown Savannah, mid-April,* *(912) 238-0248*

Great Golden *Easter Egg Hunt,* *Easter Sunday, Jekyll Island* *Historic District,* *(912) 635-3636*

Civil War Relic Show *& Sale, mid-June, Savannah* *Civic Center, (912) 897-1099*

Christmas in Savannah, *throughout December, (800)* *444-2427*

Historic St. Marys *Christmas Tour, mid-* *December, (912) 927-4976*

Blame It on the General

It's ironic that the city's founding father, Gen. James Edward Oglethorpe, may have inbred Savannah's love of hard drink. Although he tried unsuccessfully to prohibit rum (and lawyers) from his colony, Oglethorpe was the first person in the colony to brew beer. He did it, he wrote, "to keep the soliders satifisfied." Like the Puritans and Pilgrims in New England, Oglethorpe also believed that drinking beer was a far healthier and more Godly endeavor than partaking of polluted water whose very sip was an invitation to disease.

brick Italianate mansion at 429 Bull Street. Antiques dealer, social arbiter, and arts patron Jim Williams lived there until he shot his companion to death in 1984 and became fodder for John Berendt's international best-selling nonfiction book, **Midnight in the Garden of Good and Evil,** loosely made into a 1997 movie. It's not open to the public, but guided tours from the Visitors Center will take you past it and other *Midnight* sites.

Another 2 blocks and you're in Forsyth Park. The centerpiece of the twenty-acre sanctuary is an ornate, wrought-iron fountain that looks a bit like a three-tiered wedding cake decorated with swans and water-spouting tritons.

Squares east and west of Bull Street are blessed with landmarks in a variety of styles. *Isaiah Davenport House* on Columbia Square played a pivotal role in the restoration crusade. Built between 1815 and 1820 and considered one of America's most perfect Georgian mansions, the redbrick house was threatened with demolition in the 1950s to make space for a funeral home parking lot. The Historic Savannah Foundation came to the rescue and went on to help save hundreds of other imperiled structures. The restored Davenport House, (912) 235–8097, gleams with Chippendale and Sheraton furnishings, woodwork, and plaster crown moldings. It's open Monday to Saturday 10:00 A.M. to 4:30 P.M. and Sunday 1:30 to 4:30 P.M. All ages, $5.00. As for the funeral home, it's now Kehoe House, one of the city's grandest historic inns.

The Marquis de Lafayette slept at the **Owens-Thomas House,** (912) 233–9743, around the corner on Oglethorpe Square, during his 1825 farewell to America tour. He spoke to the populace from the wrought-iron side balcony. The prolific William Jay's Regency-style urban villa is filled with art, antiques, and intriguing architectural details. At 124 Abercorn Street, it's open Tuesday through Saturday 10:00 A.M. to 5:00 P.M. and Sunday and Monday 2:00 to 5:00 P.M. Adults, $6.00; senior citizens, $5.00; students, $3.00; ages 6 to 12, $2.00.

William Jay also left his mark on the Regency-style *Telfair Art Museum,* 121 Barnard Street, (912) 232–1177. Built in 1819 as the showplace home of the Telfairs, a distinguished local family, the elegant rooms house collections of English and American art, furnishings, and decorative pieces. You can also see the original *Bird Girl* statue featured on *Midnight*'s cover. Open Tuesday to Saturday 10:00 A.M. to 5:00 P.M. Adults, $5.00; senior citizens, $3.00; students, $2.00, children, $1.00.

King-Tisdell Cottage/Black History Museum, an 1890s Victorian cottage at 514 East Huntington Street, (912) 236–5161, displays documents, furniture, and artifacts of Low Country Black heritage. It's the headquarters for Negro Heritage Tours, which include landmarks of Black history going back to the first slaves. Open by appointment only. All ages $2.50.

Ships of the ***Sea Maritime Museum,*** 41 Martin Luther King Jr. Boule-

A Prophesy Fulfilled

Savannah is full of ghosts and tales of ghosts. Jack Richards, an artist fascinated by the subject, leads true-believers and the openly skeptical on "Ghost Talk, Ghost Walk" tours of the historic district. He relates tales of apparitions at the Pirates House and Olde Pink House restaurants, cemeteries, and private homes. One of his favorites is a romantic story about the mother of Girl Scouts founder Juliette Gordon Low. In the 1890s, when workmen were digging the foundation in Wright Square for the monument to William Washington Gordon, founder of the Georgia Railroad, they inadvertently dug up the remains of Tomochichi, the Indian chief who had befriended founding father Gen. James Edward Oglethorpe. They reported the discovery to Eleanor Kinsey Gordon, Gordon's daughter in-law and Juliette Gordon Low's mother.

Embarrassed by the incident, she ordered the big granite stone now on Tomochichi's grave in Wright Square. Although she asked for a bill several times, the Stone Mountain Granite Company never sent one.

After a decade of repeated requests, she finally got a bill for a dollar, "Due on Judgment Day." She sent a check for a dollar, with a curt note: "I'll be much too busy on Judgment Day to pay my debts."

On the day she died, her prophesy apparently came true. She called her deceased husband's name, as if she were seeing an apparition. He was known as "The Old Captain," his rank in the Confederate Army. Minutes later, as her daughter-in-law, Margaret, rested in the downstairs parlor, a man in a Confederate officer's uniform walked down the stairs and out the front door. He was followed by Margaret's husband who announced Mrs. Gordon's death. He hadn't seen the mysterious officer. When they walked outside, the family servant was crying. He said, "I just saw the Old Captain and he said, 'I'm taking Miss Eleanor for her afternoon ride.'" Just as she predicted, Mrs. Gordon was too busy on Judgment Day to worry about her debts.

vard, (912) 232–1511, has moved its extensive collections of sailing ship models, ships-in bottles, scrimshaw art, maritime paintings, ornamental figureheads, and other nautical artifacts into more spacious galleries in the 1819 Scarbrough House. Open Tuesday though Sunday 10:00 A.M to 5:00 P.M. Adults, $5.00; students and senior citizens, $4.00.

The role Savannahians played in the 1960s Civil Rights movement is portrayed with memorabilia, photos, documents, and displays at this new Savannah museum, the **Ralph Mark Gilbert Civil Rights Museum,** 460 Martin Luther King Jr. Boulevard, (912) 231–8900. It's open Monday through Saturday, 9 :00 A.M. to 5:00 P.M. Adults are $4.00; senior citizens, $3.00; students, $2.00. Adult groups of ten or more are $3.00 each.

City Market, once-neglected blocks of brick warehouses on West Congress, West St. Julian, and Barnard Streets, 2 blocks from River Street, has been given reviving doses of adrenalin. You can browse about two dozen artists' studios and enjoy casual dining and nighttime entertainment in a growing number of venues. Several have outdoor tables. Horsedrawn carriage tours begin and end at the Market.

Some of the city's most intriguing sights are outside the historic district. The **Mighty Eighth Air Force Museum,** I–95 at Highway 80, Pooler, fifteen minutes west of downtown, (912) 748–8888, pays tribute to the juggernaut that was born in Savannah in January 1942. Although

---

Sweet Potatoes, Mrs. Wilkes Style

*M*rs. Sema Wilkes has greeted her "friends" at Wilkes Dining Room since the 1940s. Here's one of the dishes they stand in line for rain or shine:

SWEET POTATO SOUFFLE

4 pounds sweet potatoes

1 teaspoon salt

1½ cups sugar

2 eggs

½ cup raisins

1 lemon (grated rind and juice)

½ teaspoon nutmeg

½ cup evaporated milk

½ cup chopped pecans

1 stick butter or margarine

½ cup shredded coconut

Marshmallows

Slice potatoes and boil in salted water to cover potatoes. Cook until tender. Mash and whip potatoes, mix all ingredients, and pour into greased casserole dish. Bake in oven at 350° for 30 minutes. Cover top with marshmallows just before removing from oven. Brown and serve.

its headquarters soon moved to England for the duration of the war, Savannah has always had an affectionate place in its heart for "The Mighty Eighth," which won the WWII air war over Europe. Hundreds of high-tech exhibits, artifacts, films, and dioramas take you on a time trip through harrowing years. *The Darkest Hour,* a documentary film, recounts the Battle of Britain, the Japanese attack on Pearl Harbor, the Holocaust, and other atrocities. Through a doorway, displays trace the U.S. entry into the conflict; the buildup of men, women, and war machines; and the Eighth Air Force's birth. Through another door, you're on a 1943 English airfield. In small hut, you sit in on a briefing session for crews about to take off on a bombing raid over Germany. Leaving the hut, you're in front of a two-story control tower, similar to hundreds that dotted the English countryside during the war. Original 16 mm color combat film and the sounds of flak, antiaircraft guns, and German fighter planes re-create the terrors Allied crews experienced.

A following exhibit shows the tide of war turning in favor of the Allies, the coming of D-Day, V-E Day, and the atomic bombs on Japan that brought the Pacific war to a close. Open daily 9:30 A.M. to 6:00 P.M. Adults, $7.50; children, $5.50; under age 6, no charge.

Old Fort Jackson, on Highway 80/Islands Expressway, 3 miles east of downtown, (912) 232–3945, was constructed on the Savannah River between 1808 and 1879. All shipping bound for Savannah's port had to pass by the fort's heavy guns. A tidal moat still guards the stout brick walls. Artifacts include cannon, small arms, machinery, and tools demonstrated at annual events. In summer, uniformed soliders conduct cannon firings and military drills. Open daily 9:00 A.M. to 5:00 P.M. Adults, $2.50; students and senior citizens, $2.00.

Oatland Island Education Center, off the Islands Expressway east of the Wilmington River, (912) 897–3773, is a fascinating nature experience for all ages. Operated by the Chatham County Board of Education, the center is a focus of nature education programs and special events. You can walk a nature trail and see an astonishing variety of wildlife secured in natural habitats, including gators, wolves, bobcats, bears, panthers, deer, bald eagles, egrets, and heron. Open Monday through Friday 8:30 A.M. to 5:00 P.M. Admission is $2.00 per person over age 4.

Fort Pulaski National Monument, off Highway 80, a half hour east of downtown (912–786–5787), guards the Savannah River's entrance from the Atlantic. The star-shaped fortress took eighteen years to construct. A young West Point engineering grad named Robert E. Lee lent his talents—but it surrendered to Union forces on April 11, 1862 following a devastating attack by new cannon rifles. Historical exhibits, weapons, and uniforms are displayed. Open daily 8:30 A.M. to 5:15 P.M. Extended summer hours. Admission $2.00; under age 16, no charge.

There's not one iota of chic or glamor anywhere on *Tybee Island.* In truth, it's the antithesis of rich and trendy Hilton Head Island, just across the water in South Carolina. Therein lies the charm of this comfortable old shoe of a beach and summer home retreat 20 miles east of downtown Savannah. Many Savannah families spend the torrid summers in cottages near the beach, where the mild Atlantic surf laps 3 miles of hard-packed sand.

In warm weather, you'll probably want to make a beeline for the Tybee beaches. The most popular stretch for swimming and sunbathing is the commercial area around Butler Avenue and Sixteenth Street—a quirky time-warp straight out of Coney island, circa 1940. Here's where you'll find ice cream and fudge shops, hot dog stands, beer joints, old department stores, convenience stores, chair and beach umbrella vendors, motels, condos, and public rest rooms. The handsome new Tybee Island Pier & Pavilion, jutting far out into the water, is a fine place to cast your fishing line. It was modeled after the old Tybrisa Pier, where young swains and their belles used to dance to the Dorseys and Benny Goodman.

Don't be disappointed that the Atlantic on the Georgia coast isn't Caribbean blue-green. The grayish-green surf isn't polluted—rivers like the Altamaha flowing down from Georgia's interior leave a silt bottom, rather than a sand bottom that would reflect the sunlight and create more translucent colors.

Tybee Lighthouse and Museum are must-see landmarks. You can climb 178 spiraling steps to the 154-foot top of Tybee Light, which first guided ships in between the river and ocean in 1773. Partially destroyed by Confederate raiders during the Union occupation, it was rebuilt after the war. An extensive restoration was completed in 1998. Tybee Island Museum is across from the lighthouse, inside Fort Screven, a Spanish-American War coastal artillery battery. Inside the fort's old bunkers are uniforms, weapons, and displays that reflect the fort's active service through World War II. The museum and lighthouse are open April through September, Wednesday through Monday 10:00 A.M. to 6:00 P.M.; October through March, Monday through Friday noon to 4:00 P.M. and Saturday and Sunday 10:00 A.M. to 4:00 P.M. Admission for adults is $3.00; senior citizens, $2.00; children, $1.00.

Skidaway Island, south of downtown, also has a trove of off-the-beaten-

Bill's Favorites

Savannah's National Historic District

Telfair Art Museum

Tybee Island

Midway Church

Sapelo Island

Jekyll Island

Christ Church

St. Simons Island

Little St. Simons Island

The Cloister Hotel

Cumberland Island National Seashore

Dinner at Bistro Savannah

Lunch at Mrs. Wilkes Dining Room

The Gastonian Inn

path adventures. *Skidaway Island State Park* (912–598–2300), off Diamond Causeway, is a 490-acre preserve that's relaxed and quiet even in busy seasons. The 100 tent and trailer camping sites have electrical and water connections, showers, and rest rooms. Amenities include a swimming pool, picnic shelters, nature trails, and a playground. No fishing areas or beaches are inside the park, but they are plentiful nearby. There's a $2.00 per visit parking fee. For camping reservations call (800) 864–PARK.

The Skidaway Island Marine Extension Center, McWhorter Drive, off Diamond Causeway, (912) 356–2496, operated by the University of Georgia, has a twelve-tank aquarium with an array of coastal marine life, including moray eels, barracuda, catfish, pigfish, monkfish, and fifty or so others. Open daily 10:00 A.M. to 5:00 P.M. Free admission.

At *Wormsloe State Historic Site,* 7601 Skidaway Road, (912) 353–3023, a 1½-mile avenue of live oaks leads to the tabby ruins of the colonial estate built by Noble Jones, one of the contingent of settlers who arrived with General Oglethorpe in 1733. A physician and carpenter in Surrey, Jones was one of the first Georgians to fully realize the American Dream. He became a constable, soldier, surveyor, rum agent, and member of the Royal Council. Between 1739 and 1745, he built his fortified tabby home on the Isle of Hope. Tabby was a popular building material made by pouring equal parts of water, lime, sand, and oyster shells into wooden molds. When the substance hardened, the wooden molds were removed and the next layer was poured. It was designed to last forever, but alas it didn't. You can see a model of it in the visitors center, along with artifacts found on the estate and an audiovisual show about the Georgia colony's early years.

Walk a nature trail to the Jones family grave site and the ruins of Noble Jones's great house. During Christmas season, Memorial Day, Labor Day, and Georgia Week in February, staff in period dress demonstrate colonial crafts and skills. Open Tuesday through Saturday 9:00 A.M. to 5:00 P.M. and Sunday 2:00 to 5:30 P.M. Adults, $2.00; children, $1.00.

The *Isle of Hope* is a photogenic place for a drive or walk. Go to the end of LaRoche Avenue and follow Bluff Drive along the Wilmington River.

Many lovely homes and a Roman Catholic church are set off by towering live oaks and banks of azaleas.

Fort McAllister State Historic Park, in Bryan County 25 miles south of Savannah, has some of the South's best preserved earthwork fortifications. Built on bluffs above the south bank of the Great Ogeechee River, the earthworks withstood seven Union land and sea assaults before finally surrendering in December 1864. It was the last major obstacle on General William T. Sherman's "March to the Sea" and led to Savannah's peaceful surrender a few days later. The earthworks and heavy guns have been restored to their wartime appearance. The museum and visitors center has Civil War weapons and other artifacts.

Fort McAllister's recreation area has seventy-five tent and trailer camping sites with electricity, water, rest rooms, showers, picnic tables, and grills; 5 miles of hiking trails; and boat ramps and docks. There's a $2.00 per visit parking fee. Drive Highway 144 for 10 miles east of I–95 exit 15. Call (800) 864–PARK for reservations.

As you drive Highway 17 between Savannah and Brunswick, *Midway Church* looms out of the gnarled arms of a live oak grove, like a New England meeting house that's lost its way. The white clapboard church, with its gabled roof and square belfry, traces its heritage to Massachusetts Puritans, who established the Midway Society in 1754. The church dates from 1792. Illustrious parishioners have included two signers of the Declaration of Independence and Theodore Roosevelt's great-grandfather. The fathers of Oliver Wendell Holmes and Samuel F. B. Morse have served as pastor.

Pick up the big iron church key at the neighboring *Midway Museum.* The sanctuary's unadorned interior has straightback pews and a slave galley. The churchyard across the highway is the resting place of the church's founders and Revolutionary heroes. Midway Museum has colonial furnishings, documents, and exhibits. Open Tuesday through Saturday 10:00 A.M to 4:00 P.M. and Sunday 2:00 to 4:00 P.M. Adults, $1.00; children, 50 cents.

McIntosh County, between Savannah and Brunswick, was the site of a British fort that predated Georgia's founding as a colony in 1733. Marshy bays and coastal islands are home to national marine and wildlife refuges and fleets of fishing boats and shrimping trawlers.

Stop first at the Darien Welcome Center (912– 437–6684) on Highway 17 at the Darien River bridge for general information. The *Fort King*

George State Historic Site, a mile off Highway 17, (912) 437–4770, marks an earthwork and pallisaded log fortress South Carolinians built in 1721 to fend off hostile advances by the Spanish in Florida. Most of the fort was destroyed by fire in 1726. A state visitors center and museum has displays, artifacts, and a film about the fort and early Georgia life. Open Tuesday through Saturday 9:00 A.M. to 5:00 P.M. and Sunday 2:00 to 5:30 P.M. Adults, $2.00; ages 6 to 12, $1.00. On the way to the fort, you may stop and photograph Darien's shrimp fleet and St. Cyprian's Episcopal Church (1870), McIntosh County's first Black house of worship.

For insights into McIntosh County's modern history—featuring a corrupt sheriff and the Black population's assertion of its civil rights in the 1960s and 1970s—read *Praying for Sheetrock,* Melissa Faye Greene's tell-all nonfiction book.

Unlike its neighboring states, most of Georgia's barrier islands have remained undeveloped. *Sapelo Island Tours,* conducted by the Georgia State Park system, take you through the fascinating ecology of the state's fourth largest barrier island. The boat leaves from the handsome new visitor center/museum at the little fishing community of Meridian. On the thirty-minute voyage, you'll skirt wavering stands of cord grass and scores of small islets and hammocks.

Communities get their names in many curious ways. A few years ago, I met Mrs. Lewis Graham, then in her 90s, who ran the one-room post office in the tiny McIntosh County shrimping port of Valona. Mrs. Graham's father and uncle founded the town in the 1890s and wanted to named it Shell Bluff, for all the oyster shells piled up on the river bluffs. "When they applied to Washington for a post office," she said, "they were informed that there already was a Shell Bluff, Georgia. They had to have another name. They looked around and saw an Albanian fishing boat called Valona. I believe it was named for a town over there. They reckoned there couldn't be another place in Georgia named Valona, and that's how we got our name."

Touring the 10-mile-long island on a bus or tram, you'll see marine, bird, and animal life in the Sapelo Island National Estuarine Research Reserve, the University of Georgia Marine Institute, and the R.J. Reynolds State Wildlife Refuge. You'll also pause at the exterior of the mansion North Carolina tobacco baron Reynolds got when he purchased the island from Hudson Motors executive Howard Coffin during the Great Depression. Naturalists will show you how to seine a flounder, explain some of the mysteries of the marshes, and point out deer, wild turkey, and many species of waterfowl that call the island home. You'll have time to walk the beaches and collect shells. Sapelo Island's historic lighthouse is being restored. Island facilities are limited to rest rooms, water fountains, and soft drink machines. Bring a snack and don't forget the insect repellent!

Fort King George

Tours are conducted year-round on Wednesday 8:30 A.M to 12:30 P.M. and Saturday 9:00 A.M. to 1:00 P.M. Friday tours June through Labor Day 8:30 A.M. to 12:30 P.M. From March through October, a special tour is available the last Tuesday of each month 8:30 A.M. to 12:30 P.M. Tickets are $10.00, adults; $6.00, ages 6 to 18; under age 6, free. Phone (912) 437–3224.

If you'd like to hike, bike, and fish Sapelo at leisure, reserve a room at The Weekender. Ceaser and Nancy Banks have four rooms in their stucco house for singles and couples ($38 one night, $35 multiple nights) and a three-bedroom "Family and Friends" suite for $135 for one night and $115 a night for multiple nights. Guests prepare their own breakfast in a shared kitchen with provisions they bring or purchase at a local store. The Banks prepare dinner, at extra charge, which includes fish, shrimp, ribeye, and Ceaser's "world famous" BBQ ribs. Phone (912) 485–2277, access www.gacoast.com/navigator/weekender.html, or e-mail weekend@drien.tel.net

Hofwyl-Broadfield Plantation State Historic Site, Highway 17, 6 miles south of Darien, (912–264–9263), is the last vestige of the rice culture that once flourished along the Altamaha River. Developed by South Carolinian William Brailsford in 1806–07, the plantation grew to 7,300 acres, largely on the backs of 350 Black slaves who labored in hellish conditions of heat and disease. A path takes you by the tabby ruins of the rice mill and along the top of the rice field dikes to the antebellum plantation house, furnished as it was in the early 1970s, when it was willed to the state by the last owner. Open Tuesday through Saturday 9:00 A.M. to 5:00 P.M. and Sunday 2:00 to 5:00 P.M. Adults, $2.00; children, $1.00.

"The Golden Isles" are a necklace of lush, subtropical barrier islands that serpentine languidly along Georgia's 120-mile-long Atlantic coast. Several of the principal islands are part of Glynn County. Even most developed islands—St. Simons and Jekyll—are low-key, laidback, and lightly commercialized compared to other resort islands on the Eastern Seaboard.

Blessed with long stretches of hard-packed beaches, marshes, inlets, rivers, and Spanish moss–veiled live oak trees, the islands are inviting places to get off the beaten path and commune in solitude with unsullied nature.

Brunswick, the Glynn County seat and a center of Georgia's shrimping and fishing industry (population 18,000), is the gateway to St. Simons, Jekyll, Sea Island, and Little St. Simons Island. Chartered in 1771, Brunswick was named for King George II's German ancestral home. Like Savannah, it was laid out on a precise grid of broad straight streets and public squares named for English places and nobility. Albany, Amherst, Dartmouth, Egmont, George, Gloucester, London, and Newcastle Streets, and Halifax, Hanover, and Hillsborough Squares kept their names after the Revolution. They're in the Old Town National Historic District. Queen Anne, Neo-Gothic, Italianate, Mansard, and Jacobean homes are enhanced by towering live oaks and banks of azaleas, camellias, and dogwoods. Several are charming bed-and-breakfast inns. (See Where to Stay.)

Get advance information from the Brunswick & Golden Isles Visitors Bureau, (912) 265–0620; fax,(912) 265–0629; www.bgislesvisitorsb.com. When you get here, pick up maps and information at the Brunswick-Golden Isles Visitors Center at Highway 17 and the F.J. Torras/St. Simons Island Causeway. Open daily except holidays 9:00 A.M. to 5:00 P.M., (912) 254–5337.

In downtown Brunswick, the turreted Queen Anne–style City Hall was built in 1883. Around the corner, the Glynn County Courthouse, at Reynolds and G Streets, is a good place to rest a spell. The classical, cupolaed building sits in a mini-botanical garden of moss-draped oaks, Chinese pistachio, magnolia, and swamp trees and flowering shrubbery.

Get off the beaten path and walk the *Earth Day Nature Trail,* a self-guided tour that takes you on wooden boardwalks over a wading-bird habitat. You'll also see an osprey/eagle nesting platform and wildlife observation decks. The wavering salt marshes, where your favorite seafood begins its life cycle, was immortalized in Sidney Lanier's 1878 poem, "The Marshes of Glynn," which goes in part: " . . . Sinuous southward and sinuous northward the shimmering band of the sand beach fastens the fringe of the marsh to the folds of the land." Lanier was inspired by the same view you'll see from *Marshes of Glynn Overlook*

Park. Young ladies in your group may enjoy the *Mary Miller Doll Museum,* 1523 Glynn Avenue (912–267–7569). The 4,000 dolls include pre–Civil War china heads, bisques, early vinyls, carved woodens, internationals from ninety countries, antique travel cases, and hundreds of dresses and accessories. Open Monday through Saturday 11:00 A.M. to 5:00 P.M. Adults, $2.00; age 5 to 15, $1.50; under age 5, no charge.

If you'd like to go deep-sea fishing or just get out on the open water for a spell, many charter boats are at the Brunswick docks at the end of Gloucester Street. Get information at the Golden Isles Visitors Bureau.

Jekyll Island

Jekyll Island is connected to Brunswick by a 6-mile causeway and a modern new high-span bridge ($2.00 per car) that allows boats

Try Your Hand at Brunswick Stew

Brunswick Stew was created in Brunswick. The piquant concoction goes with Georgia barbecue and seafood like Mutt goes with Jeff, ice cream with peach cobbler. No two cooks make it quite the same, so there's plenty of room for your own adjustments. A rustic version includes venison, squirrel, and other wild game. This popular recipe makes one gallon.

1 3-pound chicken

1 pound lean beef

1 pound lean pork

3 medium onions, chopped

Place meat in a large, heavy pot. Season with salt and pepper. Add onions and cover with water. Cook until the meat falls from the bones (several hours). Remove from heat and allow to cool. Tear meat in shreds and return to stock. Add:

4 16-ounce cans tomatoes

5 tablespoons Worcestershire sauce

14 ounces catsup

1 tablespoon Tabasco sauce

2 bay leaves

12 ounces chili sauce

½ teaspoon dry mustard

½ stick butter

Cook 1 hour, occassionally stirring to prevent sticking. Add:

3 tablespoons vinegar

2 16-ounce cans small limas or butter beans

2 16-ounce cans cream-style corn

1 15-ounce can small English peas

Optional: 3 small diced Irish potatoes and a box of frozen, sliced okra

Cook slowly until thick. Serve with barbecue, seafood, and corn bread.

to go under while you head unimpeded for your holiday. You can fish from the mothballed, forty-two-year-old bridge. Stop first at the Jekyll Island Welcome Center at the island end of the bridge (912–635–3636 or 800–841–6586). Open daily 9:00 A.M to 5:00 p.m.

Between 1886 and 1942, Jekyll was the winter home of many of America's richest and most famous families. From the Gilded Age until early in World War II, Astors, Pulitzers, Vanderbilts, Morgans, Rockefellers, Cranes, Goodyears, and other aristocrats lived in secluded luxury on their remote Georgia island. Shortly after Pearl Harbor, they boarded up their elegant "cottages" and left the island for the last time. After the war, the state of Georgia paid $675,000 for the island and turned it into a state park. Although the purchase price now seems a pittance, Gov. M. E. Thompson, who championed it, was widely lambasted for what political enemies labeled "Thompson's Folly."

According to the legislation creating the state park, 35 percent of the island must always remain undeveloped. That's a blessing for vacationers, who can hike and bike and bird-watch in a wilderness as pristine as when it was created, and enjoy amenities the old plutocrats could never have imagined. One side of the island is skirted by nearly 10 miles of hard-packed Atlantic beaches, washed by a usually mild surf perfect for small children and waders. Several beachfront hotels welcome pets, which have a ball chasing seagulls and each other and splashing in the waves. A rock wall intended to stop erosion prevents your Fidos from racing off the beach into woods where they're hard to find. Free showers, rest rooms, and changing rooms are at regular intervals along the beachfront. Even on the busiest holiday weekends, there's plenty of room to get away from everybody else. The island's mainland side is washed by the Intracoastal Waterway and scenic salt marshes. Deer, raccoon, armadillo, wild turkey, and many species of waterfowl roam the marshes, live oak, and pine forests.

Tours of the *Jekyll Island Historic District* start at the Visitors Center. You can see a video presentation about Jekyll's colorful history, and guided tram tours take you inside several of the millionaires' restored cottages. Indian Mound Cottage, Standard Oil director William Rockefeller's shingled Cape Cod–style cottage, has been furnished as it was when the family began wintering here in 1917. You'll probably wonder why there's no kitchen in most of the houses. The Club House, now the Jekyll Island Hotel, was the social center, where members gathered for meals, cards, and other activities. Other stops on the tour include Mistletoe Cottage, a Dutch Colonial Revival with a collection of sculpture by noted artist Russell Fiore, a long-time Jekyll resident. Cypress-shingled Faith Chapel is illuminated by Louis Comfort Tiffany and D. Maitland Armstrong stained-glass windows. Jekyll's recreational riches include sixty-three holes of golf that wind through marshes and woodlands, indoor and outdoor tennis, a fishing pier, marinas, a water slide park and wave pool, rental bikes, picnic grounds, and hiking trails.

St. Simons and Sea Island

A 35-cent toll takes you over the F.J. Torras Causeway to St. Simons Island. In the summer, you can take the St. Simons Transit Company's Water Taxi between Jekyll and St. Simons, (912) 638–5678. The most developed of the four Glynn County "Golden Isles"

Jekyll Island Club House

has seen a big increase in hotels, condos, restaurants, and shopping areas in recent years, but that hasn't dimmed the natural glories of the Manhattan-size island's salt marshes, beaches, and live oak forests wrapped in Spanish moss. You can swim and sunbathe on long strands of beach—all Georgia beaches are public domain—fish, ride horseback, play golf and tennis, and visit historic sites dating back to the early eighteenth century.

Fort Frederica National Monument, at the island's northern end, includes remnants of a tabby fortress the British built in the 1730s as a bulwark against Spanish invaders from Florida. Leading up to the fort are foundations of homes and shops once occupied by 1,500 troops and civilians. The fort was never tested. The Spanish attacked in 1742, and their defeat at the nearby Battle of Bloody Marsh kept England firmly in control of Georgia's coast. Stop first at the National Park Service Visitors Center (912–638–3639) for a film and historical displays. Bring insect repellent and don't step on the fire ant mounds! Open daily 9:00 A.M. to 5:00 P.M. Adults, $1.00; ages 16 and under, free.

Christ Church, a Gothic wooden sanctuary on the road to Fort Frederica, is the island's most beloved (and most photographed) landmark. The site of services John and Charles Wesley conducted for Frederica's garrison, the original church was built in 1820. Desecrated by Union soldiers, it was rebuilt in 1884 by the Reverend Anson Phelps Dodge, whose life was chronicled by late St. Simons novelist Eugenia Price in *Beloved Invader.* The church is framed by an arbor of live oaks, dogwoods, and azaleas. The interior is illuminated by stained-glass windows. Open daily, donations appreciated. Episcopal services are conducted every Sunday.

St. Simons Lighthouse, at the island's southern end, has been a landmark since 1872. The present 104-foot brick sentinel—still maintained as an operational beacon by the U.S. Coast Guard—stands on the site of an 1810 lighthouse destroyed by retreating Confederate troops in 1861. The old lightkeeper's cottage houses the Museum of Coastal History, with collections of colonial furniture, shipbuilding tools, and changing exhibits of coastal art.

Neptune Park, around the lighthouse, has seaside picnic tables, a playground, and steps down to the beach. You can fish from the beach or take a cooler and lawn chair onto the Municipal Pier and angle for flounder and whiting and even pull up a startled hammerhead shark or barracuda. No license is required for saltwater fishing. The pier, lighthouse, and Neptune Park are in The Village, around Mallory Street, St. Simons's original commerical area, where you'll find restaurants, shops, and lodgings.

Massengale Park, on Ocean Boulevard, between the King & Prince Hotel and the Coast Guard Station, has several miles of public beach, picnic areas, and rest rooms.

The world is truly not much with us on **Little St. Simons Island.** By the time we've made the twenty-minute launch crossing from "big" St. Simons, the world's problems have vanished in the sunlight of another glorious Low Country morning. A fortunate set of circumstances has left the island—6 miles long by 2 to 3 miles wide—very nearly as nature created it.

Through the 1800s, the 10,000 acres were the domain of one rice planter family. In 1903, a pencil company bought the island, but when the red cedars proved too wind-gnarled for writing instruments, it became an off-the-beaten-path retreat, now open to the public.

Congenial hosts Debbie and Kevin McIntyre will put you up in rustic but comfortable, recently air-conditioned guest rooms and cottages that accommodate up to thirty. At mealtime, sit at a communal table and relive your day's adventures. Things to do are bountiful: horseback riding, sunbathing, and swimming in a pool or in 7 miles of wild beaches, boating, canoeing, crabbing, birdwatching, fishing, and walking through forests inhabited by deer, raccoon, armadillos, pelicans, red-tail hawks, great blue heron, egret, and more than 200 other species of birds. Gators cruise like ironclad vessels in marshes and rivers. All meals and activities are included in double occupancy daily rates of $300 to $525; two- to four-bedroom cottages, $400 to $1,500. You can even rent the whole island for $3,400 to $5,400! Phone (912) 638–7472; fax (912) 634–1811; www.pactel.com.au/lssi.

Sea Island, linked to St. Simons Island by a small bridge over an estuary, is home of the renowned *Cloister Hotel,* one of America's legendary

Little St. Simons Low Country Boil

*O*ccasionally, the LSSI kitchen staff hauls a big iron kettle out to the beach and invites everyone to join.

½ pound keilbasa, or other smoked sausage, per person

½ pound raw shimp in shell per person

3 New potatoes per person

1 ear shucked corn per person

2 onions per person

1 box commercial shrimp boil per 2 pounds shrimp

1 teaspoon vinegar per pound shimp

½ teaspooon Tabasco sauce per pound shrimp

1 teaspoon black pepper per 4 pounds shrimp

1 carrot per person, cut in fourths

1-2 crabs per person

Boil water in a large kettle on stove or outdoor cooker. Add potatoes and all spices, bring to boil, and cook 5 minutes. Add sausage and bring back to boil for 5 minutes. Add corn, onions, and carrots and boil 5 minutes. Check ingredients, especially potatoes, for doneness. Add crabs, boil 5 minutes. Add shrimp and boil until just done—they will be bright pink. Drain and pour onto platters. Have cole slaw, cornbread, cocktail sauce, and Dijon mustard on hand. A real crowd pleaser!

resorts. (Sea Island 31561, 912–638–3611 or 800–732–4752; fax 912–635–5159). Even if you're not a guest of this gracious hotel, you may admire the Spanish-Mediterranean–style buildings Addison Mizner designed in 1928 and set in beautifully landscaped grounds, and drive past the stately homes lining Sea Island Drive. Nonguests may also play the Cloister's Sea Island Golf Course and tennis courts and have lunch and dinner in the dining room.

Dinner at The Cloister's Main Dining Room is from another era— dressy and formal, courtly and unhurried. Gents wear jacket and tie, and ladies dress pretty close to the proverbial "nines." Wednesday and Saturday nights are optional black tie. The menu ranges from traditional resort fare—prime rib, filet mignon, stuffed flounder—to more contemporary pasta, seafood, lamb, and chicken dishes. Service is extremely gracious. Breakfast and lunch are more casual, but the dress code calls for tasteful sportswear; no shorts, please. American plan rates, with three daily meals, $248 to $574, double occupancy.

Cumberland Island

Cumberland Island National Seashore is an intricate web of nature's rarest, most wondrous gifts. Maintained by the National Park Service, the island—18 miles long and 1 to 2 miles wide—preserves astonishing treasures of marshes and dunes, pristine beaches, live oak forests, lakes, ponds, estuaries, and inlets. "Natives" include great blue heron, wood storks, egrets, and dozens of other bird species, many rarely seen beyond these shores; giant sea turtles, which plod over the beaches to regenerate their endangered kind; fiddler, hermit, and ghost crabs; shrimp, oysters, and flounder; deer, armadillo, mink, wild horses, and wild boar; playful otters; and gators that cruise the waterways like ironclad men o' war.

Mankind's 4,000-year habitation began with ancient Guale Indians, followed by sixteenth-century Spanish missionaries, eighteenth-century British troops, and pre–Civil War indigo and cotton planters. Thomas Carnegie, of the Pittsburgh Carnegies, bought the entire island in the 1880s. His family's splendid estates were mostly abandoned when the "Gilded Age" gave way to the "Roaring Twenties," and high society discovered more fashionable wintering places. With only a a few intrusions, the island has passed into public trust largely as it was created.

Unless you own your own boat, the only way to enjoy Cumberland's glories is via a forty-five-minute ride on *The Cumberland Queen* from St.

Marys. With a capacity of 150, the *Queen* departs St. Marys daily from mid-May through Labor Day at 9:00 A.M. and 11:45 A.M., arriving Cumberland at 9:45 A.M. and 12:30 P.M. respectively. The rest of the year, it operates at the same times daily except Tuesday and Wednesday. Including taxes, fares are adults, $10.07; ages 65 and over, $7.95; and ages 12 and under, $5.99.

The first Sunday of each month, an extended trip to **Plum Orchard** estate on the island's north end is an additional $6.00 a person. When you arrive on the island, the National Park Service will collect a $4.00 per person user fee. For information and reservations, phone (912) 882–4336.

Bear in mind that sailing times are as precise as Swiss trains. If you miss the last ferry from the island, you'll have to hire a boat from St. Marys or Fernandina Beach. Campers have a choice of developed and primitive campgrounds available for a small cost, which varies according to the site you choose. Sea Camp, five-minute's walk from the ferry dock, has bathrooms and showers; primitive campsites, a $3\frac{1}{2}$- to 10-mile hike from the dock, have trench latrines and cold water spigots. If you're a day-tripper, you can walk several nature trails, or swim and sun and view the remains of Dungeness, the Carnegies' fabulous estate destroyed by fire in the 1950s. Park Service rangers lead history and nature walks. There's nothing at all for sale on the island, so remember to bring food, cold drinks, insect repellent, and sunscreen.

St. Marys Submarine Museum, St. Marys waterfront, (912) 882–2782, will tell you everything you ever wanted to know about submarines, with special emphasis on the nuke fish at nearby Kings Bay Submarine Base. You can also see diving equipment, research documents, uniforms, and a re-created sub interior. Looks pretty cozy, eh? Imagine spending several months in these quarters without seeing the surface of the seas you're cruising under. Open Tuesday through Saturday 10:00 A.M. to 4 :00 P.M. and Sunday 1:00 to 5:00 P.M. Adults, $2.00; ages 6 to 18, $1.00.

The ***Greyfield Inn*** is Cumberland's only hotel-type accommodation. John F. Kennedy Jr. and his wife, Carolyn, had their wedding reception in the Carnegie family's old Georgian-style mansion after taking their vows at the island's African-American chapel. Staying overnight is a one-of-a-kind experience. Guests sleep in seventeen recently air-conditioned rooms with four-poster beds, bathe in claw-footed tubs, and relax amid family portraits and mementos. All meals, boat transportation from Fernandina Beach, Florida, and walks with naturalists are included in rates of $275 to $395 per day per couple year-round. Contact Greyfield Inn, P.O. Box 900, Fernandina Beach, FL 32035-0900, (904) 261–6408.

Spanish Moss

Spanish moss, which isn't a moss at all, but an air plant loosely related to pineapple, hangs in wispy picturesque veils from live oak trees in the southern and coastal parts of the state. Lovely to look at, but the very devil to touch. Chiggers (aka redbugs) are voracious little pests that make their home in Spanish moss. They enjoy nothing better than feasting on a fresh, tasty smorgasbord of anybody unwary enough to think the moss would be picturesque in a home garden or stuffed in a pillow. Chiggers attack *en masse* and make you itch and scratch until you think you'll lose your sanity. Modern medications like Benadryl™ can relieve the torture, but many Southerners prefer old-fashioned remedies like Epsom salt baths, nail polish, and Chapstick. A couple of years ago on Little St. Simons Island, I saw a little boy come out of the forest with his arms loaded with the stuff and strands of it draped around his neck. I bet the poor kid is still itching.

The *Woodbine Crawfish Festival* takes over the tiny Camden County seat the last weekend of April. The chance to see beauty queens, marching bands, parades, and arts and crafts and put away mountains of delicious crustaceans—fried, gumbo'd, étoufféed, jambalaya'd, and boiled in savory Cajun herbs—lures crowds from all over the Georgia coast, even down into Florida. Phone (912) 576–3211 for information.

WHERE TO STAY IN COASTAL GEORGIA

SAVANNAH (HISTORIC DISTRICT)
Bed & Breakfast Inn,
117 West Gordon Street,
(912) 238–0518.

History and charm at moderate prices. A pair of 1835 Federal-style townhouses have 15 guest rooms. A garden suite and 2 cottages have kitchens and sitting areas. Full Southern breakfast included in $55 to $95 rates.

Foley House,
14 West Hull Street,
(800) 647–3708.

Danish-born Inge Svensson presides over this elegant 1896 Victorian townhouse with 19 guest rooms, several with oversize whirlpool tubs and working fireplaces. Continental breakfast, afternoon tea, and cordials included for $95 to $200.

The Gastonian,
220 East Gaston Street,
(800) 322–6603,
(912) 232–2869.

Sumptuous 17-room inn in a matched pair of 1868 townhouses. Georgian and Regency antiques and all the modern comforts. Honeymooners prefer the Caracalla Suite, with an antique four-poster bed and a draped whirlpool bath as big as Cleopatra's barge. The $240 to $350 rate includes gourmet breakfast.

Grand Toots Inn,
212 West Hall Street,
(912) 236–2911
and (800) 835–6831.

A grand three-story Victorian that plucky Dolores Ellis saved from destruction. Four distinctively furnished rooms are in the main house and a large suite in the carriage house. Each room has a fireplace, TV, and phone. Some rooms share bath. Rates are $75 to $155.

Hampton Inn,
201 East Bay Street,
(800) 576-4945
and (912) 231-9700.

Centrally located new chain motel is designed to fit into the historic surroundings. Full restaurant and bar. Rates are $89 to $149.

Mulberry Inn,
601 East Bay Street,
(912) 238-1200
and (800) 688-9198.

The 121-room historic district hotel, in a one-time Coca-Cola bottling plant, is a Holiday Inn franchise, but you'd never guess it from the antiques and other Old Savannah decor and furnishings. Full restaurant and bar. Rates are $135 to $195.

More than three dozen historic bed & breakfast inns surround you with the aura of Old Savannah. For information and reservations phone Bed & Breakfast Reservations of Savannah, (800) 729-7787 and (912) 232-7787 (RSVP), and Savannah Historic Inns and Guest Houses, (800) 262-4667. Chain hotels and motels are also abundant.

TYBEE ISLAND
Georgianne Inn,
1312 Butler Avenue,
(912) 596-5301.

Only a few steps from the beach, innkeeper Judy Hopper's inn, built in the early 1920s, has 5 units, all with cable TV and telephone. One is a two-bedroom, two-bath suite. Three have full kitchens where you can prepare your own meals, which aren't included in rates of $65 to $125.

Hunter House,
1701 Butler Boulevard,
(912) 786-7515.

Fits Tybee like a hand in a glove. Simply furnished guest rooms range from singles to four-room suites. Some have kitchens and fireplaces for brisk winter days by the sea. The upstairs restaurant and bar, with an outside deck, specializes in coastal seafood, steaks, seafood, pastas, and potent drinks. Lend an ear during afternoon happy hour, and you'll pick up the skinny on what's happening on the island. Moderate seasonal rates.

If you'd like to rent a condo or a beach house, contact Tybee Island Rentals, P.O. Box 1440 Tybee Island 31328, (800) 755-8562.

Tybee's chain motels include Days Inn, (800) 325-2525 and (912) 786-4576;

Econo Lodge Beachside, (912) 786-4535; and Best Western Dunes Inn, (912) 786-4591.

For general information, contact Tybee Island Visitor Center, (800) 868-2322.

DARIEN
Open Gates B&B,
Vernon Square,
(912) 437-6985.

An 1876 timber baron's home has been regeared with antiques and heirlooms from owner Carolyn Hodges's Philadelphia ancestors. Five guest rooms and public areas are air-conditioned. There's a swimming pool and a library with coastal books, and Hodges can point you in many off-the-beaten-path directions. Breakfast included in rates of $58 to $65.

BRUNSWICK
Brunswick Manor,
825 Egmont Street,
(912) 265-6889.

Built in 1886 as the home of a former Union Army officer, the redbrick Romanesque mansion is decorated with antiques and period furnishings. Four suites have queen-size beds and private beds. Two have kitchens and breakfast nooks. A separate cottage sleeps eight. Full breakfast and high tea are included in rates of $75 to $100.

McKinnon House,
1001 Egmont Street,
(912) 261-9100.

Victorian splendor in a handsomely restored Queen Anne mansion with elaborate woodwork and fine New Orleans and Charleston furniture. Full breakfast and afternoon refreshments. Three guest rooms with private baths. Rates are $85 to $125.

Rose Manor Guest House,
1108 Richmond Street,
(912) 267-6369.

Six guest rooms in a Victorian mansion filled with period furnishings and antiques and all the modern comforts. Gourmet breakfast and afternoon tea with a harpist to set the proper mood. Rates are $65 to $125.

Scarlett House,
902 Wright Square,
(912) 264-5902,
fax (912) 264-8187.

Two spacious rooms in a luxurious home. Full Southern breakfast. Rates are $100 to $200.

JEKYLL ISLAND
Clarion Resort Buccanneer, 85 South Beachview Drive, (912) 635-2261, fax (912) 635-3230.

There are 208 rooms and efficiencies. Rates are $85 to $175.

Comfort Inn Island Suites,
711 Beachview Drive,
(912) 635-2211,
(800) 204-0202,
fax (912) 635-2381.

There are 178 suites with refrigerators. Rates are $75 to $175.

Jekyll Island Campground, North Beachview Drive, (912) 635-3021 and (800) 841-6586.

Eighteen wooded acres with full hookups, rest rooms, showers, laundry, and camp store. Pets allowed on leash. Near beaches, fishing, and golf courses. Nightly rates are $17. Weekly and monthly rates available.

Jekyll Island Club Hotel,
371 Riverview Drive,
(912) 635-2600,
(800) 535-9547,
fax (912) 635-2818.

The millionaires' turreted, four-story former clubhouse has been transformed into a deluxe hotel graced by stained glass, plaster molding, and other rich architectural details. Swim in the outdoor pool, take carriage rides, and play croquet on the emerald lawns. The 134 guest rooms and suites have all the first-class comforts for $95 to $200.

Villas by the Sea Hotel,
Condominium &
Conference Center,
1175 North Beachview Drive, (912) 635-2521, (800) 841-6262, fax (912) 635-2569.

There are 168 1- to 3-bedroom villas with fully equipped kitchens for $75 to $240.

ST. SIMONS ISLAND
Days Inn,
1701 Frederica Road,
(912) 634-0660
and (800) 329-7466.

Complimentary continental breakfast and microwave and fridge in all 101 rooms. Bike rentals on site. Rates are $65 to $89.

Epworth-by-the-Sea,
100 Arthur Moore Drive,
(912) 638-3030.

Methodist conference center, spiritual retreat, and vacation center has 218 modern motel rooms, an inexpensive cafeteria, a swimming pool, tennis courts, and fishing piers. No alcohol or unmarried couples allowed. Rates are $39 to $78.

Queen's Court,
437 Kings Way,
(912) 638-8459.

Old-fashioned but clean and comfortable motel with some kitchenettes. In The Village, near shops, dining, the lighthouse, and Neptune Park. Rates are $50 to $82.

St. Simons Inn by the Lighthouse,
609 Beachview Drive,
(912) 638–0943.

Thirty-four modern attractive guest rooms and pool around the corner from Village shops, restaurants, pier, and lighthouse. Microwaves and fridges in every room. Rates are $50 to $115.

ST. MARYS
During the past 15 years, the Kings Bay Nuclear Submarine Base—home port for eight Trident missile nuclear subs—has mushroomed St. Mary's population from 2,000 to nearly 9,000. A flood of fast-food outlets, video rentals, and chain stores has grown up on the outskirts, but the historic old town on the St. Marys River is as quaint and unchanged as ever.

Crooked River State Park,
Highway Spur 40, 7 miles north of St. Marys,
(912) 882–5256.

Has campsites and cottages, swimming pool, fishing areas, and playgrounds. There's a $2.00 per visit parking fee. For camping and cottage reservations call (800) 864–PARK.

Goodbread House Bed and Breakfast,
209 Osborne Street,
(912) 882–3242.

Has four guest rooms with private baths in an 1870s Victorian house. Children are welcome and pets can stay in the fenced yard. Full breakfast with rates of $65 double and $50 single.

Riverview Hotel,
105 Osborne Street,
(912) 882–3242.

Has plain but comfortable guest rooms across from the Cumberland Queen docks for $40 to $60. The WWI-era hotel's restaurant serves moderately priced breakfast, lunch, and dinner. A full bar pours your favorite libations.

Spencer House Inn,
101 East Bryant Street,
(912) 882–9427.

Mary and Mike Neff's 1872 National Register House is a short walk from the Cumberland Island ferry. Fourteen rooms have private baths, claw-foot tubs, TV, and phone. Guests relax in the library and on verandas with cypress rockers. Full breakfast. Rates are $65 to $95.

WHERE TO EAT IN COASTAL GEORGIA

SAVANNAH (HISTORIC DISTRICT)
Bistro Savannah,
309 West Congress Street,
City Market,
(912) 233–6266.

Chef Mark Gaylord's fresh market cuisine is a contemporary spin on healthy, vibrant foods enjoyed in the Low Country before the Civil War. Specialties include coastal seafood bouillabaisse, crisp pecan chicken with bourbon sauce, and veal and wild mushroom meatloaf. Dinner served Monday through Saturday.

Chiang Mai Orchids Thai Cafe,
215 West Broughton Street, (912) 231–0789.

Storefront cafe among the antiques malls that are taking over the vacant spaces in downtown's former main shopping street. Thai curries, chicken, seafood, and noodle dishes are prepared to individual heat preferences. If you'd like it three-alarm Bangkok-style, just tell them and they'll send it out with prayers and a fire extinguisher. Lunch and dinner Monday through Friday.

Express Cafe,
39 Barnard Street, (912) 233–4683.

Popular City Market drop-in serves sandwiches, soups, salads, pastries, and croissants in a cheerful black-and-white tiled former drugstore.

Gryphon Tea Room, 337
Bull Street, at Madison Square, (912) 238–2481.

A century-old pharmacy has been transformed into a romantic Parisian tearoom. Sit back and enjoy your tea, coffee, soups, sandwiches, and desserts amid the beauty of Honduran mahogany, 14 original stained glass windows, Tiffany-style globes, and lace curtains. Open daily morning to night.

Il Pasticcio,
Bull and Broughton Streets, downtown, (912) 231–8888.

Fresh pastas, grilled vegetables, shrimp, risotto, oak-fired pizza, rotisserie chicken, real Italian gelato, and fresh-baked goods in a stylishly converted Art Deco women's dress shop with floor-to-ceiling windows overlooking the busy corner. Owner/artist Floriana Venetico's second-floor art gallery is a before-or-after dinner treat. Lunch and dinner daily.

Nita's Place,
140 Abercorn Street, (912) 238–8233.

A stellar little soul food palace tucked into the historic district. Owner/chef Nita Dixon is one of the city's most congenial hosts. A plate of top-notch fried chicken, crab cakes, corn bread, and Southern-style vegetables and homemade dessert is yours for a modest price. Weekday lunch.

The Olde Pink House,
Reynolds Square, 23 Abercorn Street, (912) 232–4286.

This is the ticket for a romantic, candlelit dinner. The stunning eighteenth-century mansion's dining rooms are graced by colonial paintings and decor, a perfect dress-up place for Low Country she-crab soup, crispy flounder, sauteed shrimp, country ham served over grits, and Vidalia onion stuffed with sausage. Before or after dinner, sit by the fireplace and enjoy the pianist in the cozy downstairs Tavern. Dinner daily.

Mrs. Wilkes Boardinghouse, 107 West Jones Street, (912) 233–5997.

Aka Wilkes Dining Room, this is a treasure hidden away in an historic district townhouse. You know you're there by the long lines waiting outside. Family-style lunch fills the tables with bottomless platters of fried chicken, fried fish, Southern-style vegetables, corn bread, biscuits, and dessert. Come for breakfast and you'll be treated with feather-light biscuits, eggs, sausage, and buttery grits. Very inexpensive. Monday through Friday, breakfast and lunch only. No credit cards.

TYBEE ISLAND
Cafe Loco Waterfront Bar & Grill,
Lazzaretto Creek Marina, (912) 786–7810.

The quintessential seafood shack, with wooden booths, a long bar, and an outside deck overlooking the marina, is a laid-back place for sandwiches, burgers, shrimp, crab, and steak. Way into the wee hours, the place boogies to the beat of local blues and rock bands. Open from 11:00 A.M. to 2:00 A.M. daily. Off Highway 80, the marina is also headquarters for dolphin-watching tours, deep-sea fishing excursions, and gambling cruises on the *Atlantic Star.* Phone (800) 242-0166.

The Crab Shack,
40A Estill Hammock Road, (912) 786-9857.

As the sign of the happy crab says, THE PLACE WHERE THE ELITE EAT IN THEIR BARE FEET, The Crab Shack epitomizes Tybee's laidback ambience. Sit on a big open deck by the water or in the screened-in dining room, and tuck into monster platters of fried and broiled shrimp, oysters, crabs, and fish at very moderate prices. Open continuously for lunch and dinner daily.

North Beach Grill,
41A Meddin Drive, (912) 786-9003.

Behind the Tybee Museum, across from the lighthouse, this longtime Tybee favorite delivers a flavorful blend of Southern and Caribbean cooking. Genial owner/chef George Spriggs wows his patrons with Jamaican-style jerk (marinated) chicken, pan-seared snapper, egg-

plant parmigiana, crab-cake sandwiches, Cuban-style pot roast, and many other wonderful creations. Open daily for lunch and dinner.

Snappers, off Highway 80 near Wilmington River bridge, (912) 897-6101.

A great place for family dinner, especially after a big day at the beach. Big plates of Low Country shrimp, oysters, deviled crabs, and pecan and key lime pies. Lunch Monday through Saturday.

Spanky's Beachside, across from the Tybee Pier, (912) 786-5520.

A popular drop-in for cold beer, seafood, and sandwiches and casual meeting and mingling. Open daily.

BRUNSWICK
The Georgia Pig,
I-95/Highway 17 South, exit 6, (912) 264-6664.

The place for Brunswick stew at the source, plus delectable barbecue pork plates with all the trimmings. Lunch and dinner daily.

Grapevine Cafe,
1519 Newcastle Street, (912) 265-0115.

A popular downtown Brunswick destination for local seafood, chicken, vegetarian dishes, and great desserts. Lunch Monday through Saturday.

Royal Cafe,
1618 Newcastle Street, (912) 262-1402.

Serves hamburgers, grouper burgers, soft-shell crab, pastas, and other trendy dishes in an attractive downtown setting. Lunch Monday through Friday.

JEKYLL ISLAND
Blackbeard's,
200 North Beachview Drive, (912) 635-3522.

Fresh Low Country seafood dishes are the specialties at this popular beachfront eatery.

Cafe Solterra, Jekyll Island Club Hotel, 371 Riverview Drive, (912) 635-2600.

Pick up sandwiches, salads, pizza, and desserts, and enjoy them inside or at outdoor tables.

The Grand Dining Room,
Jekyll Island Club Hotel.

Dine in the splendor of the Gilded Age, amid candlelight, fine crystal, china, and silver. The extensive menu includes innovative continental cuisine, steaks, fresh seafood, and pasta. The yards-long Sunday brunch shouldn't be missed.

SeJay's Waterfront Cafe & Pub,
Jekyll Harbor Marina, 1 Harbor Road, (912) 635-3200.

Low Country seafood,

steaks, and Brunswick stew in a casual dining room overlooking the shrimp and pleasure boats and sunset on the marshes.

ST. SIMONS

Bennie's Red Barn,
5514 Frederica Road, (912) 638–2844.

Fresh coastal seafood and steaks grilled over a wood fire have made this rustic off-the-beaten-path old barn a dining landmark since 1954.

Blanche's Courtyard,
440 Ocean Boulevard, (912) 638–3030.

Blanche's has withstood vacationers' changing tastes for nearly 25 years. In historic St. Simons Village, near the pier and lighthouse, Blanche's ongoing popularity stems from its charming tropical ambience—a 300-year-old oak tree is the center-piece—and consistently

high-quality fresh seafood and steaks. Blue crab soup and killer seafood platters are something to write home about. Dinner daily except Monday.

Fourth of May Cafe & Deli,
321 Mallory Street, at the main Village corner, (912) 638–5444.

Has daily potluck specials—meat or seafood with two fresh vegetables, for about $6.00. Also has huge deli sandwiches and desserts. Lunch and dinner daily.

J. Mac's Island Restaurant & Bistro,
407 Mallory Street, (912) 634–0403.

A cool, classy place for rack of lamb, soft shell crabs, lobster, steaks, pasta, cocktails, wine, and live musical entertainment. Dinner Monday through Saturday.

St. Simons Brewing Co.,
100 Marina Drive, (912) 638–0011.

Watch the boats on Golden Isles Marina while you sip six on-tap microbrews (Black oyster stout and Bloody Marsh red are among the selections) and enjoy Low Country seafood, sandwiches, and salads. Lunch and dinner daily.

St. Simons Island Club,
100 Kings Way, (912) 638–5132.

Operated by The Cloister Hotel, the upscale Low Country plantation-style dining room excels in Low Country seafood, steaks, quail, lamb chops, and pasta. Lunch and dinner Monday through Saturday. Sunday brunch.

Northeast Georgia

Depending on which direction you've pointed your hiking boots, the 2,015-mile *Appalachian Trail* either begins or ends with 79 miles of northeast Georgia mountainland. Many AT veterans acclaim the Georgia section as the most beautiful in all the fourteen states between here and Mount Katahdin, Maine.

The AT's southern terminus is atop 3,782-foot *Springer Mountain,* in Dawson County, 75 miles northeast of Atlanta. An 8-mile approach trail begins at Amicalola Falls State Park. There hikers may camp out, get their gear together, and have their packs weighed by park rangers.

From Springer Mountain the AT's Section I is a 22.3-mile easy-to-strenuous hike to Highway 60 at Woody Gap. Section II, 10.7 miles from Woody Gap to Neels Gap, has just one long uphill stretch and is popular with one-day and weekend hikers. At Neels Gap, the trail crosses Highway 19/129 and goes "indoors" as it passes through a covered breezeway of the *Mountain Crossing/Walasi-Yi Center.* At this stone and log legacy of the 1930s Civilian Conservation Corps (CCC), hikers can get trail information and replenish supplies of dehydrated foods and camping gear. Motorists stop by for mountain handicrafts and short hikes on the trail. Phone (706) 745–6095. From Walasi-Yi, Section III is a moderately difficult 5.7 miles to Tesnatee Gap on the Richard Russell Scenic Highway (Highway 348). Sections IV–VI carry the trail upward and onward. At Bly Gap, near the Rabun County/ Towns County border, you bid adieu to Georgia and cross into the North Carolina Great Smokies. Mount Katahdin, here we come!

Blue Ridge Mountains

I n Georgia's far northeast corner, up against the North Carolina and South Carolina borders, Rabun County is the heart of the state's dramatically rugged Blue Ridge Mountain country. About 80 percent of the county is included in national forests and state parks. Outdoor adventures range from tranquil trout fishing in mountain

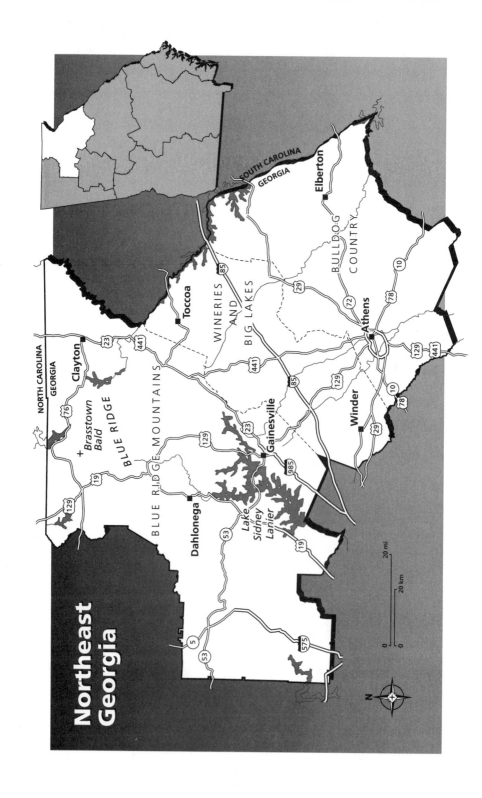

Northeast Georgia

NORTH CAROLINA
GEORGIA

SOUTH CAROLINA
GEORGIA

Clayton

Toccoa

Elberton

BLUE RIDGE

Brasstown
Bald

BLUE RIDGE MOUNTAINS

WINERIES AND BIG LAKES

BULLDOG COUNTRY

Dahlonega

Lake
Sidney
Lanier

Gainesville

Athens

Winder

20 mi

20 km

N

streams, canoeing, swimming, off-the-beaten-path hiking, and browsing for handmade crafts at country stores to the ultimate heart-pounding adventure: *Chattooga River Rafting.*

For information on the county's outdoor bounty, contact the Rabun County Welcome Center, Highway 441, Clayton 30525, (706) 782–5113, www.gamountains.com/rabun.

Until the early 1970s, when Jon Voight, Burt Reynolds, and the rest of the *Deliverance* movie crew let the world in on the secret, the Chattooga River was the remote domain of mountain folk along the Georgia–South Carolina border. Nowadays daredevils come from early spring through late fall to test their courage against the river's steep sluices, whirlpools, and roller-coaster rapids. To see that they accomplish their missions safely, the U.S. Forest Service licenses professional outfitters to conduct the trips, which are made in sturdy six-person rubber rafts and are led by guides who know every rock and rill along this tempestuous waterway.

Outfitters offer a variety of Chattooga experiences. Beginners usually test their wings on Section III, a seven-hour, 6-mile ride that sweeps them through many of the *Deliverance* landmarks. At lunchtime guides pull a small deli out of their waterproof packs and spread the feast at the foot of a waterfall.

Section III is a mere warm-up for "The Ultimate Challenge," the Chattooga's wild and woolly Section IV. Suggested only for well-seasoned whitewater hands in top physical condition, this rip-snorting seven-hour cruise carries you through swiftly moving currents; steep, wooded gorges; up and over, down and around such potential perils as Seven Foot Falls, Corkscrew, and Jawbone. At day's end, the Chattooga finally turns you loose, into the peaceful waters of Tugaloo Lake.

For those who really want to get to the heart of the river, outfitters offer two-day trips, which include overnight camping, a steak dinner, and a bountiful breakfast. Some packages offer the option of lodgings at rustic inns and cabins.

Day-trips on Section III are about $60 on weekdays, $10 higher on weekends. For Section IV, figure on paying around $70 on weekdays, $90 on weekends. You'll be supplied with all the necessary equipment and transportation to and from river access points. You'll also get a briefing on paddling techniques and safety rules, expert guide service, lunch, and a place to shower and change clothes at the end of your ride. Half-day trips are also offered (pick up names and phone numbers). Contact Nantahala Outdoor Center, (800) 232–7238; Wildwater Limited, (800) 451–9972; and Southeastern Expeditions, (800) 868–7238.

If the Chattooga sparks memories of *Deliverance*, **Lake Rabun,** near the little town of Tallulah Falls, may remind you of the film *On Golden Pond.* Ringed by the soft green humps of the Blue Ridge Mountains and unpretentious summer cottages, some dating back to the 1920s and 1930s, this small off-the-beaten-path lake is the embodiment of peace and quiet.

Built in 1922, the **Lake Rabun Hotel** is the perfect complement to the lake. New owners have spruced up the sixteen-room wood and stone lodge, polished the mountain laurel and rhododendron furniture, added baths to some rooms, and put in heat for spring and fall guests. You'll still have to go elsewhere for a television, telephone, or air-conditioning. What the Lake Rabun does offer is rare tranquility and hospitality that draws guests back year after year. In the evenings you can sit by the flagstone hearth, play parlor games, swap tips on local eateries and "secret" waterfalls, and store up energy for the next day's boating, fishing, and hiking. Doubles, with breakfast, are $65.40. The new Boar's Head Restaurant serves dinner Thursday to Monday. Major credit cards are accepted. Closed December to April. Contact Lake Rabun Hotel, Lakemont 30522, (706) 782–4946.

Fishing boats and canoes may be rented at **Hall's Boat House,** next to the hotel. **Lake Rabun Road,** which twists and turns about 15 miles between Highway 441 near Tallulah Falls, to Georgia Highway 197, is a very scenic drive. It curves around Lake Rabun and Seed Lake, with many lovely vistas of the water and woodlands. Ask the proprietors of the Lake Rabun Hotel for directions to **High Branch Falls,** also known as Minnehaha Falls. It's a little tricky to find but well worth the search. During the summer **Rabun Beach Recreation Area,** (706) 782–3320, a state-run facility, is a relaxing place to swim and have a picnic.

Old Highway 441, a curvy two-lane road running north and south between the Lake Rabun crossroads of Lakemont and the Rabun County seat of Clayton, is another picturesque drive. You may stop for a relaxing Southern-style breakfast, lunch, or dinner at the **Green Shutters Inn** (706–782–3342), a pretty little place with an antiques shop upstairs from the dining room, between Clayton and the community of Tiger.

The Clayton Welcome Center (706–782–5113), on Highway 441, can give you further tips on off-the-beaten-path adventures. You may also contact the Rabun County Chamber of Commerce, Box 761, Clayton 30525, (706) 782–4812.

Top Annual Events

Tallulah Falls Whitewater Festival, early April, (706) 754–8590

Bear on the Square Mountain Festival, mid-April, Dahlonega, (706) 864–7817

Athens Home & Garden Tour, late April, (706) 353–1801

Southworks Arts Festival, late May, Watkinsville, (706) 769–4565

Mountain Laurel Festival, mid-May, Clarkesville

Helen-to-Atlantic Hot Air Balloon Race and Festival, early June, (706) 878–2271

Oktoberfest, September and October, Festhalle, Helen, (706) 878–2271

Sorghum Festival, mid-October, Blairsville, (706) 896–5789

Mule Camp Market, mid-October, Gainesville, (770) 532–7714

Georgia Mountain Fall Festival, early to mid-October, Hiawassee, (706) 896–4191

Toccoa Harvest Festival, early November, (706) 886–2132

Alpine Helen Winter Festival, November–January, (706) 865–5356

Lighting of the Chateau, Thanksgiving weekend, Chateau Elan Winery, Braselton, (770) 932–0900

It may be difficult to imagine now, but early in this century, **Tallulah Falls** was one of the South's most popular summer resorts. Honeymooners, families, and other nature-loving city folk came to admire the cataracts of the Tallulah River, which stormed through a gorge 820 feet across and more than 1,200 feet deep. All that ended in the early 1920s, when a series of hydroelectric dams diverted water from the falls but at the same time created Lake Rabun, Lake Burton, and other recreational areas.

Tallulah Gorge Park and Terrora Park and Campground invites hikers to explore the depths of the gorge. The parks department and Georgia Power Company periodically open the floodgates and allow kayakers to experience the falls' glorious power. The Terrora Park area has a fishing pier and picnic tables on the Tallulah River. Exhibits explain Georgia Power's conservation efforts. Fifty campsites have water and electrical hookups. Phone (800) 864–PARK for reservations. If you'd like to hike the gorge, you'll need to register, free of charge, at the visitors center by the Highway 441 bridge. For general information contact Park Superintendent, P.O. Box 248, Tallulah Falls 30573, (706) 754–7970 or (800) 864–7275.

Tallulah Gallery (706–754–6020) has a beautiful selection of paintings, pottery, weaving, and other mountain handicrafts in the parlors of a Victorian mansion built by the president of the now-extinct local railroad. The two-story home is on Highway 441 in the center of the small community. Open daily.

Traveling on Highway 441 between Tallulah Falls and Clayton, Dillard, and Mountain City, you'll be sorely tempted by a raft of mountain-craft shops and art galleries. *Lofty Branch Art and Craft Village,* 6 miles south of Clayton, (706) 782–3863, is a scattered complex of studios offering mostly high-quality weaving, woodwork, leather, pottery, and glass.

Green thumbers shouldn't miss a visit to *Penny's Garden.* Look for a small sign at Highway 441 and Darling Springs Road, north of the entrance to Black Rock Mountain State Park. Follow a winding road to Penny and Don Melton's greenhouse and shop. There you can purchase fresh flowers (you can pick your own), herbs, gourmet jams and vinegars, baskets, garden ornaments, birdhouses, sachets and potpourris, and gourmet herbal foods. You can also sign up for gardening or herbal workshops. Write P.O. Box 305, Blacks Creek Road, Mountain City 30562, or call (706) 746–6918.

The *Foxfire Museum,* on Highway 441, 3 miles north of Clayton, (706) 746–5828, is a treat for all those who've enjoyed the long series of Foxfire Books. The books—in case you're not familiar with them—chronicle the research by students at Rabun Gap-Nacoochee School who were sent into the hills to preserve their endangered heritage. The small museum displays furniture, baskets, logging and woodworking tools, animal traps, farm implements, part of a gristmill, and other necessities of nineteenth- and early twentieth-century Appalachian life. Open Monday through Saturday 9:00 A.M. to 4:30 P.M. Admission is free, but donations are always welcome.

For the ultimate in rustic mountain lodgings and some of Georgia's most accomplished home cooking, head for *LaPrade's*, a cluster of cabins, a dining room, and fishing docks on Highway 197 at Lake Burton. Built in the early 1920s, the spartan pine cabins have full kitchens and bathrooms and sleep up to twelve. Meals are served family-style, all-you-can-eat, at long communal tables in the screened-in dining room.

Breakfast is highlighted by country ham and sausage, hot biscuits and sorghum syrup, and grits and eggs. Chicken and dumplings, barbecue, meat loaf, vegetables, and corn bread are served at weekday lunch. Some of the world's finest Southern fried chicken is the centerpiece of Sunday lunch and weekday dinner.

You may have all those meals—served family-style—and your cabin, for $40 a person a day; ages 3 to 9, half-price; and under age 3, free. If you're just dropping by at mealtime, breakfast is $6.75, lunch $8.75, dinner and Sunday lunch $11.75. Again, children 3 to 9 are fed for half-price and those under age 3 for free. The dining room is closed Tuesday and Wednesday. The entire place is closed from the end of November to the first of April. Contact LaPrade's, Highway 197 North, Clarkesville 30523, (706) 947–3312 and (800) 262–3313 for "The Meal Reservation Hot Line." Also www.LaPrades.com.

Beechwood Inn Bed & Breakfast, P.O. Box 120, Clayton 30525, (706) 782–5485, fax (706) 782–5485, is one of the mountain country's newest and nicest small lodgings. Innkeeper Marty Lott fastidiously restored this old Rabun County summer vacation house, originally built in 1922. On a rise, among terraced gardens, the house has dramatic views of the neighboring mountains. Five guest rooms have queen-size or twin beds. All have their own baths, and some have working fireplaces. Marty sends you off in the morning with an excellent full breakfast. The location is especially convenient to launching points for Chattooga River rafting adventures. Rates of $85 to $135 include a big mountain breakfast.

Two scenic state parks in Rabun County offer a wealth of outdoor activities and overnight lodgings. *Black Rock Mountain State Park,* 1,500 acres of brawny beauty atop a 3,600-foot elevation of the Blue Ridge Mountains, has an eighteen-acre lake, many miles of wooded nature trails, waterfalls, and campsites with electrical and water hookups and kitchens. Contact Park Superintendent, Black Rock Mountain, P.O. Drawer A, Mountain City 30562, (706) 746–2141, (800) 864–PARK.

Moccasin Creek State Park, on Lake Burton, has a boat ramp and docks, a trout hatchery, hiking trails, and campsites. For reservations phone (800) 864–PARK. Contact Park Superintendent, Moccasin Creek State Park, Route 1, Box 1634, Clarkesville 30523; (706) 947–3194.

For twelve days early every August, the normally unhurried Towns County seat of Hiawassee (population 1,985) throbs with the energy of the *Georgia Mountain Fair.* Against a backdrop of Blue Ridge Mountains, forests, and blue-green lakes, the fair takes Hiawassee and the rest of Georgia's *"Little Switzerland"* literally by storm.

The fairgrounds resound with the music of bluegrass fiddlers, gospel singers, clog dancers, and some of the very big names of the country music entertainment world. Scores of craftspeople show off their skills at woodworking, pottery, cornshuck and applehead dolls, painting, leatherwork, furniture and toy making, jewelry, basket weaving, needlework, quilting, and macramé.

Pioneer Village is like a walk through a mountain town of yesteryear. You can peruse the canned goods and bolt cloth in the mercantile store, see the hickory switch in the one-room schoolhouse, visit the smokehouse, and stop in at the hand-hewn log cabin. Elsewhere on the forty-two-acre grounds, you can taste just-squeezed apple cider and see a "moonshine" whiskey still up close. "Revenooers" keep a close guard against any free samples. For information contact Towns County Chamber of Commerce, 1140 Fuller Court, Hiawassee 30546, (706) 896–4966.

From early June to early August you can enjoy *"The Reach of Song."* Georgia's official state historic drama tells the story of the mountain folk with fiddling, gospel singing, dancing, tale swapping, and problem sharing. It's performed from late June to late August in a new auditorium on the Young Harris College Campus, Young Harris 30582, (800) 262–7664, (706) 379–4312.

Also at the college, the Rollins Planetarium has seasonal shows on Friday nights and free telescope viewings.

Most of the year *Lake Chatuge* is a great place at which to play. The 7,500-acre Tennessee Valley Authority (TVA) reservoir on the western edge of the Hiawassee is a tranquil retreat for trout and bass fishermen, waterskiers, swimmers, and boaters. Several marinas and public boat docks offer easy access to the lake. You'll also find picnic grounds, tennis courts, a sand beach, playgrounds, and camping sites at the 160-acre *Towns County Park* on the lakeside.

The *Chattahoochee National Forest* blankets much of Towns County with Georgia pines and hardwoods. Sections of four national wilderness areas in the county afford you the opportunity to get well off the beaten track. During certain times of the year, the Appalachian Trail, crossing Towns County near Brasstown Bald Mountain, gets downright busy as hikers test their stamina on the 2,000-mile Maine-to-Georgia route described at the beginning of this chapter.

Brasstown Bald Mountain, 4,784 feet, is Georgia's highest point. A steep, winding road off Highway 180 takes you to a parking area a half mile from the top, where you'll find rest rooms and a gift shop. You can hike the paved, moderately strenuous trail to the visitors center/observation platform, or take a shuttle van, $1.50 per person. There's a $2.00 parking fee in the lot. Be sure your car is up to the task before heading up the mountain. Many a vehicle has been left overheated and steaming by the roadside.

Fieldstone Inn Brings Bob Cloer Full Circle

*B*ob Cloer still remembers the morning in 1939 when a shiny black car drove up to his family's farm near Hiawassee. At supper that night, his father told the family that the Tennessee Valley Authority was going to take their farm for a dam that would create Lake Chatuge. Cloer's father reluctantly accepted the $6,500 TVA paid for the forty-acre farm and built a boat dock on the lake, which was fully filled by 1942.

"My mother told me to get out of Hiawassee and get an education," Cloer recalls. "I got a law degree at the University of Georgia but went into construction. My roots in Towns County brought me back, and the **Fieldstone Inn and Conference Center** is the result of inspiration I got from my parents."

In 1987, he built the Fieldstone on surplus land TVA sold back to his family. The sixty-six-room wood and fieldstone inn sits only a few hundred feet from his family's original homesite (now under water). Guests in comfortably furnished modern rooms can look out their windows at a panorama of the lake and surrounding mountains. They also get a view from big windows in the dining room. Big stone fireplaces in the lobby ward off the brisk mountain air. There's an outdoor heated pool, tennis courts, a whirlpool, and the lake usually rewards fishermen with catches of bass, bream. crappie, and bluegill. Doubles are $90 to $125. Phone (800) 545–3408 or (770) 446–1550.

You may follow the 5½-mile Arkaquah Trail from the crest of Trackrock Gap and the less-strenuous 2½-mile Jack's Trail Knob to the foot of Brasstown. Wagon Train Road meanders 6 miles to a pastoral valley that cradles the pretty town of Young Harris and the campus of Young Harris College.

A short drive from Brasstown Bald Mountain, *7 Creeks Housekeeping Cabins,* 5109 Horseshoe Cove Road, Blairsville 30512, (706) 745–4753, fax (706) 745–2904, is an answered prayer for anyone who's ever dreamt of "getting away from it all." In the midst of gorgeous mountain scenery, the seven cabins have baths, full kitchens, grills, and picnic tables. You can swim and fish in a private lake, pet farm animals, and play badminton and horseshoes. Furnished cabins (guests bring towels and bedsheets) sleeping four, six, and eight are $60 to $65 a day for one or two persons, $5.00 for each additional person; $350 to $375 for a week, $25.00 for each additional person.

Brasstown Valley Resort, opened in 1995 on a scenic 503-acre Blue Ridge mountainscape, has all the upscale resort bells and whistles: 134 attractively appointed guest rooms in the four-story main lodge and adjacent cottages; 18-hole, 7,000-yard Scottish links–style golf course; and tennis, horseshoes, trout fishing, horseback riding, indoor/outdoor pool, fitness center, and full-service restaurant and lounge. It's a great place to roost for a while and an excellent base while sightseeing in the surrounding mountainlands. Lodge rooms run $99 to $174 for a double, cottages $109 to $169 per bedroom. Brasstown Resort is in Young Harris 30582, (706) 379–9900.

Deer Lodge, a hideaway near the junction of Highways 66 and 75, is another heaven-sent place to park a while and savor the glories of the mountains. Hospitable proprietors Richard and Willene Haigler serve some of the biggest, best, and lowest-priced steaks and trout anywhere in these parts. Cabins secluded in the nearby woods are $25 a night for two persons and $45 for four. Contact Deer Lodge, Hiawassee 30546, (706) 896–2726.

The *Russell-Brasstown Scenic Highway,* in White and Union Counties, takes you through the heart of some of northeast Georgia's most spectacular mountain country. Designated as Highway 348, the 14-mile paved highway takes you from the outskirts of Georgia's "Alpine Village" of Helen, across the Appalachian Trail, to the state's highest mountain and a picture postcard state park. Several parking areas and overlooks give you the chance to stop and admire the rugged beauty of the Blue Ridge Mountains. The drive is especially striking in mid-October to early November, when the hardwoods turn a brilliant orange, yellow, and scarlet.

One of the Scenic Highway's "high points" is 3,137-foot Tesnatee Gap, where the Appalachian Trail crosses on its way between Maine and Springer Mountain, Georgia. You can get out of your car here and mingle a while with the earnest hikers. At its northwestern end the Scenic Highway intersects with Highway 180. If you turn right, you may explore 4,784-foot Brasstown Bald. A steep, paved road ends at a parking area 930 feet below the summit. From here either hike to the crest of Georgia's highest peak or take a commercial van up to the view of four states.

A left turn at Highway 180 will lead you to Highway 19 and **Vogel State Park.** Cradled in mountains, beside a pretty lake, Vogel is a delightful place for fishing, boating, warm weather swimming, and year-round hiking on woodland trails. The park's seventy-two campsites have

Brasstown Valley Resort's Gourmet Trout

*T*alented young Chef Steve Walsh's cuisine is a big reason Brasstown Valley Resort has quickly become one of the mountains' most popular destinations.

TROUT WITH SPICY PECAN COMPOUND BUTTER

4 whole deboned trout

2 cups crushed pecans

2 cups bread crumbs

1 cup flour

3 beaten eggs

Salt and pepper to taste

Combine pecans and bread crumbs and place in a pan. Season flour with salt and pepper and place in a separate pan; put beaten eggs in another pan. Dredge meat side of the trout in flour, then eggs, then the pecan–bread crumbs mixture. Place on an oiled

350° griddle, meat side down, for about 4 to 5 minutes. Turn skin side down and cook an additional 4 to 5 minutes or until flesh is firm.

SPICY PECAN COMPOUND BUTTER

1 pound melted butter

½ pound pecan pieces

½ teaspoon cumin

½ teaspoon cayenne pepper

¼ cup honey

1 tablespoon lemon zest

1 tablespoon orange zest

½ teaspoon vanilla extract

1 tablespoon garlic salt

Blend all ingredients and ladle over trout at serving time. Serves 4.

electricity, water, hot showers, and rest rooms; thirty-six rustic but very snug cottages, by the lake and in the adjacent woodlands, are equipped down to sheets, towels, pots, and pans. For reservations phone (800) 864–PARK. The park also has a $2.00 one-time parking fee. The park office is open 8:00 A.M. to 5:00 P.M. Contact Vogel State Park, Blairsville 30512, (706) 745–2628.

Georgia Highway 180, which joins U.S. Highway 19 north of Vogel Park, is a 22-mile scenic mountain route to the little community of Suches. Along the way stop at *Sosebee Cove Scenic Area,* where a half-mile loop trail takes you through a second growth forest with wildflowers and rhododendron. Farther along *Lake Winfield Scott Recreation Area* has a thirty-two-acre campground with showers ($6.00 a night) and an eighteen-acre fishing and swimming lake. There is a $2.00 parking fee for noncampers.

Habersham County claims some of northeast Georgia's most photogenic Blue Ridge Mountain country. These mountains and valleys, thousands of acres of Chattahoochee National Forest, and scores of lakes and streams offer limitless opportunities to take a hike, ride a bike, camp out, and fish, swim, and otherwise unwind.

Habersham is one of Georgia's major apple producers. Rich soil and a cool climate encouraged English and Canadian families to initiate the apple-growing arts here in the 1920s. In October, roadside stands overflow with Red Delicious, Stayman Winesaps, dark red Yates, and bright yellow-green Granny Smiths. You can buy 'em by the sackful or the carload and also purchase homemade apple jelly, apple butter, and ice-cold, freshly squeezed sweet apple cider by the glass and gallon jugful. As a rule Habersham owners don't allow visitors to come in and pick their own fruit.

Habersham County also produces enough grapes to merit location of one of Georgia's major wineries. *Habersham Vineyards* (706–778–WINE) at Highways 365 and 441 near the small town of Baldwin, produces more than a dozen types of wine, including pinot blanc, Chablis, chardonnay, Riesling, and sauvignon. Habersham's Georgia muscadine wine has won gold medals in international competitions. Other wines have captured silver and bronze medals here and overseas.

You may tour the winery and enjoy free samples Monday through Saturday 10:00 A.M. to 5:00 P.M. and Sunday 1:00 to 6:00 P.M.

Clarkesville, Habersham's snug little county seat, is a happy hunting ground for antiques and mountain handicrafts. Several shops around the courthouse square on Highway 441 are loaded with handcrafted furniture, pottery, paintings, weaving, leatherwork, handmade baskets and quilts, toys, dolls, jellies, jams, and preserves.

When all that browsing and decision making saps your strength, go get recharged at *The Trolley* (706–754–5565), a turn-of-the-century drugstore turned into a most attractive cafe. Owner Stephen Woodard has re-created the old soda fountain feeling with ceiling fans, country antiques, and old-timey chairs and tables. The service area is behind the marble soda fountain. The menu includes fresh mountain trout, steaks, prime rib, and Mediterranean and Mexican dishes. Prices are inexpensive to moderate at lunch and dinner Tuesday through Saturday. The Trolley is located on Highway 441 at the town square, Clarkesville 30523.

> ## "My Old War Horse"
>
> *General James Longstreet, the Confederate hero who Robert E. Lee called "My Old War Horse," survived his numerous Civil War battles and retired to Gainesville, where he lived from 1875 until his peaceful death in 1904. After he hung up his uniform and sidearms, Longstreet ran a hotel, a farm, and a vineyard and became a leader of the Republican Party. He and his family are buried in Gainesville's Alta Vista Cemetery.*

The *Glen-Ella Springs Hotel* sits on seventeen pastoral acres, off Highway 441/23 between Clarkesville and Tallulah Falls. Owners Barrie and Bobby Aycock have converted the one-hundred-year-old hotel building into a sixteen-room country inn, full of rustic touches and modern conveniences. In warm weather, enjoy the outdoor swimming pool. All the rooms have porches with rocking chairs, antiques, and heart-of-pine paneling. Some have fireplaces and whirlpools. The dining room features fresh mountain trout but varies from traditional mountain fare with veal dishes, pasta, scallops, fresh fish, and other American/continental entrees. Doubles are $115 to $175, including full breakfast. Contact the Aycocks, Route 3, Bear Gap Road, Clarkesville 30523, (706) 754–7295.

Burns-Sutton House, 855 Washington Street, Clarkesville 30523, (706) 754–5565, fax (706) 754–9698, an imposing early 1900s Queen Anne house, has been tastefully restored by innkeeper Jaime Huffman. Seven guest rooms have period furnishings, heart pine floors, and woodwork. Some have shared bath. Enjoy the mountain breezes on the wraparound front porch. Full breakfast is included in rates of $60 to $90. Jeffrey's, a restaurant by Jeffrey Bailey, of Clarkesville's former Taylor's Trolley, serves dinner Tuesday through Saturday and Sunday brunch.

Highway 197, twisting and turning north between Clarkesville and Clayton, is considered one of north Georgia's prettiest drives. The *Mark of the Potter,* 9 miles north of Clarkesville, (706) 947–3440, is a favorite stop for mountain visitors. The weathered old white frame corn-grinding mill, by the rapids of the Soque River, sells some of the finest work of Georgia's most accomplished craftspeople. Shelves are laden with superb pottery, colorful fabrics, metal, and leatherwork. Open daily.

You'll also find a feast of fine folk art at these nearby galleries: Rosehips Gallery, Highway 129 South, Cleveland, (706) 865–6345; Burton Gallery and Emporium, Burton Dam Road, Clarkesville, (706) 947–1351; Timpson Creek Gallery, Highway 76, Clayton, (706) 782–5164; and Gourdcraft Originals, Highway 384, Sautee, (706) 865–4048. You can check out many of the artists on the Internet at www.rosehipsart.com.

Browsing inevitably will take you onto the porch overhanging the Soque to throw treats to the fat, pampered trout swimming in the river's pools. Mark of the Potter (706–947–3440) is open daily. If you follow Highway 197 another 8 miles north, you'll be at the dining room of LaPrade's, one of the mountains' most famous eateries (see page 165). Habersham also shares Tallulah Falls and Tallulah Gorge with Rabun County.

South of Clarkesville, the little town of **Demorest,** on Highway 441, is worth a visit. A couple of antiques shops are on the short main street, and you may stroll through the peaceful campus of Piedmont College.

When your children pose that age-old question—"Where do babies come from?"—take them to Cleveland and show them. At Cleveland's **Babyland General Hospital** (706–865–2171) some very special "babies" come from a cabbage patch. Originally a doctor's turn-of-the-century clinic, the white frame "hospital" at 19 Underwood Street/Highway 129 is where the soft-sculpted Cabbage Patch Kids, created by White County's own Xavier Roberts, first see day's light. Uniformed "nurses" lead you through the nursery, day-care center, and delivery room. At the magic moment, a "doctor" in surgical garb plucks a new-born Kid from a patch of sculpted cabbage leaves to "oohs" and "aahs" all around. You can take home a cuddly Cabbage Patch Kid of your very own. Just remember, they're "babies," not "dolls"; not "bought," but "adopted." The hospital is open Monday through Saturday 9:00 A.M. to 5:00 P.M. and Sunday 10:00 A.M. to 5:00 P.M. Free admission.

Cleveland's town square has lots of places to buy pottery, weaving, paintings, and other mountain handicrafts. For a taste of the mountains, head for **Ma Gooch's** (706–865–2023), a cafe and social center where locals meet to eat and exchange the day's news over breakfast, lunch, and dinner. It's in front of the Gateway Motel at Highways 192 and 17.

If the sheer granite escarpments of *Mount Yonah,* off Highway 75 north of Cleveland, set your rock-climbing juices flowing, make plans to scale the heights with commercial outfitters in Atlanta. High Country Outfitters (404–434–7578) will put you in the proper climbing gear and send you up Yonah's 150- to 300-foot cliffs with experienced guides. Mount Yonah is also one of Georgia's best and most popular hang-gliding points.

Driving up to the *Old Sautee Store* (706–878–2281) at the junction of Highways 17 and 255, you might imagine an old-time mercantile stocked with bolts of cloth, seeds, farm implements, and sacks of cornmeal. Walk inside and what do your wondering eyes behold, but an array of tempting goods from Scandinavia: Norwegian and Icelandic sweaters, jackets, and coats; crystal, dinnerware, needlework, gourmet foods, jewelry, and unique gifts from Sweden, Denmark, and Finland. On special occasions, owner Astrid Fried appears in her ornate Norwegian wedding dress. The adjacent log cabin sells Christmas ornaments year-round. The store is open daily.

You can spread a picnic by the *Stovall Covered Bridge,* in a small park by Chickamauga Creek on Highway 255. Only 33 feet long, the bridge is one of the shortest anywhere in Georgia.

The *Stovall House,* nearby on Highway 255, is one of the nicest country inns anywhere in the state. Built in 1837, the handsome two-story frame house is in the heart of the scenic Sautee Nacoochee Valley. Five guest rooms are decorated with country antiques and all the modern comforts. The dining room features Southern and continental cooking and is one of the best anywhere in the mountains. For pure, sweet relaxation, settle yourself into a porch swing and listen to the absolute peace of this lovely countryside. Rates are $50 single, $80 double, all with private bath and breakfast. Contact the Stovall House, Route 1, Box 103-A, Sautee 30571, (706) 878–3355.

Highway 17 cuts a most picturesque path through the Sautee-Nacoochee Valley as it meanders westerly toward Helen. You may want to stop for a picture—or attend Sunday services—at *Crescent Hill Baptist Church,* on a wooded hillock near the intersection of Highways 17 and 75. The pretty Carpenter Gothic church was built in the 1870s by the same well-off gentleman who built the grand Victorian house and gazebo atop the Indian mound at Highways 17 and 75.

Going north on combined Highway 17/75, stop off at *Nora Mill Granary & Store* (706–878–2927). Founded in 1876 on the banks of the Chattahoochee River, the mill's current owners still grind corn into meal and grits in the tried and true old-fashioned way. It's open daily.

Don't try to pinch yourself awake as you drive by the WILKOMMEN signs of *"Alpine Helen."* You haven't wandered onto a Disney film set. About twenty years ago this then-humble mountain hamlet underwent a wholesale transformation into a make-believe Alpine village. Nowadays, the red-tile roofs, flower boxes, biergartens, and stucco-fronted shops selling cuckoo clocks, Christmas ornaments, Tyrolean hats, and loden coats put the once-quiet village very much on the well-beaten path. Outlet stores, with all the usual suspects, are amassed on the south end of town.

Like it or disdain it, Helen's worth at least a short stroll and a browse. The many inns and "hofs" around town are good bases for more off-the-beaten-path adventures, such as the Appalachian Trail, Russell-Brasstown Scenic Byway, and Chattahoochee National Forest. In trout season, you can don your waders and cast in the Chattahoochee River, which rises near here and wends its bonny way through the middle of town.

More Blue Ridge than Bavarian, *Betty's Country Store* (706– 878–2943), on the north end of town, has grown into a full-blown supermarket. The modern store with some rustic ambience is loaded with jams and jellies, fresh vegetables, gourds, cookbooks, canned goods, cheeses, fresh meat and fish, gourmet coffee, apple cider, and other goods.

Hofer's of Helen, across from Betty's, 8758 North Main Street, (706) 878–8200, fits tongue-in-groove with Helen's Bavarian motif. Walk in the door and you'll be intoxicated by the aromas of fresh-baked breads, cakes, cookies, and strudels. In the cozy dining room, treat yourselves to Belgian waffles with maple syrup and whipped cream, Alpine French toast, and a variety of bountiful omelets; the lunch menu includes bratwurst and sauerkraut, German-style meatloaf, smoked pork chops, grilled and deli sandwiches. Breakfast and lunch daily.

At *Troll Tavern,* Castle Inn, Main Street, Helen, (706) 754–5566, sit on an outdoor terrace by the Chattahoochee and watch the tubers float gently through Helen. The menu includes bratwurst, smoked pork chops, chicken, fish, deli sandwiches, German beer and wine. Lunch and dinner is served Monday through Saturday.

If you've never made it to Munich for Oktoberfest, Helen has a scaled-down replica. In late September and early October, the town's pavilion resounds to oompah bands and thousands of folk-dancing feet. In late October and early November, the mountain hardwoods change their colors as brilliantly as those in New England, making this an especially worthwhile time to visit. It's also prime season for freshly squeezed apple cider and boiled peanuts. Simmered in brine in huge iron kettles, the goobers are warm, salty, sticky, and a special mountain delicacy that not everyone goes for, but that should at least be experienced.

Unicoi State Park, just north of Helen, is a treat that everyone can enjoy. With 1,081 acres of highlands and woodlands, threaded by streams, lakes, and waterfalls, there's plenty of off-the-beaten-path solitude.

Swimming, canoeing, and fishing focus on a picture-postcard fifty-three-acre lake. You may take solitary walks on 12 miles of trails and take part in nature walks led by park naturalists. Craftspeople share the secrets of pottery, quilting, dulcimer- and furniture-making, and other mountain arts. The handicraft shop in the Unicoi Lodge sells an array of beautiful items.

Also in the lodge the cafeteria-style dining room serves excellent breakfast, lunch, and dinner at extremely low prices. The park's accommodations include ninety-six camping sites, with water, electricity, nearby showers, and rest rooms; and two- and three-bedroom, completely furnished cottages. For reservations call (800) 864–PARK. Contact Park Superintendent, P.O. Box 849, Helen 30545, (706) 878–2201.

Anna Ruby Falls is the awesome showpiece of a 1,600-acre Chattahoochee National Forest recreation area that neighbors Unicoi. From the parking area follow a moderately strenuous half-mile trail through the woodlands bordering a swift-flowing stream. An observation platform sits at the base of Anna Ruby's two cascades, dropping dramatically 153 and 50 feet over the edge of Tray Mountain. Back at the parking area, restore your energy with a picnic by the water's edge. A handsome new visitors center has an excellent gift shop and a porch from which you can toss treats to some of creation's fattest trout. A Trail for the Blind identifies trees and plants in Braille. There is a $2.00 per car parking fee.

Two remarkable donations of land have enhanced Helen's attraction to nature and wilderness lovers. *Smithgall Woods Conservation Area* west of town, and the Hardman Farm, south of town, are peaceful counterpoints to the hyper Alpine Village.

In 1994, north Georgia publisher Charles Smithgall made his pristine 5,600 acres of woodlands and streams a gift-purchase to the state. Although it's administered by the state park system, the similarities to other parks are few. Virtually no car traffic is allowed. Visitors who wish to hike the preserve's three wilderness trails and catch-and-release trout in 4-mile Duke's Creek sign in at the Visitors Center and take a free shuttle bus to their destinations. Mountain bikers may use 12 miles of improved roads. On the Martin's Mine Historic Trail, hikers can stop at the site of an 1893 gold mine, with a 125-foot deep shaft and a 900-foot-long tunnel. Groups of eight or more can stay overnight in furnished cottages, including Charles Smithgall's almost-palatial former home, fashioned from mammoth lodgepole pines. If you want to fish, reserve a place at least a couple of weeks in advance. In order to give everybody casting room, only fifteen are allowed on the creek at the same time. A $2.00 parking pass is the only charge. Open daily, it's located at Highway 75-Alt, 3 miles west of Helen, and just south of the Richard B. Russell Scenic Highway (Highway 348). Phone (706) 878–3087.

The 170-acre **Hardman Farm** was developed in the late 1860s. In 1902, Gov. Lamartine G. Hardman, a farmer and medical doctor, purchased the property and experimented with crop rotation, soil testing, and other new ideas. His heirs donated the property to the state in 1997. By late 1999 or early 2000, the Italianate villa (built in 1870) and twenty-one historic buildings in the Chattahoochee River's picturesque Nacoochee Valley will be transformed into a living museum. Blacksmiths, bakers, farm workers, and country tradesmen will provide a window to nineteenth- and early twentieth-century life. Guides will interpret the villa's many antiques and architectural features. The site also includes one of the mountains' most photographed landmarks, an ancient Indian mound crowned by a century-old Victorian gazebo. Look for it at the junction of Highways 17 and 75, on Helen's southern outskirts. For information contact Trust for Public Land, 1447 Peachtree Street, Atlanta 30309, (404) 873–7306, fax (404) 875–9099.

The Nacoochee Valley gets its name from a Native American version of *Romeo and Juliet*. According to legend, Cherokee Princess Nacoochee fell in love with a warrior from an enemy tribe. Her father captured the suitor and had him executed. In her grief, Nacoochee leapt to her death from Mont Yonah on the western end of the valley. Some say her tearful laments can still be heard on moonlit nights.

In 1828 a trapper named Benjamin Parks allegedly stubbed his toe on a rock in **Dahlonega** and shouted the north Georgia version of "Eureka!" as he gazed at a vein of gold that soon sent prospectors streaming into these hills. *Dahlonega* is a Cherokee Indian word meaning "precious yellow," and until the War Between the States, the substance flowed into a major U.S. Mint right here. Although it's no longer a major industry, enough gold is still mined to periodically releaf the dome of Georgia's state capitol and intrigue visitors who pan for it at reconstructed camps. The *Dahlonega Visitors Center* on the square has rest rooms and information on anything you could possibly be interested in. Phone (706) 864–3711 or access www.dahlonega.org.

True to its heritage, the *Dahlonega Courthouse Gold Museum,* in the center of the little town of 2,800, chronicles the gold rush and the numerous mines that flourished in these parts. A twenty-eight-minute film upstairs in the old courtroom is especially worthwhile. Operated by the Georgia Department of Natural Resources, the Gold Museum, Dahlonega 30533, (706) 864–2257, is open Tuesday through Saturday 9:00 A.M. to 5:00 P.M. and Sunday 2:00 to 5:30 P.M. Adults are $2.00; ages 6 to 18, $1.00; under age 5, no charge.

Buildings around the square have a rustic frontier look. Shops purvey gold-panning equipment, ice cream, fudge, mountain handicrafts, gold jewelry, and antiques. Many people make the 70-mile drive north from Atlanta just to feast at the famous *Smith House.* It's off the square at 202 South Chestatee Street, Dahlonega 30533, (706) 864–3566. The Smith House puts out huge family-style spreads with fried chicken, chicken and dumplings, beef stew, shrimp, numerous vegetables, biscuits, relishes, and dessert for about $12 a person. They also serve breakfast and have a cafeteria line for those not up to the full board. It's open daily except Monday.

You can stay close to the chow line in the Smith House's sixteen guest rooms, all with private baths, for $59 to $129. Many other restaurants, inns, and motels are close to the square.

Gainesville's Spanish Accent

*M*exican and other Latin American immigrants who've flocked to Gainesville to work in scores of poultry processing plants have given the northeast Georgia city a bilingual accent. As they comprise about 20 percent of the town's 20,000 population, Latinos have their own newspaper, radio shows, churches, restaurants, specialty stores, and other businesses. Gainesville is the center of the Georgia poultry industry, which annually produces about eight million pounds of chickens for tables around the world. Latinos are also highly visible in Dalton's carpet making plants, agriculture, and other labor-intensive industries around the state.

The **Worley Homestead Inn,** at 410 West Main Street, Dahlonega 30533, (706) 864–7002, is a short stroll from the Gold Museum, restaurants, and shops on Dahlonega's square. Seven guest rooms in the mid-nineteenth-century Victorian house are full of antiques and pictures of Worley family ancestors. Each has a private bath, some with claw-foot tubs. There are even rumors of a friendly resident haint. The $85 double weekdays, $95 Friday and Saturday, tariff qualifies you for a huge country breakfast.

Mountain Top Lodge has a wealth of creature comforts including air-conditioning, contemporary-country furnishings, private baths, and outdoor patios. An outdoor hot tub eases the aches of a hard day on the craft-shopping trail. Doubles, with a huge breakfast, are $60 to $125. Located down a winding farm road and atop a wooded hill 5 miles southwest of the Dahlonega square, the Mountain Top has thirteen guest rooms in its main lodge and adjacent cottage. Route 7, Box 150, Dahlonega 30533; or phone (706) 864–5257.

Gold Rush Days, the third weekend of October, celebrates the gilded heritage with arts and crafts, clog dancing, and lots of bluegrass fiddling and singing. You can pan for gold year-round at **Crisson's Mine,** Wimpy Mill Road, Dahlonega 30533. You'll feel some of old Benjamin Park's excitement and might even whoop out "Eureka!" when you spot a few grains gleaming amid the mud in your pan. Phone (706) 864–6363.

You can also take a guided walk through the tunnels of the old **Consolidated Mine.** At the turn of the century, it was the largest and richest gold mine in the eastern United States. It went mysteriously bankrupt in 1906, and much of the old equipment is still in place. Phone (706) 864–8473.

Dahlonega is a popular gateway to the northeast Georgia mountain vacation areas. From here Highway 19 snakes north toward Vogel State Park, while other roads aim toward Helen, Cleveland, and Amicalola State Park.

Two of north Georgia's most interesting and unusual dining and lodging places are off the beaten path among the green hills and marble quarries of Pickens County. The Woodbridge Inn at Jasper and the Tate House at Tate depart joyously and deliciously from the culinary path most often trod in rural Georgia.

German-born Joe Rueffert and his Georgia-born wife, Brenda, have been the hospitable proprietors of the **Woodbridge Restaurant and Inn** for more than fifteen years. On the surface, the rustic pre–Civil War inn, with the checkered tablecloths and big windows with panoramic views of the mountains, gives few hints of surprises. It's only when Joe dons his chef's hat and parades from the kitchen with grilled swordfish steaks, fresh grouper, and mahi-mahi with rich creamy sauces; chateaubriand forestière and steak au poivre; veal dishes with silken béarnaise and hollandaise sauces; roast duckling with orange sauce; bananas Foster and other luscious desserts, that the wealth of this "find" finally sinks in.

You may select American or European wines and beers from the Woodbridge list. After your feast, you're only a few steps from your lodgings in the inn's chalet-style rooms. Comfortably furnished and air-conditioned, the eighteen large rooms come with complimentary mountain views for $50 to $80. The dining room serves lunch on Sunday and dinner Tuesday through Saturday. Prices are moderate, and major credit cards are accepted. Contact Woodbridge Inn, 411 Chambers Street, Jasper 30143, (706) 692–6293.

The inn is, true to its name, across a wooden bridge, at the northern edge of the bucolic small town of Jasper. If you've forgotten how sweet and peaceful a town of 5,000 can be, take a leisurely constitutional on Jasper's main street, and chat with the folks in the stores and around the Pickens County Courthouse. The Ruefferts don't serve breakfast, so you may wish to indulge in the grits and eggs at one of Jasper's hometown cafes.

A driving tour of Pickens County is a nice way to spend a day. *John's Mill*, a nineteenth-century water-powered mill, is a picturesque place to picnic and to buy a sackful of stone-ground cornmeal. From the junction of Highway 53 and I–575, drive west on Highway 53 about 7 miles and turn right on the road between the Hinton Milling Co. and a service station. Continue ¼ mile to the John's Mill sign and turn left; the log cabin mill and stone dam are at the bottom of the hill. There's no phone, but the mill is usually in operation on weekdays and Saturdays.

Amicalola Falls State Park and the *Appalachian Trail approach trail* are a scenic half-hour drive from Jasper, in neighboring Dawson County. The 400-acre park, centered on a majestic 729-foot waterfall has hiking trails above and below the falls, picnic areas, fishing, campsites—with electricity, water, hot showers, and rest rooms—and furnished cottages with fireplaces. The handsome *Amicalola Falls Lodge* has fifty-seven guest rooms with spectacular views and all the modern comforts. For reservations phone (800) 864–PARK. Contact the park at Star Route, Box 215, Dawsonville 30534, (706) 265–8888. The Appalachian Trail is described at the beginning of this chapter.

The mountain may not have come to Mohammed, as the old saying goes, but in 1957, an inland sea came to northeast Georgia's Hall

County. The U.S. Army Corps of Engineers closed the Buford Dam on the Chattahoochee River and created Lake Sidney Lanier. Nowadays about 25,000 of the lake's 38,000 acres and some 380 miles of its green and hilly 550-mile shoreline cover former Hall County farmlands and forests.

Lake Lanier Islands is the huge waterway's biggest recreational package. Developed by the state on wooded hilltops that bobbed above the water after the dam was closed, the islands have a lifeguarded, Florida-sand swimming beach; an 850,000-gallon wave pool; mild and hair-raising water slides; miniature golf and championship golf; all kinds of rental boats, such as houseboats, pontoon boats, sport boats, ski boats, sailboats, fishing boats, and paddleboats; horseback riding; picnic grounds; campgrounds; and two deluxe resort hotels. *Renaissance Pine Isle Resort* (770–945–8921 or 800–468–3571) has 250 guest rooms, three restaurants, indoor and outdoor tennis, and an indoor/outdoor swimming pool. Stouffer PineIsle Resort Golf Course wraps 8 of its 18 holes around the lakeshore. *Lake Lanier Islands Hilton Resort* (770–945–8787 or 800–221–2424), with 224 guest rooms and full amenities, invites guests and nonguests to challenge its par-72 championship-style Emerald Pointe golf course.

While you're admiring the scenery, beware of thirteen water holes! The Islands' 300 lakeside campsites are equipped with water, electricity, and some sewer hookups. Campers also have their own fishing pier, outdoor pavilion, and boat launch ramp. For reservations phone (770) 932–7270. Admission to the Islands' wave pool and water slides, including the swimming beach, is $18.95 for adults and $11.95 age 3 to 47 inches tall; ages 2 and under, free. For information contact Lake Lanier Islands, 6950 Holiday Road, Lake Lanier Islands 30518, (770) 932–7200 or (800) 840–5253; and *Gainesville-Hall County Convention and Visitors Bureau,* 830 Green Street, Gainesville 30501, (770) 536–6206.

At the end of a big day of fishing, boating, and swimming, join famished natives at *Major McGill's Fish House,* an unpretentious and always busy set of dining rooms in the small community of Flowery Branch, just off Highway 13, (770) 967–6001. Specialties are fried and broiled Lake Lanier catfish, oysters, shrimp, mountain trout, steaks, and chicken.

Gainesville, the Hall County seat (population about 20,000; Hall County, 95,000), is a popular gateway to the northeast Georgia vacationlands. Before heading for the hills, enjoy a leisurely stroll through the **Green Street Historical District.** The wide, tree-lined thoroughfare, also designated as Highway 129, holds a wealth of late nineteenth- and early twentieth-century Victorian and Neoclassical Revival residences.

Also in the Green Street Historical District, the *Quinlan Art Center* (770–536–2575) shows the works of state, regional, and national artists Monday through Saturday 10:00 A.M. to 4:00 P.M. and Sundays 2:00 to 5:00 P.M. at no charge.

The *Georgia Mountains Museum,* 311 Green Street, (770) 536–0889, fills an old two-story fire station with history and memorabilia of Georgia's hardy mountainfolk. One of the most popular exhibits is the "Ed Dodd Room," dedicated to the Gainesville native son who created the "Mark Trail" comic strip adventurer. You'll also see excellent displays on Native Americans, Black history, textiles, Gainesville's vital poultry industry, spinning, weaving, and pioneer life. Two blocks from the main museum, the affiliated *Railroad Museum* houses memorabilia in a renovated baggage car. Open Tuesday to Saturday. Free admission.

Elachee Nature Science Center, at 2125 Elachee Drive, (770) 535–1976, is a great place to get lost in the woods for a while and learn something about the world around us. The heavily wooded, 1,200-acre preserve's many fascinating experiences include please-touch fish, amphibians, reptiles, and a 300-gallon trout tank. The interactive, computer, and contemporary music–enhanced "If Everyone Lived Like Me" exhibit looks at the effects of our lifestyles on our environment. Enjoy the tranquil beauty of the Chicopee Woods Nature Preserve on 2½ miles of nature trails, where you can take a close look at animal and plant habitats. Open Monday to Saturday 10:00 A.M. to 5:00 P.M. Adults, $3.00; children, $1.50.

All the buildings around *Roosevelt Square,* in the center of Gainesville, have a distinctive 1930s Art Deco look. That's because all the older buildings in the area were lost, along with many lives, in a monster tornado in 1936. President Franklin D. Roosevelt's New Deal programs rebuilt the devastated town, and he spoke here at dedication ceremonies in 1938.

If you enjoy unusual monuments, bring your camera to *Poultry Park,* where a rooster atop a granite obelisk hails Gainesville's distinction as "Poultry Capital of the World." Some 2.6 million broilers leave here every week for kitchens around the world.

Wineries and Big Lakes

Created by U.S. Army Corps of Engineers impoundments of the Savannah River, *Lake Hartwell* is a vast inland sea whose 55,000 acres offer limitless off-the-beaten-path opportunities for fishing, boating, swimming, and nature hikes. You can headquarter at two state parks on the lake and play another park's 9-hole golf course. While meandering the green, hilly backroads of Hart, Stephens, and Franklin Counties, you can rest a while at an eighteenth-century stagecoach inn and reminisce with old-timers, who sill remember baseball's "Georgia Peach," Ty Cobb.

Hart State Park, 1525 Hart Park Road, Hartwell 30643, (706) 376–8756, reservations (800) 864–PARK, spreads 417 acres along the lakeshore. Set up housekeeping in eighty-three camping sites, with utility hookups, adajcent rest rooms, and showers, and in furnished cottages. Enjoy swimming, boating, waterskiing, hiking, and fishing for largemouth bass, bream, black crappie, walleye pike, and rainbow trout.

Tugaloo State Park, on a wooded peninsula jutting into Lake Hartwell, 1763 Tugaloo State Park Road, Lavonia 30553, (706) 356–4352, is another motherlode of bass and other fish fry favorites. Nonfisherfolk can play tennis and miniature golf, swim and waterski from a sand beach, and hike and bike on trails threading though the woodlands. Lodgings include twenty furnished cottages and 122 tent and camper sites.

After driving all day, are you tantalized by thoughts of a round of golf, a swim, maybe some late-afternoon fishing? *Victoria Bryant State Park,* off I-85 near Royston, 1105 Bryant Park Road, Royston 30662, (706) 245–6270 or (800) 864–PARK, (706) 245–6770 for golf, may be the answer to your search. The park's 3,288-yard, par-34, 9-hole course is hardly a monster, but clusters of Georgia pines, hills, and plenty of water hazards will keep you on your toes. Rental clubs and pull carts are available at the clubhouse, which also has showers, changing rooms, and a snack bar.

Nongolfers can enjoy the swimming pool and angle for bass, bream, and catfish in stocked ponds. The park's twenty-five camping sites have utility hookups, with access to rest rooms and showers.

If you're a real baseball fan, drive down to *Royston* and see the little town that gave the world the "Georgia Peach." Gloves, balls, bats, plaques, newspaper clippings, and other artifacts are displayed at City Hall.

In the 1830s and 1840s—more than a century before Ty Cobb headed to the majors—travelers enduring the bone-jarring stagecoach trip through the north Georgia wilderness took solace in the thought that by and by they'd reach *Travelers Rest,* off Highway 123, 6 miles northeast of Toccoa, (706) 886–2256.

The sturdy, fourteen-room plank structure was built in 1833 as the plantation home of wealthy planter Devereaux Jarrett. As more and more travelers streamed through the region, the enterprising Jarrett turned his home into an eighteenth-century B & B. South Carolina statesmen John C. Calhoun was a guest and Joseph E. Brown, Georgia's Civil War governor, spent his honeymoon here.

Now a state historic site maintained by the Georgia Department of Natural Resources, the fourteen rooms are furnished with four-poster beds, rocking chairs, vanities, marble-topped tables, goose feather mattresses, spinning wheels, china, cutlery, glassware, and memorabilia of Travelers Rest's days as a post office. The grounds are shaded by a huge white oak tree, believed to be well into its third century, and several century-old crape myrtle trees. Open Tuesday through Saturday 9:00 A.M. to 5:00 P.M. Admission for adults is $2.00; ages 6 to 18, $1.00; under 6, free.

Approaching the Winder/Chestnut Mountain exit (48) on I–85, 30 miles north of metro Atlanta's I–285 Perimeter Highway, what appears to be a sixteenth-century French castle, surrounded by vineyards, rises from the piney landscape. It's no mirage. *Chateau Elan Winery & Resort,* 100 Rue Charlemagne, Braselton 30517, (770) 932–0900 or (800) 233–9463, was established in 1982 as Georgia's first major winery since the end of Prohibition. Inside the Chateau's "castle," you're welcome to stroll around a movie-set French marketplace and purchase jams, mustards, wine guides, cookbooks, picnic hampers, and other gourmet foods and gifts. Before purchasing the Chateau's grape, take the winery tour, followed by a free tasting. In a short time, cabernet sauvignon, chardonnay, Riesling, pinot noir, zinfandel, and other varieties bearing the Chateau Elan label have won more than fifty-five awards in national competitions. Southerners are partial to the sweet, fruity Summerwine, a blend of peaches and muscadine grapes. Wines are about $6 to $12 a bottle.

Six restaurants include the Marketplace Cafe with quiche, pâté, chicken breast, salads, cheeses, and other light luncheon fare. Candlelit Cafe Closs serves a five-course dinner with appropriate wines (and appropriate prices). For a taste of another old country, stop in the Chateau's Paddy's Irish Pub. Constructed in Ireland, dismantled, and shipped to Georgia, it was reassembled by Irish craftsmen and staffed with smiling young lasses and laddies. The rough-hewn timber ceiling, beer barrel tables, slate floors, and stacked stone fireplace—and a menu that includes Irish lamb stew, Irish whiskey mousse, and Irish ales, stouts, and whiskeys—make the pub seem like a cozy corner of Eire transplanted to the north Georgia hills.

Chateau Elan Winery

The 3,100-acre resort also has three championship golf courses with sixty-three stem-winding holes, tennis, and an indoor heated pool. You can overnight in the deluxe 245-room Chateau Inn, in furnished *Golf Villas,* and at the moderately priced Days Inn–Chateau Elan. The *Chateau Elan Spa* has diet and nutrition services, smoking cessation programs, massages, mineral baths, herbal wraps, saunas, and fourteen guest rooms.

Fort Yargo State Park, at nearby Winder, takes its name from a still-standing log blockhouse that white settlers built in 1792 as protection against hostile Creeks and Cherokees. The park's big green lake is an inviting place to swim and fish and to rent paddleboats, rowboats, and canoes. You can also enjoy tennis and miniature golf, hike nature trails, and set the youngsters loose on the playground. *Will-A-Way Recreation Area,* inside the park, has facilities for handicapped persons, including specially equipped, furnished cottages. There are also furnished cottages and campsites not so equipped. For reservations phone (800) 864–PARK. Contact Park Superintendent, Winder 30680, (770) 867–3489.

At Christmas season, many people bring their holiday mail to the post office in the nearby little community of Bethlehem for that special postmark.

The *Crawford W. Long Museum,* 28 College Street, (706) 367–5307, in Jefferson honors the physician who first used ether for surgical anesthesia. Dr. Long, then a young Jackson County practitioner, performed the first painless surgery on March 30, 1842. The museum displays his personal papers and a diorama depicting the first operation. An 1840's doctor's office and apothecary and a general store are also part of the museum. The outdoor herb garden grows many plants commonly used in nineteenth-century medicine. Open Tuesday to Sunday; free admission.

Bulldog Country

Elbert County proudly hails itself "The Granite Capital of the World." The county's more than forty quarries and 150 monument manufacturing plants produce a third of the granite used in memorials and monuments in this country, and much of it is shipped overseas. The **Elberton Granite Museum**'s exhibits and taped programs will tell you how granite is formed, how it's quarried, the many types it comes in, and the geological differences between it and marble. You'll also see a short film about the Georgia Guidestones. The museum is on Highway 17/77, a block from downtown Elberton, (706) 283–2551. Open daily 2:00 to 5:00 P.M. Free admission.

Georgia Guidestones, on Highway 77, 7 miles north of Elberton, (706) 283–5651, may remind you of England's Stonehenge, and their origin is almost as mysterious. No one's quite certain who commissioned the Guidestones, or why. But there they are: four massive granite tablets, 19 feet, 3 inches high, arranged in a spokelike pattern, with a smaller stone in the center and another across the top. Astrological readings may be made through slots and holes drilled in the stones. The Ten Commandments are etched in eight living languages, including English. Four dead languages bear the message: LET THESE BE GUIDESTONES TO AN AGE OF REASON. Other maxims inscribed on the stones include: BE NOT A CANCER ON THE EARTH—LEAVE ROOM FOR NATURE. Free admission.

Two state parks on the Savannah River are happy hunting grounds for bass and trout fishing. **Bobby Brown State Park,** Box 232, Elberton 30635, (706) 213–2046, has boat ramps, picnic areas, a swimming pool, and campsites on 70,000-acre Clarks Hill Lake. Just upriver, **Richard B. Russell State Park,** Box 118, Elberton 30635, (706) 213–3045, also has campsites, cottages, a swimming beach, boat ramps, and fish that aim to please. Both parks have a $2.00 per visit parking fee. For camping reservations call (800) 864–PARK.

Athens throbs with the vitality of 30,000 **University of Georgia** students, who almost balance "The Classic City's" 45,000 townies. Founded in 1785, America's oldest chartered state university existed only on paper for sixteen years before the legislature provided funds for land and academic buildings in 1800. The first classes met in 1801. That same year Athens was founded on hills above the Oconee River—hopeful of Olympian inspiration, the rude little settlement was named for Greece's hub of classical learning. Planters and literati embellished the campus and Athens's elm- and oak-lined thoroughfares with Greek

Revival, Georgian, and Federal architecture. Over the ensuing decades, "town and gown" have coexisted in peace and harmony only seriously disrupted when 85,000 Bulldog football fanatics shake the skies over Sanford Stadium with exhortations of "Go-oooo Dawgs!"

Stop first at the Athens Welcome Center in the *Church-Waddel-Brumby House,* 280 East Dougherty Street, (706) 353–1820. The fine Federalist house was built in 1820 for Alonzo Church, who became one of UGA's early presidents. Dr. Moses Waddel, who succeeded him in the president's chair, also lived in the house, believed to be the city's oldest surviving residence. You may view the lovely rooms and pick up walking and driving tours of the Athens Historic District and information about other attractions.

As Athens and the university have grown, much of the city's antebellum heritage has been lost. Many antebellum homes have been torn down, others turned into UGA sorority and frat houses, funeral homes, commercial offices, and academic buildings. Only the *Taylor-Grady House,* 634 Prince Avenue, (706) 549–8688, is open as a museum. It was built in 1845 by General Robert Taylor. In 1863, Major William S. Grady purchased the house and his son, Henry W. Grady, lived in it while studying journalism at UGA. Grady went on to become the nationally renowned editor of *The Atlanta Constitution* and spokesman for the post–Civil War "New South." UGA's journalism school is named for him.

The *State Botanical Garden,* 2450 South Milledge Avenue, (706) 542–1244, is a serene oasis 3 miles from UGA's high-energy campus. The three-story glass and steel Visitors Center and Conservatory is the gateway to the 313-acre sanctuary, which UGA created in 1968 as a "living laboratory" for the study and enjoyment of plants and nature.

"Just in Case"

*I*f you fancy Civil War oddities, don't miss the "Double-Barreled Cannon," a whimsical piece of memorabilia that was a spectacular failure. Cast in Athens in 1862, each barrel was to be loaded with cannonballs connected to each other by an 8-foot chain. When fired, the missiles were supposed to exit together, pull the chain tight, and sweep the cannon across the battlefield like a scythe. In reality, the barrels weren't synchronized, and instead of devastating Yankees, the errant shots went in different directions, plowing up a corn field, knocking down a tree and a log cabin chimney, and killing a cow. It was permanently retired and rests today on the City Hall grounds, pointing north, "just in case."

After a 10-minute audiovisual introduction, stroll among orchids, ferns, bamboo, bougainvillea, birds of paradise, and other lush tropical and semitropical plants that flourish along man-made streams and ponds. You can have lunch in the sunny indoor/outdoor **Garden Room Cafe** and browse among plants, books, and gardening paraphernalia in the gift shop. Revolving exhibits highlight botanical and horticultural paintings by regional and national artists.

"The Tree That Owns Itself" is a quirky landmark. The 50-foot oak, at Dearing and Findley Streets in Athens, was granted its autonomy and 8 feet of land on all sides by a UGA professor many years ago.

Five miles of color-coded trails wind through hardwood forests and along ravines of the Middle Oconee River. As you admire azaleas, wildlfowers, rhododendron, 125-year-old beech trees, and other plants and trees native to the Georgia piedmont, you might spot white-tailed deer, rabbits, foxes, opossum, and a remarkable variety of birds.

Theme gardens display roses, dahlias, mums, camellias, hollies, ornamentals, and other seasonal plants. There are plenty of spots for quiet musings. Eleven collections in the three-acre International Garden follow history and culture of botany back to the beginnings of civilization. Grounds are open daily 8 A.M. to sunset. Visitors Center hours are 9:00 A.M. to 4:30 P.M. Monday through Saturday and 11:30 A.M. to 4:30 P.M. Sunday. Free admission.

UGA's contemporary vitality is a dichotomy with antebellum Athens. Stop at the **UGA Visitors Center,** Four Towers Building, College Station Road, (706) 542–0842, in a refurbished dairy barn on the edge of UGA's new East Campus, for infomation about campus landmarks and activities. Open Monday through Friday 9:00 A.M. to 5:00 P.M.; Saturday 9:00 A.M. to 5:00 P.M.; and Sunday 1:00 to 5:00 P.M. The campus is a crazy-quilt of classical and modern architecture. According to tradition, freshmen may not walk under the three-columned **University Arch,** which was forged in cast iron in 1857 and is the centerpiece of Georgia's Great Seal, representing WISDOM, JUSTICE AND MODERATION. Walk under it and you're on the historic **North Campus.** Listed on the National Register of Historic Places, "Old North's" landmarks include Phi Kappa Hall, an 1836 Greek Revival; Federal-style Waddel Hall, 1820; Palladian-style Demosthenian Hall, 1824; Greek Revival University Chapel, whose bells clamor joyously when the Bulldogs win one on the gridiron; and Old College, where Crawford W. Long, a Georgian who pioneered the use of anesthesia for surgery, was the 1832 roommate of Alexander Hamilton Stephens, who became vice president of the Confederacy.

The *Georgia Museum of Art,* 90 Carlton Street, (706) 542–4662, exhibits more than 7,000 paintings, sculptures, and other works by regional, national, and international artists. It hosts more than twenty annual special exhibits and educational programs and film series. Open Tuesday to Saturday 10:00 A.M. to 5:00 P.M. and Sunday 1:00 to 5:00 P.M. Free admission.

With its thousands of perpetually ravenous students, finding a place to eat is no problem. Restaurants, casual cafes, coffeehouses, and snack bars line Broad Street across from the University Arch and spill over onto adjacent streets.

When it comes to music, Athens is a spawning ground for modern rock groups. The *40 Watt Club,* 285 West Washington Street, (706) 549–7879, still lives on its reputation as the launching pad for REM and the B-52s back in the seventies. Widespread Panic is the latest Athens group to make the big time. Local bands and touring groups play at the early 1900s *Morton Theater,* 199 West Washington Street. Once the state's most famous Black vaudeville theater, the Morton has recently been restored to its former glory.

Oconee County

Knock on a farmhouse door down a rutted dirt road in the back- woods of Oconee County, or stop by a tidy house on a shady street in *Watkinsville,* the 200-year-old county seat, and don't be sur- prised when an artist invites you in. The rural, but rapidly suburban- izing county of 25,000, just south of Athens, boasts what people here proudly claim is one of Georgia's most extraordinary congregations of creative talent. From Watkinsville (population 2,100) down pasture roads and in the woods around Farmington, Bishop, and Bogart, 100 or more virtuosos are painting, throwing pottery, and making jew- elry; metal, marble, and papier-mâché sculptures; decorative wood- craft; calligraphy; ceramics; woven rugs; forged iron; folk art; custom furniture; and blown and fused glass and fabric wall hangings that sell in shops from here to Alaska.

The five-year-old *Oconee Cultural Arts Foundation* (OCAF) fosters many of the county's visual and performing arts programs. With the enthusiastic support of local governments and a wellspring of donated time, labor, and money, a 1902 redbrick school building has been regeared as a setting for exhibitions, plays, and educational workshops.

Works by Oconee's artists span the spectrum from representational to anarchic, folkloric to contemporary. There are Christmas ornaments that would fit in your pocket and steel and marble sculptures that require an army to move—and a philosopher to interpret. Some artists are homegrown, but many move here initially to study in the University of Georgia's nationally respected visual arts programs.

A few artists work in close communities, but most prefer to labor alone in barns, cabins, old industrial buildings, and refitted farmhouses around the county. You can search for them by riding through the rolling piedmont countryside, a patchwork of pecan and peach orchards, cornfields, covered bridges, pine forests, and cattle farms, but many artists live and work hidden away on isolated roads, with no clue to the creative endeavors transpiring behind the trees.

The surest way to locate them is to stop first at the *Eagle Tavern Welcome Center,* across from the courthouse on Watkinsville's 1-block, back-in-time Main Street, (706) 769–5197. The tavern has been a landmark since 1820, when it was a frontier stagecoach stop. "The Oconee County Guide to the Arts," a free foldout guide, lists more than fifty artists, and director Bonnie Murphy will point you in the right directions. To get an idea of what's out there, walk across the street to *Art Masters Gallery,* (706) 769–4450. Owner Peggy Holcomb represents about sixty artists in Oconee and neighboring counties. Her cheerful, pine-floored shop is in a refashioned nineteenth-century mercantile store, in the middle of a block that also houses antiques, clothing, home accessories, engraving, and gift shops. Down the street, Teresa Ruggiere's Red Door Folk Art Gallery, (706) 769–7247, sells whimsical creations by artists all over the South. Next door, the companion Ruggiere, A Gallery, represents contemporary Southern artists.

Most people trace the arts community's birth to 1970, when Jerry and Kathy Chappelle came down from Minnesota to teach pottery at the University of Georgia. The Chappelle's *Happy Valley Pottery,* a collection of old farm buildings and workshops 9 miles south of Watkinsville, (706) 769–5922, is one of the county's largest one-stop arts sources and one of the few that keeps regular hours. Their high-fire stoneware is characterized by colorful fruit, flowers, and mountainscapes. Other members of the Happy Valley community include glassblower Loretta Eby, an Indiana native nationally known for her Christmas ornaments, oil lamps, perfume bottles, and paperweights. You can purchase their wares in the Happy Valley shop. Discounted seconds are also for sale.

WHERE TO STAY IN NORTHEAST GEORGIA

GAINESEVILLE
The Dunlap House Bed & Breakfast Inn,
635 Green Street,
(770) 536–0200.

Here is another gracious Green Street landmark. Built in 1910, the ten-room mansion was turned into a luxury bed and breakfast in 1985. Each uniquely decorated guest room has either a queen- or king-size bed, private bath, telephone, TV, designer linens, oversize towels, and terry cloth robes. Some rooms have working fireplaces. Continental breakfast is included in the double rates of $75 to $95 weekdays and $105 to $155 weekends.

Whitworth Inn Bed & Breakfast,
6593 McEver Road,
Flowery Branch 30542,
(770) 967–2386.

Has ten light, airy guest rooms, all with private baths, a few minutes from Lake Lanier. Enjoy the cool mountain air on open porches. Innkeepers Ken and Christine Jonick send you off in the morning with a full country breakfast. Doubles are $65.

HARTWELL
The Skelton House,
97 Benson Street,
(706) 376–7969.

An excellent B & B alternative to state park cottages and campgrounds. The Skelton family's 1896 home, fully restored in 1997, has eight guest rooms, all with private baths, TV, balconies, and porches and full breakfast. Rates are $85 to $100.

ATHENS
Magnolia Terrace Guest House,
277 Hill Street,
(706) 548–3860
or (800) 891–1912.

The handsome Colonial Revival mansion, built in 1912, is close to downtown and the UGA campus. Innkeeper Sheila Hackney's eight guest rooms have claw-foot tubs and modern fixtures. There's a spacious front veranda and outdoor seating for breakfast. Doubles are $50 to $125.

Nicholson House,
6295 Jefferson Road,
(706) 353–2200.

On the edge of town, Nicholson House has four guest rooms with Victorian antiques, private baths, TV, and phone. Rates for doubles are $75, including breakfast.

Oakwood Bed & Breakfast,
4959 Barnett Shoals Road,
(706) 546–7886.

This 1850s Victorian house on 5½ acres has three guest rooms and two others in an adjacent cottage. Full breakfast. Rates are $75 to $150.

WATKINSVILLE
Ashford Manor Bed-and-Breakfast, 5 Harden Road,
(706) 769–2633.

This B & B was opened in 1997 by two Chicago brothers and a partner. They've beautifully decorated and furnished seven rooms in an 1893 Victorian mansion, which sits on five acres of lawns, gardens, and woods within walking distance of downtown shops. Pets are welcome at an adjacent cottage. Rates are $85 to $95, including breakfast.

Watson Mill Bridge State Park, on Highway 22,
6 miles south of Comer,
(706) 783–5349; (800)
864–PARK for camping reservations.

The site of Georgia's longest covered bridge. The century-old bridge's four spans stretch 236 feet over the South Fork of the Broad River. It's an idyllic place for a picnic, canoeing, and an overnight stay in the campgrounds.

WHERE TO EAT IN NORTHEAST GEORGIA

GAINESVILLE
Poor Richard's,
1702 Parkhill Drive,
(770) 532–0499.

Gainesville's choice for steaks, prime rib, chateaubriand, baby back ribs, shrimp, lobster, and chicken since 1977. They'll also serve you a hefty hamburger, salads, sandwiches, and wine. Dinner is served Monday to Saturday.

Rudolph's On Green Street, 700 Green Street, (770) 534–2226.

This is a baronial English Tudor rich with dark, exposed beams, stained-glass windows, Oriental carpets, and Duncan Phyfe furnishings. Lunch and dinner entrees are equally impressive: broiled baby salmon, chicken Florentine, roast duckling, several veal dishes, and Georgia mountain trout complemented by wines from California, Georgia, and Europe. Dinner Monday through Saturday and Sunday brunch.

ATHENS
Athens Brewing Company,
312 East Washington Street,
(706) 549–0027.

Bulldog town's only brewpub. House-brewed beers and ales are complemented by steaks, sandwiches, pizza, salads, and soups. Continuous lunch and dinner service Monday though Saturday.

East West Bistro,
351 East Broad Street,
(706) 546–4240.

Serves Athens's most adventurous international cuisines. It's really two restaurants in one. The casual street-level dining room, with big comfortable booths and a large bar area, serves Spanish tapas, pastas, seafood, and Asian, Southwestern, and Mexican dishes and great desserts. The more formal white-tablecloth upstairs dining room has a classical Italian menu. Continuous lunch and dinner service daily.

The Grit, 199 Prince Avenue, (706) 543–6592.

REM's Michael Stipes owns the building, but native Brit Mark Dalling rules the kitchen of this "renegade vegetarian" restaurant that's so good even nonvegans wait in line for tofu chicken salad, lentil and roasted garlic soup,

Helpful Web Sites

Athens Welcome Center,
www.visitathensga.com

State Botanical Garden of Georgia,
www.uga.edu/botgarden

University of Georgia Performing Arts Center,
www.uga.edu/pac/

Dahlonega-Lumpkin County Chamber of Commerce,
www.dahlonega.org

Union County Chamber of Commerce,
www.blairsvillechamber.com

Fieldstone inn,
www.fieldstoneinn.com

Towns County Tourism,
www.townscountytourism.com

Helen & White County Information,
www.whitehelengeorgia.net

Oconee County Arts Foundation,
www.ocaf@athens.net

and other specialties. Lunch and dinner daily.

Harry Bisset's New Orleans Cafe,
279 East Broad Street, (706) 353–7065.

The place for Cajun and New Orleans Creole-style cooking. Favorite dishes include soft-shell crab, jambalaya, oysters, shrimp, crawfish étouffée, and bread pudding. Lunch Tuesday to Friday, dinner Monday through Saturday, Sunday brunch.

The Grill,
171 College Avenue, (706) 543–4770.

Fills up those hungry students and townies with great hamburgers, fries, shakes, egg muffins, bagels, and other tasty stuff around the clock daily.

The Varsity,
1000 West Broad Street, (706) 548–6325.

For a bite-on-the-run, dive into the chili dogs, burgers, shakes, wonderfully greasy French fries and onion rings, sandwiches, and ice cream at this landmark fast-food emporium. Open continuously daily.

Otherwise, just follow your nose and ask a friendly Bullldog for his/her suggestion.

WATKINSVILLE
Gautreau's Cajun Cafe,
downtown, (706) 769–9330.

Serves moderately priced jambalaya, gumbo, crawfish étouffée, fried shrimp and oysters, red beans and rice, blackened steaks, chicken and catfish, po' boy sandwiches, and bananas Foster at lunch and dinner Tuesday to Saturday.

Hot Thomas on Highway 15, 5½ miles
south of Watkinsville, (706) 769–6550.

The old-timey roadside place is a local favorite for barbecue, Brunswick stew, and homemade sandwiches. Lunch and dinner are served Monday through Saturday 10:00 A.M. to 7:00 P.M. Eat in or picnic down by the nearby Elder Covered Bridge.

Index

INDEX

Special Indexes

Festivals and Folk Plays

Museums

National Parks and Historic Sites

State Parks and Historic Sites

INDEX